A Legal Guide to
Starting and Managing
A Nonprofit Organization

NONPROFIT LAW, FINANCE, AND MANAGEMENT SERIES

A Legal Guide to Starting and Managing A Nonprofit Organization

Second Edition

BRUCE R. HOPKINS

John Wiley & Sons, Inc.
New York • Chichester • Brisbane • Toronto • Singapore

References for discussion in Chapter 21 are: Alvin Toffler, *Future Shock* (New York: Random House, 1970); John Naisbitt, *Megatrends: Ten Directions Transforming Our Lives* (New York: Warner, 1982).

This text is printed on acid-free paper.

Library of Congress Cataloging in Publication Data:

Hopkins, Bruce R.
    A legal guide to starting and managing a nonprofit organization / Bruce R. Hopkins. — 2nd ed.
        p.   cm. — (Nonprofit law, finance, and management series)
    Rev. ed. of: Starting and managing a nonprofit organization. c1989.
    Includes index.
    ISBN 0-471-58507-6 (cloth : acid-free paper). — ISBN 0-471-58506-8 (paper : acid-free paper)
    1. Nonprofit organizations—Law and legislation—United States. 2. Nonprofit organizations—Taxation—Law and legislation—United States. I. Hopkins, Bruce R. Starting and managing a nonprofit organization. II. Title. III. Series.
    KF1388.H66   1993
    346.73'064—dc20
    [347.30664]   93-9858

Printed in the United States of America

10 9 8 7 6

To my parents, Frederick and Jane,
who, as teachers, professional and otherwise,
encouraged me, in their own way and
in ways they may not realize, to write this book,
with love.

Preface

This book was conceived a few years ago, during a speech before managers of relatively small nonprofit organizations. I had been assigned some esoteric topic on the law of tax-exempt organizations and was about five minutes into my presentation when I suddenly realized, from the glazed-over looks, that few people in the audience had even the faintest idea what I was talking about. Preservation instincts took over. The assignment was hopeless, so I abandoned my intended remarks. Instead, we talked about what my audience wanted to hear: some of the basics of the laws affecting nonprofit organizations.

The experience was not a measure of the level of intelligence of that particular audience. A massive gap exists between the wish-lists and the legal expertise of those responsible for nonprofit organizations. The law can either help them achieve their goals or prevent them from succeeding.

I was struck by the thought that there was a need for a summary of the laws that affect the operation of nonprofit organizations. The summary I envisioned would have no citations or footnotes—just readable text.

I had no shortage of questions, from my practice, speeches over the past 24 years, and 19 years of teaching a law school course on tax-exempt organizations. I began recalling and noting these questions, and was surprised to realize how the same ones are asked again and again. This book has been written to provide answers to those basic questions.

The questions are fundamental and important, but they reveal tremendous confusion. The confusion is understandable: the law in this field is confusing—even overwhelming. The ultimate purposes of this book are: to decipher the Internal Revenue Code as it affects nonprofit organizations; to translate the intricacies of the law in these areas and try to make them understandable to nonlawyer-managers of "nonprofits";

and to otherwise help to close the gap between goals and knowledge in nonprofit organizations.

Lawyer-managers or others who want more detail should refer to one of the books listed on page ii.

The law affecting nonprofit organizations is volatile. Ongoing change is inevitable, and many changes lie ahead during the Clinton years. I have tried to make the book sufficiently general to withstand most of this change. Yet, once the basics in this field are grasped, some readers may want more detail and more current information. My monthly newsletter, *The Nonprofit Counsel* (Wiley), is a useful resource for keeping up with legal developments that affect nonprofit organizations.

For some readers, there may be more in the book than they need at this time, particularly if they are just beginning to establish a nonprofit organization or are thinking about doing so. Let me offer this perspective for the newcomer to the world, and the law, of nonprofit organizations. There are many types of nonprofit organizations. Nearly always, those who start a nonprofit organization want it to be tax-exempt. At a minimum, they want it to be eligible to receive tax-deductible contributions. They equate "nonprofit" organizations with "tax-exempt" organizations and perhaps with "charitable" organizations.

For those who already know that they want a "charitable" entity, Chapter 4 can be just skimmed as a review. For others, Chapter 4's inventory of the various types of tax-exempt organizations is the place to begin.

A fictional "Campaign to Clean Up America" is used throughout as an illustration of how to organize and qualify a tax-exempt charitable organization. Most individuals, when planning to establish a nonprofit organization, are thinking in terms of a charity, even if that thinking is only subconscious. Rarely have they selected between a "public" versus a "private" charity. Usually, they are thinking about the establishment of a "foundation."

There is more to the universe of nonprofits than charity. The first question for an individual interested in establishing a nonprofit organization should be: What is the nonprofit organization going to do? Just like starting a business, the first step is to determine the organization's functions, then match the category of tax-exempt status (if any) to the organization's purposes and functions. Too often, individuals start with a round-peg nonprofit organization (usually, a charitable one) and try to force it into the square-hole requirements of the law imposed on that type of organization.

A *charity* will not fit the requirements of all. Here are some of the other choices:

- *Advocacy organizations.* These groups attempt to influence the legislative process and/or the political process, or otherwise champion particular positions. They may call themselves "social welfare organizations" or perhaps "political action committees." Not all advocacy is lobbying and not all political activity is political campaign activity. Some of this type of program can be accomplished through a charitable organization, but that outcome is rare where advocacy is the organization's primary undertaking. In some instances, two nonprofit organizations are used, to have it both ways—a blend of charitable and advocacy activities.

- *Membership groups.* Some nonprofit organizations—associations, veterans' groups, and fraternal organizations—are structured as membership organizations. This is not to say that a charitable organization may not be structured as a membership entity; it can, but there are other categories of membership groups. Frequently, these are "business leagues."

- *Social or recreational organizations.* Nonprofit organizations may be organized as formal "social clubs" (like country clubs, and tennis and golf clubs), or hobby, garden, or sports tournament organizations. The key factor is their primary purpose; some social activity can be tolerated in charitable groups. There is some overlap with other categories, for example, a social organization can be structured as a membership entity.

- *Satellite organizations.* Some nonprofit organizations are deliberately organized as auxiliaries or subsidiaries of other organizations. Examples of these organizations include title-holding companies, the various types of cooperatives, and retirement and other employee benefit funds. The "parent" organization may be a for-profit entity, such as a business corporation with a related foundation.

- *Employee benefit funds.* The world of compensation is intricate, regardless of whether the employer is a for-profit or nonprofit organization. Various current and deferred benefits for employees are provided, including retirement and profit-sharing programs. When properly organized and operated, these funds are tax-exempt entities.

Once the category of tax-exempt organization is decided, the reader can use Chapter 5, which discusses the concept of "private inurement," as a brief review. Among other things, it offers an explanation of the basic distinctions between nonprofit and for-profit organizations. An understanding of these distinctions may well avoid some difficulties later on, and, at some point, an understanding of the private inurement doctrine will be necessary.

If the organization will engage in attempts to influence legislation, a jump ahead, for a reading of Chapter 13, is essential. If the organization is to engage in efforts to intervene or participate in political campaign activities, a perusing of Chapter 14 is necessary.

For charitable organizations, another jump ahead in the book may be in order. Because all charitable organizations are presumed to be "private foundations" and because there is little advantage in being so classified, most charitable entities strive to avoid private foundation status if they can. A review of the basic differences between "public" and "private" charities, included in Chapter 11, is important at the outset.

In addition to being tax-exempt, an organization may have charitable donee status. Not every tax-exempt organization can receive tax-deductible gifts, but many can. Chapter 4 identifies those that are charitable donees; Chapter 8 provides the basic charitable giving rules. Hopefully, the new charitable giving program will include at least the rudiments of a planned giving program; this type of giving is described in Chapter 17. If a charitable gift solicitation program is planned, the organization must keep in mind the state and federal laws pertaining to fund raising. These laws are summarized in Chapter 9.

Charitable organizations must obtain a ruling from the Internal Revenue Service (IRS) that they are tax-exempt and eligible to receive deductible gifts. Most other categories of tax-exempt organizations may wish to obtain IRS rulings but are not required to do so. The process of obtaining such a ruling is the subject of Chapter 6, a necessary chapter for newcomers. Readers will find it helpful to have a copy of IRS Form 1023 on hand when they reach this chapter.

Another key chapter is Chapter 7, which outlines the various returns and reports that a tax-exempt organization must file, under both federal and state law.

Chapter 19 may be the most riveting chapter for those who are serving (or are thinking of serving) on boards of directors and/or as officers in nonprofit organizations. The chapter deals with personal liability and how to avoid it.

The balance of the book can be read when the topics are relevant for particular situations. Chapter 10 focuses on compensation programs other than basic salaries, Chapter 15 deals with the use of subsidiaries, and Chapter 16 details involvements in partnerships. Let's assume that newcomers read the initial four chapters of the book, and then only Chapters 6 through 9. The rest of the book will be more valuable after this basic learning and when dealing with specific areas.

The final chapters (20 and 21), which look at the future of nonprofit organizations, are not critical or immediate reading for newcomers. However, these chapters provide some insight on the federal tax law in this area and can be reviewed from that perspective as time allows.

An inherent dilemma faces those involved with start-ups of nonprofit organizations: How is an organization to progress if it does not absorb and act on new information? Yet how can it avoid stagnating in frustration and not progressing at all, if it is overwhelmed with unnecessary detail, particularly in the beginning stages?

The trick, of course, is balance, and that balance lies in understanding the basics. As an example, take the topic of Chapter 18, planned giving. Assume that, against all advice, the management of a charitable organization refuses to entertain even a preliminary thought about launching a planned giving program at this time. Hopefully, there will be an employee or a trustee who has tried at least to understand what planned giving is, and has become aware of the basic terms. Even if the management of a charitable organization elects to turn down a planned giving program for now, at least they will have some idea of what they are turning down.

Those who are tempted to spurn Chapter 18 should spend a few minutes reviewing the topics it covers:

- The basic concept of planned giving
- The likelihood of securing a planned gift immediately
- The reasons for not postponing the advent of a planned giving program
- The "charitable remainder trust"
- The "charitable gift annuity"
- The "pooled income fund"
- The "charitable lead trust"
- The use of insurance as the basis for a charitable gift
- The integration of estate planning and charitable giving
- The need for an endowment for the organization
- The existing fund-raising resources that might more productively be devoted to a planned giving program

Someday, someone may ask a trustee, officer, or employee of a charitable organization: "Do you have a pooled income fund?" It would be nice for the potentially hapless respondent to have some idea of what a "pooled income fund" is.

The same may be said for the definitions of subsidiaries and/or partnerships. (See Chapters 15 and 16.) Those starting a nonprofit organization may believe (and rightly so) that the use of a taxable subsidiary or an involvement in a joint venture is the farthest thing from their minds. Yet, it would be nice to know at least the basics regarding the use of a subsidiary. For example:

- Would the tax-exempt status of the organization be disturbed, enhanced, or preserved if one or more activities were housed in a separate organization?
- Aside from tax considerations, do management or other types of factors dictate the use of a subsidiary?
- How is the subsidiary to be funded, for initial capitalization and/or ongoing operations?
- How does the "parent" organization maintain control over the subsidiary?
- What circumstances might cause the activities of the subsidiary to be attributed back to the tax-exempt parent?

Regarding partnerships, a wise newcomer will learn such fundamentals as:

- The purpose of using a partnership (frequently simply a financing device)
- The difference between a "general partnership" and a "limited partnership"
- When property is best acquired by a partnership rather than by a participating nonprofit organization
- When to use (and when not to use) a for-profit partner
- How and why it may be beneficial for a nonprofit organization to lease property from a partnership in which it is a partner
- When to become involved in a joint venture—and when not to
- The circumstances where involvement by the exempt organization in a partnership might cause the organization to forfeit its tax-exempt status

Chapters 20 and 21 offer a short-run and a long-run look ahead. Unlike the other chapters, these two chapters are not intended to be a discussion of basic legal principles; they describe the changing environment in which the new exempt organization will be functioning. The chapters are not crucial reading, but a review of them along the way may enhance the value derived from the "mandatory" chapters.

Thus, each chapter is designed to have some practical import, and, for newcomers, some chapters are of greater necessity than others. This Preface serves as a guide to the must-read chapters and pleads with readers not to abandon the rest. When in doubt on the meaning of a word or phrase, the glossary is available.

No book is a substitute for good legal or other professional advice. Some managers of nonprofit organizations are afraid to seek advice—out of embarrassment for asking "dumb questions" or fear of the costs involved. An operator of a nonprofit organization may not even realize the presence of a legal problem. This book is intended to ease those fears and close those gaps.

BRUCE R. HOPKINS

Washington, DC
July 1993

Acknowledgments

This book is possible because of the contributions of many people: clients, participants at conferences and seminars, students, and colleagues. There are five individuals who warrant particular mention. Three of them reviewed drafts of the manuscript of the first edition and offered many very helpful suggestions. They are Robert Smucker, Vice-President for Government Relations at Independent Sector; Carolyn Fazio, Chairman of Fazio International; and Charles Fazio, President of Fazio International. I very much appreciate their assistance; the book is better because of their efforts. Any mistakes of fact, law, or judgment are, of course, mine.

The fourth individual is Jeffrey W. Brown, Publisher, at John Wiley & Sons, Inc. Jeff has been involved in all of my projects with Wiley and has offered more help and overall support over the years than I can possibly describe. Working closely with me on this book and the others, and the newsletter *The Nonprofit Counsel,* has been Marla J. Bobowick, Acquisitions Editor at Wiley. Marla offers great encouragement and frequent assistance; working with her is a delight, except around deadline time. I acknowledge the contributions of both of them with thanks.

Finally, I acknowledge a considerable debt to the copyeditor for this book, Maryan Malone of Publications Development Company. Practicing law and writing legal documents for over twenty years has not aided my book-writing style; to compensate, Maryan worked tirelessly to rid the text of its "lawyerese." Thanks, Maryan; I do not envy you your job.

B. R. H.

Contents

PART ONE

Starting a Nonprofit Organization

CHAPTER ONE

Why Start a Nonprofit Organization?

One of the most striking features of the twentieth century's closing years has been the awesome sweep of reforms around the world. Freedom of thought and action is now permitted in societies that previously knew only totalitarianism and suppression. Almost daily, yet another country earns the label "emerging democracy" by introducing startling economic and political changes. The collapse of the former U.S.S.R. and the struggles toward freedom and economic betterment in the several countries that were once part of it is a prime example of these reforms.

Those who are planning transitions to a democratic state are discovering a fact that some Western countries learned a long time ago: to create and maintain economic and political freedom, which is the essence of a truly democratic state, the power to influence and cause changes cannot be concentrated in one sector of that state or society. There must be a "pluralization of institutions" in society, a fancy way of saying that the ability to bring about changes and the accumulation of power cannot belong to just one sector—inevitably, the government.

A strong democratic state has three sectors: a government sector, a private business sector, and a nonprofit sector. Each sector must function effectively and must cooperate with the others, to some degree, if the democracy is to persist for the good of the individuals in the society. A democratic society must be able to make and implement policy decisions with the participation of all three sectors. Ideally, a democratic society can solve some of its problems with minimal involvement of government if there is a well-developed and active nonprofit sector—charitable, educational, and religious organizations; associations and other membership organizations; advocacy groups; and similar private agencies.

Of all the countries in the world, the United States has the most highly developed sector of nonprofit organizations. The U.S. national and state governments are often limited by the activities of nonprofit organizations, but that is a prime mark of a free and otherwise democratic society. The federal and state governments acknowledge this fact (sometimes grudgingly) by exempting most nonprofit organizations from taxes and, in some instances, allowing tax-deductible gifts to them. These tax permissions are crucial for the survival of many nonprofit organizations.

When an individual perceives either a personal problem or one involving society, he or she does not always have to turn to a government for the problem's resolution. The individual, acting individually or with a group, can attempt to remedy the problem by turning to a nongovernmental body. There are exceptions to this sweeping statement: Governments provide a wide range of services that individuals acting together are not likely to create. Still, in U.S. culture, more so than in any other, an individual is often likely to use nongovernmental means to remedy, or at least to attack, personal and social problems.

A BIT OF PHILOSOPHY

For most Americans, this mind-set stems from the very essence of our political history: distrust of government. We really do not like government controls; we prefer to act freely, as individuals, to the extent it is realistic and practical to do so. As the great political philosopher Alexis de Tocqueville wrote in 1835, "Americans of all ages, all conditions, and all dispositions constantly form associations" and "[w]henever at the head of some new undertaking you see the government in France, or a man of rank in England, in the United States you will be sure to find an association." About 150 years later, John W. Gardner, founder of Common Cause, observed: "In the realm of good works this nation boasts a unique blending of private and governmental effort. There is almost no area of educational, scientific, charitable, or religious activity in which we have not built an effective network of private institutions."

This "effective network of private institutions"—the nation's nonprofit organizations—is called the *independent sector*, the *voluntary sector*, or the *third sector* of U.S. society. For-profit organizations are the business sector, and the governmental sector is made up of the branches, departments, agencies, and bureaus of the federal, state, and local governments.

Nonprofit organizations, particularly charitable ones, foster pluralization of institutions (described earlier) and encourage voluntarism. Society benefits not only from the application of private wealth to specific public purposes but also from the variety of choices that individual philanthropists, making gifts of all sizes, make available for support. Choice making is decentralized, efficient, and more responsive to public needs than the cumbersome and less flexible government allocation process. As John Stuart Mill once observed, "Government operations tend to be everywhere alike. With individuals and voluntary associations, on the contrary, there are varied experiments, and endless diversity of experience."

Contemporary writing is replete with statements of these fundamental principles. Here are some examples:

. . . the associative impulse is strong in American life; no other civilization can show as many secret fraternal orders, businessmen's "service clubs," trade and occupational associations, social clubs, garden clubs, women's clubs, church clubs, theater groups, political and reform associations, veterans' groups, ethnic societies, and other clusterings of trivial or substantial importance.—Max Lerner

. . . in America, even in modern times, communities existed before governments were here to care for public needs.—Daniel J. Boorstein

. . . voluntary association with others in common causes has been thought to be strikingly characteristic of American life.—Merle Curti

We have been unique because another sector, clearly distinct from the other two [business and government], has, in the past, borne a heavy load of public responsibility.—Richard C. Cornuelle

The third sector is . . . the seedbed for organized efforts to deal with social problems.—John D. Rockefeller

. . . the ultimate contribution of the Third Sector to our national life— namely, what it does to ensure the continuing responsiveness, creativity and self-renewal of our democratic society . . . .—Waldemar A. Neilsen

. . . an array of its [the independent sector's] virtues that is by now fairly familiar: its contributions to pluralism and diversity, its tendency to enable individuals to participate in civic life in ways that make sense to them and help to combat that corrosive feeling of powerlessness that is among the dread social diseases of our era, its encouragement of innovation and its capacity to act as a check on the inadequacies of government.—Richard W. Lyman

The problems of contemporary society are more complex, the solutions more involved and the satisfactions more obscure, but the basic ingredients are still the caring and the resolve to make things better.—Brian O'Connell

AN ILLUSTRATION: A NEW ORGANIZATION

Enough of philosophy. Let's reduce the role of nonprofit organizations to a more practical level. What problems in society trouble you? How you would solve these problems if:

- Sufficient money was available to fund the programs you feel are needed?
- No governmental agency was to become directly involved?

Suppose you decide that something must be done nationwide about littering. You intensely dislike the environment's being cluttered with an assortment of bottles, cans, and other trash, and you resent those who do the littering. You realize that this is not a problem that you can conquer singlehandedly, and you suspect (correctly) that there is not much money in the coffers of your town, county, state, or federal treasuries to be used for more trash control. Yet you suspect (also correctly) that others in your community and around the nation feel the same about accumulating litter as you do.

In the best tradition of problem solving in the United States, you decide to form an organization to "do something." In your opinion, the trash problem can be solved in two basic ways: pickup and disposal, and public education. You envision scores of volunteers who will comb the streets, parks, and other areas of their communities, picking up trash and distributing anti-litter literature. Your hope is that greater sensitivity to the trash problem will inhibit littering and encourage citizens to be more willing to clean up their communities and keep them clean.

Being not one of the rich and famous, you begin thinking about how you will fund this organization and the specific nature of its programs. As your plans take shape, you mention your ideas to a neighbor, who is a labor relations lawyer. She has only a vague idea of what to recommend, but she helps you contact one of her law partners who practices in the field of corporate and tax law.

While you are driving to the first appointment, your car radio delivers a fund-raising message on behalf of a charitable organization that has a catchy name and some memorable slogans. Suddenly, you realize that your organization-to-be must likewise be a charitable one (to be exempt from taxes and to receive deductible gifts) and that it needs a suitable name. By the time you reach the lawyer's office, you know what the name will be: "Campaign to Clean Up America."

The lawyer is a specialist in the field of nonprofit, tax-exempt organizations. He takes down from his bookshelf a 1977 report by a body known then as the Commission on Private Philanthropy and Public Needs, and reads this passage:

> The practice of attending to community needs outside of government has profoundly shaped American society and its institutional framework. . . . This vast and varied array is, and has long been widely recognized as part of the very fabric of American life. It reflects a national belief in the philosophy of pluralism and in the profound importance to society of individual initiative.

Next, he produces a copy of congressional testimony in 1973, when George P. Shultz, then Secretary of the Treasury, said that charitable organizations "are an important influence for diversity and a bulwark against overreliance on big government."

Then, as befits a lawyer, he reaches into the casebooks. A federal court of appeals, in the context of explaining the rationale for tax-exempt status for nonprofit organizations, had this to say:

> [O]ne stated reason for a deduction or exemption of this kind is that the favored entity performs a public service and benefits the public or relieves it of a burden which otherwise belongs to it.

For further backup, the lawyer turns to a U.S. Supreme Court decision:

> The State has an affirmative policy that considers these groups as beneficial and stabilizing influences in community life and finds this classification [tax exemption] useful, desirable, and in the public interest.

He then reads from a federal district court opinion concerning the charitable contribution deduction. The court stated that the reason for the deduction has "historically been that by doing so, the Government relieves itself of the burden of meeting public needs which in the absence of charitable activity would fall on the shoulders of the Government."

By this time, your enthusiasm and vision are nearly boundless. Here you are, thinking and acting in the finest American traditions: approaching and solving a problem, invoking the principles of pluralism and voluntarism, demonstrating your care and "resolve to make things better"—all without government help. You're relieving government of a responsibility that society must assume. You feel that, almost single-handedly, you are ensuring the "continuing responsiveness, creativity and self-renewal of our democratic society."

Twenty minutes later, however, your soaring enthusiasm for ridding the United States of its litter has plummeted into deep confusion. What seemed like such a wonderful concept has been quickly and repeatedly punctured with swirls of advice about state corporate law intricacies, warnings of personal liability, gobbledygook about the law of deductible charitable giving, babble about related and unrelated activities, something about state regulation of fund-raising, talk of a Form 1023 and Form 990, and—here the lawyer has totally lost you—a discourse on the distinctions between private foundations and public charities.

Discouraged, and rapidly abandoning any more thoughts about saving your country from the onslaught of more rubbish, you dejectedly mumble something about paying a fee for the consultation and prepare to leave. Sensing your dejection and despair, the lawyer assures you that, although the startup may be more complex than you thought, you have a good idea and he can help you (for a reasonable fee) through the maze of laws to your goal. Implicitly trusting him, you agree to proceed. In a few short months, you have a successful, nationwide, multimillion-dollar charitable organization to combat the blight of trash in the American environment. In fact, you have quit your job and are now the full-time, paid president of the Campaign to Clean Up America.

AN INITIAL CHECKLIST

Looking back, you review the questions that you and the lawyer resolved:

- What should be the form of the organization? Why? In what jurisdiction should it be formed?
- Who should be its directors and officers? Why? What about their personal liability? Should there be employees? Consultants? Compensation arrangements?
- What will be the organization's programs? Will they be related or unrelated?
- How will the organization achieve its goals at the community level? Will it have chapters? Members? In either case, what will be the criteria?
- How can the organization be exempt from federal and state taxation?
- How will the organization be funded? Gifts? Grants? Income from the performance of exempt functions? Endowment income? Unrelated income?

- Will the organization be "public" or "private"?
- To what extent will gifts to the organization be deductible?
- What reports must be filed with federal and state governmental agencies?
- What are your state's laws on fund-raising requirements?
- Can or should the organization engage in lobbying or political campaign activities?

You're aware that there are subquestions within each of these categories. Tens of other questions have come up since you became president. Some are on your desk now, and you know that many others lie ahead.

CHAPTER TWO

Getting Started

Being enthusiastic, imaginative, and creative about establishing a nonprofit organization is one thing. Actually forming the entity and making it operational is another.

For better or worse, the exercise is much like establishing one's own business. It is a big and important undertaking, and it should be done carefully and properly. The label "nonprofit" does not mean "no planning." Forming a nonprofit organization is as serious as starting up a new company.

Many nonprofit organizations are started on a shoestring; the individuals involved do jobs they would never do if they were starting a commercial enterprise. One of the reasons is a widespread "nonprofit mentality"—a belief that because the undertaking is nonprofit, it need not pay for services rendered. Encumbered with this view, the sponsors of the organization will, in abundant good faith and with the best of intentions seek—or even expect—free assistance. Sometimes, this attitude carries over to the acquisition of equipment and supplies.

In some instances, this nonprofit mentality is wonderful. It enables a skilled manager to parlay a horde of earnest volunteers into a magnificent service-providing organization. However, truly skilled managers are rare, and anyone considering organizing and operating a nonprofit organization is well-advised not to skimp on hiring three consultants: a lawyer, an accountant, and a fund-raiser. The professional services of these individuals are crucial. The old adage, "You get what you pay for," is amply applicable here.

The basic components of forming and operating a particular nonprofit organization may go beyond those listed in this chapter. In keeping with the scope of this book, the considerations that *must* be confronted are described.

LOCATION AND LEGAL FORM

What form should a prospective nonprofit organization take? A lawyer may say, "It must be a separate legal entity." What does that mean?

Any nonprofit organization legally must be one of three types: a corporation, a trust, or an "other" (usually an unincorporated association). (Occasionally, a nonprofit organization is created by a legislature.) A common element in each is that there should be a creating document (articles of organization) and a document containing operational rules (bylaws).

Keep in mind that before an organization can be tax-exempt, it must be a nonprofit organization. Nonprofit organizations are basically creatures of state law; tax-exempt organizations are basically subjects of federal tax law.

Location

The starting point for organizing a nonprofit organization is the law of the state. But which state? Although it can operate in more than one jurisdiction, an organization can be created or formed under the law of only one jurisdiction (at a time).

In most instances, selecting the jurisdiction where the organization is to be created is easy: It will be the jurisdiction in which the organization will be headquartered. For example, if you (the founder of the Campaign to Clean Up America) live and work in the state of Michigan, chances are that you will form the CCUA under Michigan law. Some people feel that a national organization should be formed under the law of a jurisdiction such as New York, the District of Columbia, or Delaware (the for-profit corporate mecca). However, no matter what state the organization is created in, it will still have to meet the requirements of any jurisdiction in which it operates. If you plan to operate the CCUA in Michigan, you can incorporate it in, for example, the District of Columbia, but you will also have to qualify the organization to "do business" in Michigan.

Because the process of qualifying an organization to do business in a state is about the same as incorporating it, there usually is no point in forcing the organization to comply with the laws of two different states. There are exceptions to this rule: a stock-based nonprofit organization may be appropriate, or perhaps only one director is desired. If an organization is formed in one state but has offices in one or more other states, this duplication of effort is unavoidable. Thus, if the CCUA is formed in Michigan and has offices in other states, it must be registered to function in each of the other states.

A caution: If a nonprofit organization is formed in one jurisdiction and the plan is to qualify it in another, be certain that the organization will meet the requirements of the law of the state of qualification. For example, not all states allow a nonprofit organization formed as a corporation with stock to qualify.

Legal Form

Once the headquarters jurisdiction of the nonprofit organization is selected, or the place of formation is otherwise determined, the legal form of the organization must be considered. This is basically a matter of state law, and the laws of the state in which the headquarters is based will govern this decision.

Assuming that the nonprofit organization is expected to qualify as a tax-exempt organization under both federal and state law, it is essential to see whether a particular form of organization is dictated by federal tax law. In most cases, federal law is neutral on the point. However, in a few instances, a specific form of organization is required to qualify as a tax-exempt organization. For example, a federal government instrumentality and a title-holding organization must, under federal tax law, be formed as corporations, while entities such as supplemental unemployment benefit organizations, Black Lung benefit organizations, and multiemployer plan funds must be formed as trusts. A multibeneficiary title-holding organization can be formed as either a corporation or a trust. On occasion, a federal law other than the tax law will have a direct bearing on the form of a tax-exempt organization. For example, under the federal political campaign regulation laws, corporations cannot make political campaign contributions. A political committee must avoid the corporate form.

These are relatively technical types of nonprofit organizations; the vast majority need not be created by a mandated form. Thus, in the absence of a federal (or state) law requiring a particular form for the organization, the choice made by those who are establishing the entity is acceptable.

There are several factors to take into account in selecting the form of a nonprofit organization. Given the reality of our litigious society, personal liability looms as a major element in the decision. Personal liability means that one or more managers of a nonprofit organization (its trustees, directors, officers, and/or key employees) may be found *personally* liable for something done or not done while acting on behalf of the organization.

The Four "I"s. Some of this exposure can be limited by one or all of the following: indemnification, insurance, immunity, and incorporation.

Indemnification occurs (assuming indemnification is legal under state law) when the organization agrees (usually by provision in its bylaws) to pay the judgments and related expenses (including legal fees) incurred by those who are covered by the indemnity, when those expenses are the result of a misdeed (commission or omission) by those persons while acting in the service of the organization. The indemnification cannot extend to criminal acts and may not cover certain willful acts that violate civil law. Because an indemnification involves the resources of the organization, the real value of an indemnification depends on the economic viability of the organization. In times of financial difficulties for a nonprofit organization, an indemnification of its directors and officers can be a classic "hollow promise."

Insurance is similar to indemnification. However, instead of shifting the risk of liability from the individuals involved to the nonprofit organization, the risk of liability is shifted to an independent third party—an insurance company. Certain risks, such as criminal law liability, cannot be shifted via insurance. The insurance contract will likely exclude from coverage certain forms of civil law liability, such as libel and slander, employee discrimination, and antitrust matters. Even where adequate coverage is available, insurance can be costly; premiums can easily be thousands of dollars annually, even with a sizable deductible.

Immunity is available when the law provides that a class of individuals, under certain circumstances, is not liable for a particular act or set of acts or for failure to undertake a particular act or set of acts. Several states have enacted immunity laws for officers and directors of nonprofit organizations, protecting them in case of asserted civil law violations, particularly where these individuals are functioning as volunteers.

Incorporation, an additional form of protection against personal liability, may be desired. A corporation is regarded as a separate legal entity. Liability is generally confined to the organization and does not normally extend to those who manage it. For this reason alone, a nonprofit organization should probably be incorporated.

Incorporation has another advantage. The law may provide answers to many of the questions that inevitably arise when forming and operating a nonprofit organization. Here are some examples:

- How many directors must the organization have? What are their voting rights? How is a quorum ascertained? How is notice properly given? What is the length and number of their terms of office?

- What officers must the organization have? What are their duties? What is the length and number of their terms of office? Can more than one office be held by the same individual?

- How frequently must the governing board meet? Must they always meet in person, or can the meetings be by telephone conference call or video teleconferencing? Can the board members vote by mail or unanimous consent? Can they use proxies?

- If there are members, what are their rights? When must they meet? What notice of the meetings must be given? How can they vote?

- What issues must be decided by members (if any)? Directors?

- May there be an executive committee of the governing board? If so, what are its duties? What limitations are there on its functions?

- What about other committees, including an advisory committee? Which are standing committees?

- How are the organization's governing instruments amended?

- How must a merger of the organization with another occur?

- What is the process for dissolving the organization? For distributing its assets and net income upon dissolution?

Nearly every state has a nonprofit corporation act. The answers to these and many other questions may be found in that law. If the organization is not a corporation, these and other questions are usually unanswered under state law. The organization must then add to its rules the answers to all the pertinent questions (assuming they can be anticipated) or live with the uncertainties.

There is a third reason for the corporate form: More people will know what the entity is. People are familiar with corporations. The IRS knows corporations. Private foundations understand corporations as potential grantees. In general, the world in which the nonprofit organization will be functioning is comfortable with the concept of a corporation.

In contrast to the three advantages of incorporation—limitation against personal liability, availability of information concerning operations, and the comfort factor—what are the disadvantages of incorporation? Generally, the advantages far outweigh the disadvantages. The disadvantages stem from the fact that incorporation entails an affirmative act of the state government: It "charters" the entity. In exchange for the grant of corporate status, the state usually expects certain forms of compliance by the organization, such as adherence to rules of operation, an initial filing fee, annual reports, and annual fees. However, these costs are frequently nominal and the reporting requirements are usually not extensive.

A nonprofit organization that is a corporation is formed by preparing and filing articles of incorporation, with its operating rules embodied in bylaws. The contents of the articles of incorporation, established by state law, will usually include:

- The name of the organization
- A general statement of its purposes
- The name(s) and address(es) of its initial director(s)
- The name and address of its registered agent
- The name(s) and address(es) of its incorporator(s)
- Language referencing the applicable federal tax law requirements

The bylaws of an incorporated nonprofit organization will usually include provisions with respect to:

- Its purposes (it is a good idea to restate them in the bylaws)
- The election and duties of its directors
- The election and duties of its officers
- The role of its members (if any)
- Meetings of members and directors, including dates, notice, quorum, and voting
- The role of executive and other committees
- The role of its chapters (if any)
- The function of affiliated organizations (if any)
- The organization's fiscal year

Some organizations adopt operational rules and policies stated in a document that is neither articles of incorporation nor bylaws. These rules may be more freely amended than articles or bylaws. They may not, however, be inconsistent with the articles or bylaws.

The Trust. A nonprofit organization may be formed as a trust. This is rarely an appropriate form for a nonprofit organization other than a charitable entity or some of the funds associated with employee plans. Many private foundations, for example, are trusts (those created by a will are known as testamentary trusts).

However, most nonprofit organizations, particularly those that will have a membership, are ill-suited to be structured as trusts.

The principal problem with structuring a nonprofit organization as a trust is that most state laws concerning trusts are written for the regulation of charitable trusts. These rules are rarely as flexible as contemporary nonprofit corporation acts, and frequently impose fiduciary standards and practices that are more stringent than those for nonprofit corporations.

A nonprofit corporation that is to be a trust is formed by the execution of a trust agreement or a declaration of trust. Frequently, only one trustee is necessary—another reflection of the usual narrow use of trusts.

The trustees of a trust *do not* have the protection against personal liability that is afforded by the corporate form.

Although a fee to the state is rarely imposed upon the creation of a trust, most states impose on trusts an annual filing requirement for the trust agreement or declaration of trust.

It is unusual—although certainly permissible—for the trustee(s) of a trust to also adopt a set of bylaws.

The Unincorporated Association.   The final type of nonprofit organization, labeled "other," is the *unincorporated association*.

To the uninitiated, a nonprofit corporation and a nonprofit unincorporated organization might look alike. For example, a membership association has the same characteristics, whether or not incorporated. However, the shield against individual liability provided by the corporate form is unavailable in an unincorporated association.

An unincorporated association is formed by the preparation and adoption of a constitution. The contents of a constitution are much the same as the contents of articles of incorporation, and the contents of bylaws of an unincorporated association are usually the same as those of a nonprofit corporation.

The directors of an unincorporated association *do not* have the protection against personal liability that is afforded by the corporate form.

It is relatively uncommon for an unincorporated association to have to register with and annually report to a state (other than for fundraising regulation purposes; see Chapter 9).

Occasionally, nonprofit organizations will have articles of incorporation, a constitution, and bylaws. This is technically improper. For an incorporated nonprofit organization, the constitution is a redundancy.

Trusts and unincorporated associations are likely to have less contact with the state than nonprofit corporations, but this advantage is usually overshadowed by more substantive disadvantages.

In some states (such as California and New York), the nonprofit corporation and trust law is far more refined than in others. Careful examination of these and other relevant laws is essential when an organization is to be formed in, or operate in, one or more of these states. In addition, some states have far more stringent laws concerning mergers and dissolutions.

In summary, as a general rule, a nonprofit organization has clear advantages if it is organized as a corporation. Nonetheless, the facts and circumstances of each situation must be carefully examined to be certain that the most appropriate form is selected.

CHECKLIST

☐ Form of organization:
   ☐ Corporation
   ☐ Unincorporated association
   ☐ Trust
   ☐ Other
☐ Type of articles of organization:
   ☐ Articles of incorporation
   ☐ Constitution
   ☐ Declaration of trust
   ☐ Trust agreement
   ☐ Other
☐ Date organization formed _____
☐ Place organization formed _____
☐ States in which qualified to do business _____
☐ Date(s) of amendment of articles _____
☐ Date operational rules (e.g., bylaws) adopted _____
☐ Date(s) of amendment of rules _____
☐ Membership: Yes _____ No _____
☐ If yes:
   Annual meeting date _____
   Notice requirement _____
☐ Chapters: Yes _____ No _____
☐ Affiliated organizations _____
☐ Committees:
   ☐ Executive
   ☐ Nominating
   ☐ Development
   ☐ Finance

☐ Long-Range Planning
☐ Other(s)
☐ Fiscal year _____

FOCUS: Campaign to Clean Up America

After consideration of all of the relevant factors, the decision is made (in conformance with the lawyer's advice) to form the Campaign to Clean Up America (CCUA) as a nonprofit corporation. The aspect of limited personal liability is of particular interest and you can see few disadvantages to incorporation of the entity. (Regarding personal liability, the lawyer advises the use of an indemnification provision and points out that in some instances, under Michigan law, directors and officers of nonprofit organizations are immunized from personal liability.) You instruct the lawyer to prepare the articles of incorporation for the CCUA and to incorporate it in your home state of Michigan.

BOARD OF DIRECTORS

Every nonprofit organization—irrespective of form—must have at least one director (or trustee). However, few nonprofit organizations have just one "manager." (In tax-law language, directors, officers, and key employees are managers.)

The directors are those who generally administer the organization. The word "generally" is used here because day-to-day management is supposed to be the province of the employees and, sometimes, the officers. The directors are the policymakers of the organization—they develop plans for the organization and oversee its affairs. In reality, it is very difficult to set a precise line of demarcation where the scope of authority of the board of directors stops and the authority of the officers begins. The authority of directors and officers in relation to the authority of employees is equally hard to separate. All too frequently, authority or "territory" is resolved on an occasion-by-occasion basis—in the political arena, not the legal one—by the sheer force of personalities.

Many state nonprofit corporation laws require at least three directors; however, many nonprofit organizations have far larger governing boards. State laws never set a maximum number of nonprofit organization directors. The optimum size of a governing board of a nonprofit organization depends on many factors. We will not enumerate them all here.

One factor that affects the size of a nonprofit organization's governing board is the manner in which its membership is elected. If there are bona fide members of the nonprofit organization, it is likely that these members will elect some or all of the members of the governing board. This election may be done by mail ballot or by voting at an annual meeting. In some instances, the board may include some ex officio positions (such as one or more of the officers, one or more past-presidents, or individuals who hold positions in a separate but related organization). It is quite possible, however, for a nonprofit organization with a membership to have a governing board that is not elected by that membership.

In the absence of a membership (or if the membership has no vote on the matter), the governing board of a nonprofit organization may be called a "self-perpetuating board." In this case, the initial board may continue with those whom it elects and with subsequent boards. Again, there may be one or more ex officio positions.

In many nonprofit organizations, the source of the membership of the governing board is preordained. Some examples include the typical membership organization that elects the board (for example, a trade association, a country club, or a veterans' organization); a hospital, college, or museum that has a governing board generally reflective of the community; and a private foundation that has one or more trustees who represent a particular family or a corporation.

Politics is a dominant factor in board elections. Some membership organizations, for example, may appear to have an "open" election system, yet the process is controlled by a small group that functions as the nominating committee. Some advocacy groups may feature a membership that is not a true membership at all and a governing board that is tightly controlled by a small group of insiders.

The combinations of ways to generate members of a governing board are numerous. One fundamental principle to keep in mind is that no one "owns" a nonprofit organization. Control of a nonprofit organization, however, is another matter. A membership may control a nonprofit organization without owning it; more frequently, the board of directors controls a nonprofit organization, regardless of the presence of a membership.

The selection of directors and the control of a nonprofit organization are of particular consequence in a single-purpose organization that is started by one individual or a close-knit group. The people who launch a nonprofit organization do not want to put their blood, sweat, tears, and dollars into the organization, only to watch others assume control over it. Yet these founders usually want a "representative" governing board, which, if created, would clearly put them in a minority, without control.

One solution to this problem may be an advisory committee—a group of individuals who do not substitute for the board of directors but provide technical input on the organization's programs. Because the members of an advisory committee lack voting rights, their number is governed only by what is practical. Committee members serve without the threat of personal liability that may accrue to directors and officers and without incurring the larger set of responsibilities held by the directors. By having an advisory committee, an organization can surround itself with prominent names in the field. The roster can lead to some impressive stationery!

The board of directors may decide to have a chair (or chairperson or chairman) of the board. This individual presides over board meetings. The chair position is not usually an officer position (although it can be made one). The position may (but need not) be authorized in the organization's bylaws.

A board of directors (or trustees) of a nonprofit organization usually acts by means of in-person meetings (a quorum must be present). Where state law allows, the members of the board can act at a meeting held via a conference telephone call (where all participants can hear each other) or by unanimous written consent. These alternative procedures must also be authorized in the bylaws. Unless there is a specific authorization in the law, directors of a nonprofit organization may not vote by proxy, mail ballot, or telephone calls (other than a conference call). (These limitations do not normally apply to voting by members, which is why some nonprofit organizations have a membership composed solely of the board of directors.)

CHECKLIST

☐ Board of directors (trustees):

Origin _____

Number _____

Quorum _____

Voting power _____

Terms of office _____

Annual meeting date _____

Notice requirement _____

☐ Chair of board: Yes _____ No _____

How should the Campaign to Clean Up America organize its governing board? Assume that you wish to retain control and that the state law under which the CCUA is formed requires at least three directors (recall that the CCUA was formed as a nonprofit corporation). You are one of the three. The other two spots may be filled by your spouse, best friend, lawyer, accountant, or someone else whom you trust. Thus, as a matter of fact (but not necessarily of law), you presumably are in control of the CCUA.

This approach has some deficiencies. Because loyalties can shift, you can never be certain that you are in fact always in control. Your ability to advance the cause may be hindered in the absence of a "public" board. Or, the Internal Revenue Service (IRS) may allege the presence of private benefit or private inurement if the governing board is too small and incestuous.

Here are some options:

- Form the CCUA in a state that requires only one director, then become qualified to function in the state from which it will operate.

- Form the CCUA in a state that allows nonprofit corporations to issue stock. You become the sole stockholder, the bylaws are written so that the directors of the CCUA are selected by the shareholder, and the CCUA then becomes qualified to function in the state from which it will operate.

- Create an intimate, small (for example, three-person) board, to be accompanied by a separate advisory committee composed of "outsiders"; the advisory committee has no binding vote as to corporate policy.

- Elect the governing board of the CCUA by a membership vote or by some other means that is representative of those interested in the cause, and trust your political skills to enable you to retain operational control.

After due consideration, you doubt your political skills and you incorporate the CCUA in the state where you live (Michigan). You name as the three initial board members yourself, your spouse, and a close personal friend. (You invited your lawyer to be on the board but he declined on the grounds of potential personal liability and a conflict of interest.) The bylaws of the CCUA are written to provide for a self-perpetuating board and to create an advisory committee that is generally representative of the antitrash cause. You resolve that you will, someday, make the governing board of the CCUA more representative of its constituency.

In the meantime, you are not interested in a membership with full voting rights. You begin thinking about how a nonvoting membership would enable you to build a network of individuals who could serve the CCUA as volunteers at the local level. These individuals could become the heart of a very important group: the CCUA's regular donors.

OFFICERS

Nearly every nonprofit organization has officers. The classic exception is the trust, which usually has only one or more trustees (and no officers).

As with the board of directors, levels of authority of officers are difficult to articulate. In a nonprofit organization that has members, directors, officers, and employees, setting a "clear" distinction as to who has the authority to do what is nearly impossible. General principles can be stated but will usually prove useless in practice. For example, it can be stated that the members set basic policy and the board of directors sets additional policy, but within the policy parameters established by the membership. The officers then implement policy; the employees also implement policy albeit more on a day-to-day basis. Yet the reality is that, at all four levels, policy is established. Worse, at all four levels, policy is implemented.

In a typical nonprofit organization, for example, who decides: what new programs will be undertaken, who is hired and fired as employees, the nature of the retirement plan arrangements, who the lawyers and accountants will be, the type of fund-raising program, the format of the journal, or the organization's physical location? Depending on the circumstances, the answer may be: the members, the board, the chair of the board, the president, the vice-president, the executive director, or any number of others!

For the most part, the answers to these questions relate to politics and personalities. A nonprofit corporation statute may spell out the duties of directors and officers, but these are broad ranges of responsibilities. Who is to stop a board majority that wants a green tint to an organization's newsletter rather than a blue one? Or the board majority that wants the organization to use the services of a particular bank, lawyer, or pension plan administrator? Yet, in many a nonprofit organization, the directors and officers are mere putty in the hands of the executive director. Too many nonprofit organizations have volunteer members of the board of directors, each of whom believes it is his or her duty to delve deeply into the day-to-day management of the organization.

One cannot generalize on the origins of officers, except to say that they are usually elected, whether by the membership and/or by the board of directors. Some may be appointed by other officers who are elected.

The common patterns are:

- A membership elects the directors and the officers.
- A membership elects the directors and the directors elect the officers.
- A self-perpetuating board elects the officers.
- In any of the foregoing combinations, some of the officers may be appointed.

The governing instruments of the organization (usually the bylaws) should identify the offices of the organization, state the duties and responsibilities of the officers, provide for the manner of their selection, state the terms of the offices, address the matter of reelections to office, and so forth. Some organizations find it useful to stagger the terms of office so that only a portion of the board is up for election at any one time, thereby providing some continuity of service and expertise. In some states, the nonprofit corporations law imposes some requirements for officers, terms of office, and the like.

For example, in a typical pattern, a membership elects a board of directors. The directors elect a president, secretary, and treasurer. The president appoints an assistant treasurer, an assistant secretary, and an executive director. A variation is to have the members directly elect the officers. Another common pattern is for an organization to have a self-perpetuating board of directors that elects the officers. For the most part, the law allows a nonprofit organization to use whatever governing structure it wants.

Normally, a chair of the board is not a corporate officer. He or she is selected by the board of directors as its leader. In many nonprofit organizations, the chair of the board and the president are the same individual. In others, the chair of the board assumes the responsibilities normally expected of a president. Sometimes, the person normally termed an executive director is labeled the president. Here, too, the possibilities are numerous. How can the roles of a chair of the board and a president be differentiated? What is the difference between an executive director and an executive vice-president?

Can a strong, aggressive chair dominate the board of directors, the officers, and the staff? Can a strong, aggressive executive director dominate the other staff members, the officers, and the board of directors? The answer to both questions is yes.

Particularly if the organization is a corporation, state law usually will require at least certain officers. In general, the same individual can hold more than one office; the positions of secretary and treasurer are commonly combined. However, the president and the secretary should not be the same person. This duality is prohibited in many states. Frequently, legal documents will require these two officers' separate signatures.

Officers are officers of the organization. They are not officers of the board of directors or board of trustees.

CHECKLIST

☐ Officers:

Origin _____

Titles:

   ☐ President

   ☐ Other title for President

   ☐ Vice President(s)

   ☐ Treasurer

   ☐ Secretary

☐ Other(s)

Terms of office _____

FOCUS: Campaign to Clean Up America

The Campaign to Clean Up America decided to have its board of directors elect the officers. The officers must be members of the board. You are elected the president and your spouse is elected the secretary-treasurer. Given the size of the organization at this time, there is no need to have a chair of the board or a vice president.

ORGANIZATIONAL MINUTES

Another document—in addition to the articles of organization and the bylaws—that is important when forming a nonprofit organization is the organizational minutes. If there is a membership, there must be organizational minutes of that body. The same is true with respect to the board of directors. If there is no membership, the only organizational document will be that of the board of directors.

In this document (or documents), the following actions, at a minimum, will be reflected: ratification of the adoption of the articles of organization; adoption of the bylaws; election of the officers; passage of the requisite resolution(s) for the establishment of a bank account (or accounts); passage of resolutions selecting legal counsel, an accountant, and perhaps a fund-raising consultant; and authorization of reimbursement of expenses incurred in establishing the entity. (The bank that is selected will provide the form of the resolution(s) that it wishes passed.) Organizational minutes may reflect other actions, such as a discussion of program activities and/or development of the fund-raising program.

All minutes of meetings concerning a nonprofit organization are important, but the organizational minutes have particular significance. Minutes need not be filed with the IRS when pursuing recognition of tax-exempt status (see Chapter 6) but are important documents in other settings, such as an audit.

Minutes should be kept in a minute book, along with other important documents (including the articles of organization and bylaws). Minute books can be purchased commercially. A simple ring binder will suffice, but the formality of a true minute book seems to get an organization's record keeping off to a good start. To be useful, a minute book needs to be maintained, although there is nothing inherent in a good minute book that will cause an organization's operations to be successful.

IDENTIFICATION NUMBER

Every nonprofit organization must have an "employer identification number." This number is assigned by the IRS and is acquired by filing a properly completed Form SS-4. This form may be filed as soon as the entity is formed or with the application for recognition of tax-exempt status. (The bank will want the number as part of the process of opening the organization's account.)

There is much confusion about the employer identification number, also known as the "taxpayer identification number." Part of the confusion comes from its names. The number is required even though the organization does not have any employees and is not a "taxpayer."

As discussed in Chapter 3, a "tax-exempt number" is a myth. A tax-exempt organization must have an IRS-assigned identification number, but the number has nothing to do with tax-exempt status. An identification number is required of every entity, whether it is a corporation, a trust, a partnership, an estate, or some other type of venture.

CHAPTER THREE

Debunking Some Myths and Misperceptions

Those who manage and consult with nonprofit organizations all too frequently misunderstand the nature of the entities they are working with and the law that applies to them. This chapter is offered with the hope that it will, at least for the readers, put an end to these myths and misunderstandings.

MYTH 1

Nonprofit and Not-for-Profit Are the Same

Nonprofit is the proper term. Many laws and lawyers (and others) use the term *not-for-profit* when they mean nonprofit. This is understandable, because of the confusion surrounding what the term "nonprofit" means (see myth 2). The term not-for-profit is properly used to refer to an activity that is engaged in without a profit motive (that is, a hobby), where the expenses involved do not qualify for the business expense deduction.

MYTH 2

Nonprofit Organizations Cannot Earn a Profit

Nothing could be further from the truth. A nonprofit organization can enjoy a profit (more income than expenses); no organization can operate in the red for very long. The difference between nonprofit and for-profit organizations is what is done with the profit. Nonprofit organizations use profits to advance their programs. For-profit organizations distribute their profits to their owners; in a corporation, dividends are paid to stockholders. (See Chapter 5.)

MYTH 3

An Organization Must Be Incorporated to Be Tax-Exempt

In general, this is not the law. As discussed in Chapter 2, a tax-exempt organization may be one of three forms. Incorporation may be (and usually is) desirable, but generally it is not mandatory. However, the federal tax law mandates that certain tax-exempt organizations be incorporated, such as instrumentalities of the United States and single-parent title-holding organizations.

MYTH 4

Every Nonprofit Organization Qualifies as a Tax-Exempt Organization

This is not the case. Nearly every tax-exempt organization is a nonprofit organization, but not all nonprofit organizations are eligible to be tax-exempt. The concept of a nonprofit organization is broader than that of a tax-exempt organization. (See Chapter 5.) Some types of nonprofit organizations (such as mutual, self-help type entities) do not, as a matter of federal law, qualify for tax-exempt status.

MYTH 5

Being Tax-Exempt Means That the Organization Does Not Have to Pay Any Taxes

As Chapters 11 to 14 indicate, this is certainly not the case—and those chapters relate only to federal income and excise taxes. Even with complete exemption from federal taxation, an organization may still have exposure to state and/or local income, sales, use, and/or property taxation.

Moreover, several civil law penalties (not really taxes, but payments to a government nonetheless) are applicable to nonprofit organizations.

MYTH 6

All Tax-Exempt Organizations Are Eligible to Receive Contributions That Are Deductible for Federal Income Tax Purposes

Not true. Just as nonprofit organizations are a larger universe than tax-exempt organizations, tax-exempt organizations are a larger universe than charitable organizations.

MYTH 7

A Tax-Exempt Organization Must Have a Ruling from the IRS Stating That It Is Tax-Exempt

For the most part, this *is not* the law. First, the IRS does not grant tax-exempt status—Congress does that; the IRS grants recognition of tax-exempt status. (See Chapter 6.) Second, this grant of recognition from the IRS is generally made by means of a *determination letter*, which technically is not a ruling. Third, only four types of tax-exempt organizations are required to have a determination letter: charitable organizations, voluntary employees' beneficiary associations, supplemental unemployment benefit trusts, and prepaid legal service organizations. For other tax-exempt organizations, the pursuit of recognition of tax-exempt status is optional. This is not to say that a tax-exempt organization should not seek a determination letter if it does not have to (since in many cases that is advisable); the point simply is that, generally, a determination letter is not mandatory.

MYTH 8

There Is Something Called a "Tax-Exempt Number"

This is not true. As discussed in Chapter 2, every nonprofit organization (tax-exempt or not) must have an IRS-assigned identification number, but that number has nothing to do with tax-exempt status.

MYTH 9

Only Charitable Organizations Are Eligible to Receive Contributions That Are Deductible for Federal Income Tax Purposes

Not true. Congress has provided charitable donee status for organizations in addition to those that are normally regarded as charitable organizations. Besides organizations that are charitable, educational, religious, scientific, and the like, deductible charitable gifts may be made to governmental bodies, veterans' organizations, fraternal organizations, and cemetery companies. (See Chapter 8.)

MYTH 10

A Charitable Organization Cannot Engage in Legislative Activities

False. A charity is permitted to engage in far more lobbying efforts than most people realize. Indeed, under some circumstances, a charitable organization can spend more than one-fifth of its funds for legislative ends. (See Chapter 13.)

MYTH 11

A Charitable Organization Cannot Engage in Political Activities

Again, not true. A charity cannot engage in political campaign activities without loss of its tax-exempt status (and eligibility to receive deductible contributions), but it can engage in certain types of political activities. This practice may trigger a tax—but not loss of exemption. Also, a charity can use a political action committee to engage in political activities that are not political campaign activities. (See Chapter 14.)

MYTH 12

Only the States Regulate the Process of Fund-Raising by Charitable Organizations

This is not true. There is no federal charitable solicitations act (at least not yet), but the federal authorities have figured out a variety of ways to regulate charitable fund-raising (see Chapter 9), mostly through the federal tax system.

MYTH 13

State Regulation of Fund-Raising for Charitable Purposes Has Declined

Wrong. This is a boom area of the law. States that previously lacked fund-raising regulation statutes now enact them, and states that have them are finding ways to make them tougher. (See Chapter 9.)

MYTH 14

Nonprofit Organizations Have Fewer Reporting Obligations Than For-Profit Organizations

Of all the myths, this one might seem—on its face—to make the most sense. However, it is certainly wrong. Despite the favoritisms the law frequently bestows on nonprofit organizations, the reporting requirements are not one of them, particularly when the organization is tax-exempt. The annual information return that most tax-exempt organizations have to file with the IRS (see Chapter 7) is far more extensive than the tax returns most commercial businesses must file. Then, there may be several state annual reports (if the organization is doing business in more than one state) and the state annual charitable solicitation act reports (perhaps over 40 of them). (See Chapter 9.)

MYTH 15

A Nonprofit Organization Must Be Represented by a Professional (Lawyer or Accountant) to Secure Recognition of Tax-Exempt Status from the IRS

Although the professionals may wish it otherwise, there is no requirement that a professional be involved in this process. A nonprofit organization may secure recognition of tax-exempt status on its own. However, in complex circumstances (and circumstances may be more complex than most people may realize), a nonprofit organization usually will be far better off using the services of a competent professional who charges a reasonable fee to see the task done correctly. (The lawyer or other professional involved should be asked, in advance, for an estimate of total fees and expenses.) If mistakes are made, it is more costly to undo them and otherwise rectify the situation than it is to pay a fair fee to do the tax exemption properly from the beginning.

MYTH 16

All Lawyers and Accountants Are Competent to Represent a Nonprofit Organization

As society becomes more complex and as fields of practice become correspondingly more specialized, this statement is becoming more and more a myth. A lawyer, for example, may be an excellent practitioner in the field of labor law, securities law, patent law, admiralty law, or domestic relations law, but that does not mean that he or she is competent to represent a nonprofit organization. Even a corporate or tax lawyer may not have the requisite expertise. Just as you would not go to a brain surgeon for a coronary bypass operation, you should not go to a divorce lawyer when you need help with a nonprofit or tax-exempt organization.

MYTH 17

It Is Easy to Find a Lawyer or Accountant Who Is Competent to Represent Nonprofit, Tax-Exempt Organizations

Related to myth 16, this myth is too frequently untrue. There is no convenient master list of these specialists. Some lawyers and accountants who do not practice in this field are not shy about referring nonprofit organizations to practitioners who specialize in this area of the law. Other professionals, however, are not that self-confident: they are unwilling to lose a client or prospective client to someone else, even if it is in the best interest of the organization. To contact a lawyer or accountant serving nonprofit organizations on a regular basis, you must talk to those involved with other nonprofit organizations and learn whom they rely on for legal and accounting services. Most lawyers and accountants who are good at what they do will tell you that referrals are their best source of new business.

MYTH 18

All Fund-Raisers Are Equal in Competence

This untruth rivals and magnifies myths 16 and 17. Not only are there good and bad, ethical and unethical fund-raisers, there are good ones with important subspecialties. Fund-raising consultants can be excellent when it comes to direct mail, special events, capital campaigns, fee-for-service projects, or planned giving, but rarely will one consultant have any true expertise in more than one or two of these areas. Your direct mail consultant probably knows nothing about planned giving. Look for a fund-raiser with expertise in working with comparable types of organizations, such as colleges, hospitals, symphonies, or professional societies. A "fund-raiser" may in reality be a "solicitor," and you'll be faced with other types of problems.

MYTH 19

The IRS Is Always Right

Usually, the IRS is right, at least in the tax-exempt organizations context. Once in a while, nonetheless, the IRS will err. As an example, the IRS has been known to take an erroneous position on an issue at the district office level, only to be overruled by its National Office in Washington, DC. Generally, the quality of IRS personnel is good; it is exceptionally high at the National Office. The point is that, although the IRS is usually correct, an answer received from the IRS in response to a particular inquiry may be less than fully accurate. With few exceptions, IRS personnel do not provide tax planning services.

MYTH 20

There Is No Humor in the Federal Tax Law Bearing on Tax-Exempt Organizations

Actually, this myth comes closer to the truth than any of the others. However, there are exceptions.

The federal tax law definition of the term *agricultural* includes the art or science of "harvesting . . . aquatic resources." The comparable definition under the postal laws includes the art or science of "harvesting . . . marine resources." It is not clear why this distinction is made, but, because the word "aquatic" means "pertaining to water" and the word "marine" means "pertaining to the sea," an organization engaged in or associated with the harvesting of fresh waters can acquire classification as an "agricultural" organization for federal tax purposes but will fail to do so under postal law, which emphasizes salt waters.

Maybe this one will spark more mirth. A variety of types of organizations are exempt from the unrelated income rules. One of them is a category of radio station operated by a nonprofit organization that satisfies certain criteria. The three basic tests that must be met under these rules are worded so that only one radio station qualifies. The criteria are phrased in such a way that the first letter of each of the three tests identifies a call letter of the beneficiary radio station (WWL, operated by Loyola University in New Orleans, Louisiana).

MYTH 21

Only Technical Personnel (Like Lawyers and Accountants) Need to Know the Information in This Book

This may be the greatest misperception of all. Too many professionals serving nonprofit organizations are functioning without this necessary information. This book is designed to provide the basics of the law of the various subjects covered, in the belief that *everyone* seriously serving one or more nonprofit organizations—particularly directors and officers, but also fund-raisers, managers, employees, and consultants—must understand the points of law surveyed.

Indeed, if a lawyer or accountant is using this book to gain information, the nonprofit organization–client could be on the brink of serious trouble. The technical person hired by the nonprofit organization should be researching and studying some of this author's other books. (The list of publications found at the front of the book includes several titles that have annual updates.) This book surveys the basics of nonprofit law for everyone else.

PART TWO

Being Nonprofit . . . Legally

CHAPTER FOUR

Nonprofit Organizations: Much More Than Charity

T rue or false?

- The concept of the nonprofit organization and the tax-exempt organization is the same.
- Nonprofit/tax-exempt organizations mean charitable organizations.

Neither statement is true. As explained in the next chapter, the idea of a nonprofit organization is much broader than that of a tax-exempt organization. This chapter summarizes the different types of tax-exempt organizations. The charitable entity is the best known type of exempt organization, but there are many other types.

Because they are so popular, charitable organizations will be discussed first. The federal tax law uses the term *charitable* in two ways. The broader definition means all organizations that are eligible to receive deductible contributions. Used this way, charitable includes entities that are religious, educational, scientific, and the like, as well as certain fraternal, cemetery, and veterans' organizations. To get technical for just a moment, most of these organizations (not the fraternal, cemetery, and veterans' groups) are "501(c)(3) organizations"—they are governed by Section 501(c)(3), probably the most widely recognized provision of the Internal Revenue Code.

In the narrower definition, the term charitable organization is restricted to organizations that match the descriptions of that type of entity under the law.

CHARITABLE ORGANIZATIONS

The federal tax law definition of a charitable organization contains at least 15 different ways for a nonprofit entity to be charitable. These characteristics, found in the income tax regulations, IRS rulings, and federal and state court opinions, include: relieving the poor and distressed or the underprivileged; advancing religion, education, or science; lessening the burdens of government; beautifying and maintaining a community; preserving natural beauty; promoting health, social welfare, environmental conservancy, arts, or patriotism; caring for orphans or animals; promoting, advancing, and sponsoring amateur sports; and maintaining public confidence in the legal system. Those most widely claimed are discussed here.

The *relief of poverty* is perhaps the most basic and historically founded form of charitable activity. Originally, it meant largely the distribution of money or goods to the poor. In contemporary times, particularly as government has assumed some of this function, it means more the provision of services. This type of charitable entity might feed the homeless and/or provide them shelter, operate a counseling center, provide vocational training, supply employment assistance, provide low-income housing, or offer transportation services.

The *advancement of religion,* as a charitable entity, frequently pertains to collateral activities of churches. For example, charitable organizations of this nature may maintain church buildings, monuments, or cemeteries; distribute religious literature; or supplement salaries. These organizations may conduct programs unique to a particular religion, operate a retreat center, or maintain a religious radio or television station.

The *advancement of education,* as a charitable activity, includes providing student assistance, advancing knowledge through research, or disseminating knowledge by means of publications, seminars, lectures, and the like. This type of charitable function may be a satellite activity of a particular educational institution, such as a university, library, or museum.

The *advancement of science,* as a charitable activity, includes activities devoted to the furtherance or promotion of science and the dissemination of scientific knowledge. Frequently, this type of charitable function involves conducting and/or disseminating the results of research.

The characteristic of *lessening the burdens of government* includes the erection or maintenance of public buildings, monuments, or works. This type of organization's activities must parallel those that a governmental unit considers to be its burden and must actually diminish that burden. Charitable organizations of this type, for example, help finance assistance to police and firefighters, public transportation, recreational centers, and internship programs. They may provide public parks, preserve a lake, or beautify a city.

The charitable activity of *community beautification and maintenance*, and the preservation of natural beauty, somewhat overlaps the concept of lessening the burdens of government. An organization that is charitable under this definition is one that may maintain community recreational facilities, assist in community beautification activities, or work to preserve and improve public parks.

The *promotion of health* is a separately recognized charitable purpose; in this context, public and mental health are included. This function includes the establishment and maintenance of institutions and organizations such as hospitals, clinics, homes for the aged, and similar treatment or residential centers. Other illustrations of health-providing (or -promoting) organizations are health maintenance organizations, drug abuse treatment centers, blood banks, hospices, and home health agencies. The advancement of medical and similar knowledge through research, and, generally, the maintenance of conditions conducive to health are included. Classification of an organization as a "hospital" or a "medical research organization" is an automatic pathway to avoidance of private foundation status. (See Chapter 11.)

The *promotion of social welfare* is one of the most indefinite categories of charitable endeavors. In the law of trusts, the concept of promotion of social welfare can include such purposes as the promotion of temperance or national security, and the erection or maintenance of tombs and monuments. In the federal tax law context, the term embraces activities designed to accomplish charitable purposes, lessen neighborhood tensions, eliminate prejudice and discrimination, defend human and civil rights secured by law, and combat community deterioration and juvenile delinquency.

An organization that endeavors to *promote environmental conservation* might engage in a range of activities to preserve and protect the natural environment for the benefit of the public. The IRS has recognized an express national policy of conserving the nation's unique natural resources; this type of organization serves to implement that policy.

The *promotion of patriotism* is a charitable objective; organizations that, in the words of one IRS ruling, "inculcate patriotic emotions" are charitable. This type of organization may assist in the celebration of a patriotic holiday, provide a color guard, or underwrite flag-raising ceremonies.

The *promotion of the arts* includes activities such as operating a theater (for plays, musicals, concerts, and the like), working to encourage the talent and ability of young artists, promoting filmmaking, sponsoring festivals or exhibits, or otherwise promoting public appreciation of one of the arts.

The purposes and activities of a nonprofit organization may involve more than one of these various ways to be charitable. For example, your hypothetical Campaign to Clean Up America has been formed to beautify communities, preserve natural beauty, lessen the burdens of government, and advance education. In addition, it promotes social welfare, protects the natural environment, and, in some instances, promotes health. (See Chapter 6 for the CCUA's programs.)

When the IRS classifies an organization as a tax-exempt entity because it is charitable (using that term in its broader sense), it does not specifically determine the type(s) of charity it may be. However, the categories just discussed enable an organization to describe its charitable activities to the IRS (and others) in terms that conform to the federal tax law requirements.

EDUCATIONAL ORGANIZATIONS

Educational organizations include schools, colleges, universities, libraries, museums, and similar institutions. To be a "formal" educational institution, an organization must have a regularly scheduled curriculum, a regular faculty, and a regularly enrolled body of students in attendance at the place where the educational activities are carried on.

Formal educational entities are, by reason of their very programming, exempted from classification as private foundations. (See Chapter 11.) Beyond these formal educational institutions, however, are a wide variety of organizations that are educational in nature.

One way to be educational, for federal tax law purposes, is to instruct or train individuals for the purpose of improving their capabilities. Within this category are organizations that provide instruction or training on a particular subject (although they may not have a regular curriculum, faculty, or student body). For example, organizations that operate apprentice training programs, correctional or rehabilitation centers, internship programs, or seminars, conferences, and lectures are educational. In addition, educational entities can include those that engage in study and research.

Another way to be educational is to instruct the public on subjects that are useful to the individual and beneficial to the community.

Within this classification are organizations that provide counseling services, offer instruction on various subjects, endeavor to instruct the public in the field of civic betterment, publish materials for distribution, or engage in study and research. For publishing activities to be considered educational functions, the content of the publications must follow methods generally accepted as educational in character, the distribution of the material must be necessary or valuable in achieving the organization's tax-exempt purposes, and the manner in which the distribution is accomplished must be distinguishable from ordinary commercial practices.

There can be a fine line of distinction between an educational activity and a taxable business. (See Chapter 12.) Sometimes it is difficult to distinguish between an educational undertaking and one that amounts to propagandizing—the zealous endorsement of a particular idea or doctrine in a manner that is not reasonably objective or balanced. (See Chapter 13.) It is often impossible (and unnecessary) to differentiate between organizations that are charitable because they advance education and those that are educational. Your Campaign to Clean Up America would be both charitable (it advances education) and educational (it instructs the public on subjects that are beneficial to the community).

RELIGIOUS ORGANIZATIONS

Religious organizations are the oldest form of tax-exempt organization. Unlike other areas of the law of tax-exempt organizations, religious organizations defy definition. This is due in large part to the First Amendment to the U.S. Constitution, which bars Congress from making any law that would establish religious organizations or prohibit the free exercise of religion.

The U.S. Congress, the Department of the Treasury, and the IRS have all backed away from attempting to define the word "religion" (or "religious"). The courts are supposed to steer clear of definitions of the term as well. The U.S. Supreme Court has written that freedom of thought and religious belief "embraces the right to maintain theories of life and of death and of the hereafter which are rank heresy to followers of the orthodox faiths," and that, if judges undertake to examine the truth or falsity of religious beliefs, "they enter a forbidden domain."

With this in mind, one federal district court said that it will not consider the "merits or fallacies of a religion," nor will it "praise or condemn a religion, however excellent or fanatical or preposterous it may seem." The U.S. Tax Court observed that it is "loathe to evaluate and judge ecclesiastical authority and duties in the various religious disciplines." One aspect of the matter is clear: for tax and other law purposes, religious belief is not confined to "theistic" belief. Another district court noted that "an activity may be religious even though it is neither part of nor derives from a societally recognized religious sect."

Some courts have ventured into the "forbidden domain." One wrote that religious belief is "a belief finding expression in a conscience which categorically requires the believer to disregard elementary self-interest and to accept martyrdom in preference to transgressing its tenets." Another court found an activity to be religious because it was centered around belief in a higher being "which in its various forms is given the name 'god' in common usage." Even the U.S. Supreme Court has placed emphasis on belief in a "supreme being," and has looked to see whether "a given belief that is sincere and meaningful occupies a place in the life of its possessor parallel to that filled by the orthodox belief in God" and whether the belief occupies in the life of the individual involved "'a place parallel to that filled by . . . God' in traditional religious persons."

There are many kinds of religious organizations; the most common form is referred to as a church. But, here again, the federal tax law lacks a crisp definition of the word "church." The IRS has informally defined a church as an organization that satisfies at least some of the following criteria: a distinct legal existence, a recognized creed and form of worship, a definite and distinct ecclesiastical government, a formal code of doctrine and discipline, a distinct religious history, a membership not associated with any other church or denomination, a complete organization of ordained ministers ministering to their congregations and selected after completing prescribed courses of study, a literature of its own, established places of worship, regular congregations, regular religious services, Sunday schools for the religious instruction of the young, and schools for the preparation of its ministers.

Some courts are building on these informal criteria. For example, the U.S. Tax Court has concluded that, to be a church, an organization must have, at a minimum, "the existence of an established congregation served by an organized ministry, the provision of regular religious services and religious education for the young, and the dissemination of a doctrinal code." On another occasion, the Tax Court concluded that a "church is a coherent group of individuals and families that join together to accomplish the religious purposes of mutually held beliefs" and that a "church's principal means of accomplishing its religious purposes must be to assemble regularly a group of individuals related by common worship and faith."

Other types of religious organizations, for tax purposes, include conventions of churches, associations of churches, integrated auxiliaries of churches, religious orders, apostolic groups, missionary organizations, bible and tract societies, and church-run organizations, such as schools, hospitals, orphanages, nursing homes, publishing entities, broadcasting entities, and cemeteries.

The law has become clouded in this area, because of the tax abuses involved in the establishment of alleged "churches." Many entities have been declared to be nonexempt on the finding that they are "personal churches."

In recent years, the IRS has had difficulty administering the law in this area because a substantial amount of fraud and other abuse in the nonprofit world is done in the name of religion. Charlatans pose as clergy and phony churches are being peddled as tax shelters. (One alleged religious organization held "worship services" on a boat in the middle of a beautiful bay, and the worshippers spent much time in the water. The organization's name formed the acronym SCUBA.) New religions (some genuine), mail-order ministries, and the rise of televangelism are making IRS agents' lives difficult.

SCIENTIFIC ORGANIZATIONS

A scientific organization engages in scientific research or is otherwise operated for the dissemination of scientific knowledge. A tax-exempt scientific organization must be organized and operated to serve the public interest.

No definition of the term "scientific" has come from Congress, the Department of the Treasury, or the IRS. One dictionary states that "science" is a "branch of study in which facts are observed, classified, and, usually, quantitative laws are formulated and verified; [or which] involves the application of mathematical reasoning and data analysis to natural phenomena." One federal court has stated that the term "science" means "the process by which knowledge is systematized or classified through the use of observation, experimentation, or reasoning."

In this area, the focus is largely on the concept of "research." This term lacks precise definition in this setting as well. Generally, the concept differentiates between "fundamental" and "basic" research, as opposed to "applied" or "practical" research. While all research may be scientific for purposes of the law of tax-exempt organizations, applied or practical research is suspect. Thus, scientific research does not include activities ordinarily carried on in connection with commercial operations—for example, the testing or inspection of materials or products, or the designing or construction of equipment or buildings.

Certain nonprofit organizations—principally universities and independent research institutions—are today engaging in research activities that have significant commercial applications. The law is having difficulty distinguishing between activities that are truly "research" and those that are more in the nature of testing products for marketing. As businesses, nonprofit organizations, and governments team up to make and commercially market discoveries (known as "technology transfer"), the law will have to sort out tax-exempt from taxable activities.

OTHER CHARITABLE ORGANIZATIONS

A nonprofit organization may be charitable, for federal tax purposes, because it is a literary organization. Or, it may be charitable by reason of the fact that it operates to prevent cruelty to children or animals, or because it qualifies as an amateur sports organization.

Some organizations operated as cooperatives can qualify as charitable entities—for example, cooperative hospital service organizations and cooperative educational service organizations. These types of organizations are subject to strict rules, to maintain their eligibility for tax-exempt status.

Organizations that test for public safety are eligible for tax-exempt status as charitable organizations. However, this type of charitable organization is ineligible to receive contributions that are deductible as charitable gifts.

Social Welfare Organizations

Traditionally, a social welfare organization is one that, in the language of the tax regulations, functions to advance the "common good and .general welfare," and seeks "civic betterments and social improvements." This type of organization is expected to engage in activities that benefit the community in its entirety, rather than merely its own membership or other select groups of individuals or organizations.

A contemporary use of the social welfare organization is as an advocacy entity. The term *social welfare* can be broader than the term *charitable* (even though, as discussed above, the concept of *charitable* includes the promotion of social welfare). Social welfare organizations can engage in an unlimited amount of legislative activity without endangering their tax-exempt status, and they can permissibly engage in some political campaign activity. Consequently, some charitable organizations link up with related social welfare organizations as a means of engaging in more lobbying activities than the charitable organizations are allowed to undertake directly.

Like many other tax-exempt organizations, social welfare entities may not engage in transactions that constitute private inurement (see

Chapter 5) and may not operate unrelated businesses as a primary activity. The only type of social welfare organization to which contributions are deductible is a veterans' organization (see later section).

Business Leagues

The federal tax law uses the anachronistic term *business leagues* to describe what are known today as trade, business, and professional associations. The private inurement doctrine expressly applies to them.

A business league is a group of persons (an "association") who have some common business interest; the purpose of the league is to promote that common interest. Its activities (if it is to be tax-exempt) are directed to the improvement of business conditions of one or more lines of business, as distinguished from the performance of particular services for individual persons.

A unique category of association is accorded specific mention as a tax-exempt entity in the Internal Revenue Code: professional football leagues.

Chambers of Commerce

A tax-exempt chamber of commerce is an organization that has a common business interest—the general economic welfare of a community. The organization's efforts are directed at promotion of the common economic interests of all of the commercial enterprises in a given trade community. Similar to the exempt chamber of commerce is a "board of trade" or a "real estate board."

Social Clubs

Social clubs are basically tax-exempt, although, unlike most forms of exempt organizations, their investment income is taxable. A social club is a nonprofit organization, operated for pleasure, recreation, and social purposes, that is usually principally supported by membership dues, fees, and assessments. The exempt club must have an established membership, personal contacts, and fellowship.

The private inurement doctrine is expressly applicable to tax-exempt social clubs. Also, the law limits the extent to which an exempt social club can make its facilities available to the general public.

Tax-exempt social clubs include country clubs, golf and tennis clubs, college and university fraternities and sororities, clubs promoting an interest in specific sports, garden clubs, and hobby clubs.

Labor Organizations

Federal tax law provides tax-exempt status for labor organizations. The purposes of these organizations are: to better the conditions of workers, to improve the grade of their products, and to develop a higher degree of efficiency in particular occupations. The most common example of this type of organization is a labor union, which bargains collectively with employers to secure better working conditions, wages, and similar benefits.

The private inurement doctrine is expressly applicable to labor organizations.

Agricultural Organizations

Like labor organizations, tax-exempt agricultural organizations must have as their purposes the betterment of the conditions of those engaged in the exempt pursuit, the improvement of the grade of their products, and the development of a higher degree of efficiency in the particular occupation.

For this purpose, the term *agricultural* includes (but is not limited to) the art or science of cultivating land, harvesting crops or aquatic resources, or raising livestock. However, the IRS will not grant agricultural status to an organization whose principal purpose is to provide a direct business service for its members' economic benefit. The private inurement doctrine is applicable in this context.

Horticultural Organizations

The definition of a horticultural organization is much like that of the labor and agricultural organizations. For tax purposes, the term *horticultural* means the art or science of cultivating fruits, flowers, and vegetables. The private inurement doctrine is applicable.

United States Instrumentalities

A corporation that is organized pursuant to an act of Congress, is an "instrumentality" of the United States, and is specifically classified as an instrumentality under federal tax law, is an exempt organization. Certain federal credit unions are exempt under this rule.

Single-Parent Title-Holding Corporations

A corporation that is organized for the exclusive purposes of holding title to property, collecting income from the property, and turning the net income over to a tax-exempt organization is itself tax-exempt. An organization is ineligible for tax exemption under this rule if it has two or more unrelated parents.

Title-holding corporations generally may not engage in any business other than that of holding title to property. These organizations can be particularly useful in holding title to property that may attract liability, such as swimming pools and parks.

Local Employees' Associations

A local association of employees, with membership limited to the employees of a designated employer or employers in a particular municipality, is a form of tax-exempt organization. The private inurement doctrine is expressly applicable.

Fraternal Beneficiary Societies

Federal tax law provides tax-exempt status for fraternal beneficiary societies, orders, or associations operating under the lodge system or for the exclusive benefit of the members of a fraternal organization that operates under the lodge system. The purpose of such groups is to provide for the payment of life, sick, accident, or other benefits to the members of the society, order, or association, or their dependents.

Contributions to a fraternal beneficiary society are deductible where the gift is to be used exclusively for charitable purposes.

Domestic Fraternal Societies

Tax exemption is available for domestic fraternal societies, orders, or associations operating under the lodge system, if their net earnings are devoted exclusively to charitable purposes and if they do not provide for the payment of life, sick, accident, or other benefits to members. An organization not providing these benefits but otherwise qualifying as a fraternal beneficiary society qualifies as a domestic fraternal society.

Voluntary Employees' Beneficiary Associations

The law of tax-exempt organizations and the law of employee benefits are intertwined in many ways. Thus, pension funds and other funds that are part of an employee benefit program are forms of tax-exempt organizations. There are several of these exempt entities, including the next six types of tax-exempt organizations.

Federal tax exemption is available for voluntary employees' beneficiary associations (VEBAs) that provide for the payment of life, sick, accident, or other benefits to members or their dependents or designated beneficiaries. The private inurement doctrine is expressly applicable to VEBAs.

A VEBA is an increasingly popular vehicle for the provision of benefits to employees (usually of a common employer). Eligibility for membership may be restricted by geographic proximity or by objective conditions or limitations reasonably related to employment. Eligibility for benefits may be restricted by objective conditions relating to the type or amount of benefits offered.

Most VEBAs are subject to certain nondiscrimination requirements.

Supplemental Unemployment Benefit Trusts

Tax exemption is available for certain trusts forming part of a plan providing for the payment of supplemental unemployment compensation benefits (SUB). Among other requirements, a SUB must be part of a plan that does not discriminate in favor of supervisory or highly compensated employees and that requires determination of benefits according to objective standards. SUBs are intended to provide benefits to laid-off (and perhaps ill) employees, frequently in conjunction with other payments such as state unemployment benefits.

Black Lung Benefits Trusts

Income tax exemption is available for a qualifying trust used by a coal mine operator to self-insure for liabilities under federal and state Black Lung benefits laws. A coal mine operator may be located in a state deemed to not provide adequate workers' compensation coverage for pneumoconiosis. Under federal law, the operator must secure, via commercial insurance or self-insuring, the payment of benefits for which the operator may be found liable under the Black Lung statute.

Multi-Employer Pension Plan Trusts

Also tax-exempt under federal law is a trust established by the sponsors of a multi-employer pension plan as a vehicle to accumulate funds in order to provide withdrawal liability payments to the plan.

Teachers' Retirement Fund Associations

Federal tax law allows tax-exempt status to teachers' retirement fund associations of a purely local character, if there is no private inurement (other than through the payment of retirement benefits) and the income consists wholly of amounts received from public taxation, amounts received from assessments on the teaching salaries of members, and income from investments.

Benevolent or Mutual Organizations

Exemption is available for benevolent life insurance associations of a purely local character, mutual ditch or irrigation companies, mutual or cooperative telephone companies, or similar organizations, if 85 percent or more of the income is collected from members for the sole purpose of meeting losses and expenses.

Cemetery Companies

A cemetery company is exempt from federal income taxation if it is owned and operated exclusively for the benefit of its members and if it is not operated for profit. The private inurement doctrine is expressly applicable. A tax-exempt cemetery generally is an entity that owns a cemetery, sells lots in it for burial purposes, and maintains these and the unsold lots in a state of repair and upkeep appropriate to, in the words of the IRS, a "final resting place."

Contributions to tax-exempt cemetery companies are deductible for federal income tax purposes.

Credit Unions

Credit unions that do not issue capital stock and that are organized and operated for the mutual benefit of members and not for purposes of profit are tax-exempt under federal law. Usually these organizations are chartered under state law. As noted earlier, those formed under federal law are likely to be tax-exempt as "instrumentalities" of the United States.

Mutual Insurance Companies

Tax exemption is available for insurance companies or associations (other than life insurance companies or associations) if their net written premiums (or, if greater, their direct written premiums) for the year do not exceed $350,000. This category of tax-exempt organization is available not only to qualified mutual property and casualty organizations but also to qualified stock property and casualty organizations.

Crop Operations Finance Corporations

Federal tax law provides exemption for corporations that are organized by a tax-exempt farmers' cooperative, or its members, for the purpose of financing the ordinary crop operations of the members or other producers, and that are operated in conjunction with this type of a cooperative. Under certain circumstances, this entity may issue capital stock.

Veterans' Organizations

Federal tax law provides exemption for a post or organization of veterans, or an auxiliary unit or society, or a trust or foundation formed for the entity, as long as it is organized in the United States or any of its possessions. At least 75 percent of its members must be past or present members of the armed forces of the United States and substantially all of the other members must be individuals who are cadets or spouses, widows, or widowers of such past or present members or of cadets. The private inurement doctrine is expressly applicable.

A special provision in the unrelated income tax rules exempts from taxation income derived from members of these organizations and attributable to payments for life, accident, or health insurance coverage for members or their dependents, where the profits are set aside for charitable purposes. (See Chapter 12.)

Contributions to veterans' organizations are generally deductible. Some veterans' groups are tax-exempt as social welfare or charitable entities.

Farmers' Cooperatives

Farmers' cooperatives are exempt from federal income tax. These cooperatives are farmers', fruit growers', or similar associations organized and operated on a cooperative basis for (1) marketing the products of members or other producers and returning to them the proceeds of sales, less the necessary marketing expenses, on the basis of either the quantity or the value of the products furnished by them; or (2) purchasing supplies and equipment for the use of members or other persons and turning over the supplies and equipment to them at actual cost plus necessary expenses.

One of the many other requirements, if a farmers' cooperative seeks tax-exempt status, is that any excess of gross receipts over expenses and payments to patrons must be returned to the patrons in proportion to the amount of business done for them. If a farmers' cooperative issues stock and wishes to remain tax-exempt, substantially all of the capital stock must be owned by producers who market their products or purchase their supplies and equipment through the cooperative.

Shipowners' Protection and Indemnity Associations

Federal tax law provides that gross income does not include the gross receipts of nonprofit shipowners' mutual protection and indemnity associations. The private inurement doctrine is expressly applicable. These organizations are, however, taxable on income from interest, dividends, and rents.

Political Organizations

Tax exemption is basically available for a political organization. This entity is a political party, committee, association, fund, or other organization formed and operated primarily for the purpose of directly or indirectly accepting contributions and/or making expenditures for an *exempt function.* An exempt function includes influencing or attempting to influence the selection, nomination, election, or appointment of any individual to any federal, state, or local public office in a political organization, or the election of presidential or vice-presidential electors. The political organization thus includes political action committees (PACs) or, more technically, separate segregated funds.

Income of a political organization, other than income from an exempt function, is taxable. This type of taxable revenue includes investment income.

Homeowners' Associations

A homeowners' association is tax-exempt if it satisfies these basic requirements:

- It must be organized and operated to provide for the acquisition, construction, management, maintenance, and care of association property.
- At least 60 percent of the association's gross income for the year must consist of exempt function income.
- At least 90 percent of the annual expenditures of the association must be used to acquire, construct, manage, maintain, and care for or improve its property.

- Substantially all of the dwelling units in a condominium project, or the lots and buildings in a subdivision, development, or similar area, must be used by individuals for residences.
- The private inurement doctrine is expressly applicable.

Only the exempt function income of a homeowners' association escapes taxation; the remainder (including investment income) is fully taxed. This exemption must be elected.

Multi-Parent Title-Holding Organizations

Tax exemption is available for a multi-parent title-holding organization. This is an entity organized and operated for the exclusive purposes of acquiring and holding title to real property, collecting income from the property, and remitting the entire amount of income from the property (less expenses) to one or more qualified tax-exempt organizations that are shareholders of the title-holding corporation or beneficiaries of the title-holding trust. This category of tax-exempt organization was created in response to an IRS position. The IRS holds that a title-holding company that is otherwise eligible for tax exemption under preexisting law cannot be exempt if two or more of its parent organizations are unrelated.

Other Tax-Exempt Organizations

This chapter has taken a fast sweep through the various types of organizations that are conventionally described as tax-exempt. Many other entities, under federal law, are also exempt from taxes.

Governmental entities, such as states, political subdivisions of states, and other governmental bodies, whether termed "agencies," "bodies," or "instrumentalities" have tax-exempt status because of the doctrine of intergovernmental immunity.

Tax-exempt status is accorded the funds underlying employee benefit plans, such as retirement and profit-sharing plans.

Other organizations that, in effect, are tax-exempt are partnerships (see Chapter 16), certain small business corporations, some cooperatives (other than those discussed above), and planned giving vehicles (see Chapter 17) such as charitable remainder trusts and pooled income funds.

This brief survey of tax-exempt organizations illustrates the vast array of nonprofit entities that Congress has decided merit tax-exempt status. These organizations range far beyond the charitable entities and similar groups that are commonly thought of as nonprofit organizations.

FOCUS: Campaign to Clean Up America

The facts surrounding the Campaign to Clean Up America illustrate the application and interrelationship of at least some of these rules. The CCUA is a charitable organization, in the broader sense of that term; it is actually both a charitable and an educational entity.

Suppose you were to decide that the CCUA should engage in a greater degree of legislative activities than is allowed to charitable organizations. You could establish a related social welfare organization to conduct those activities. The social welfare organization might then establish a political action committee (PAC). Alternately, the CCUA could establish a PAC to engage in political activities other than political campaign activities.

Still other tax-exempt organizations may be involved. In launching its planned giving program, the CCUA will be establishing at least one pooled income fund and (hopefully) many charitable remainder trusts. (See Chapter 17.) As it grows, it will have retirement and other benefits programs for its employees (see Chapter 10); the underlying funds of those programs will be tax-exempt. The time may come when a title-holding organization is appropriate.

As discussed throughout the chapter, today's tax-exempt organization is often part of a group of related organizations, some nonprofit (and tax-exempt) and some for-profit.

CHAPTER FIVE

Nonprofits and Private Benefit

One of the fundamental requirements for qualification as a nonprofit organization is also one of the most misunderstood. There is enormous misperception of the term *nonprofit*. An entity must be nonprofit before it can be tax-exempt, so it is important to understand what the ramifications of *nonprofit* are. The meaning of the term is found in another confusing term: *private inurement.* Most nonprofit organizations are subject to the *private inurement doctrine,* which deals with the unique difference between nonprofit and for-profit organizations.

A nonprofit organization is best understood through a comparison with a for-profit organization. In many respects, the characteristics of the two categories of organizations are identical: both require a legal form, have a board of directors and officers, pay compensation, face essentially the same expenses, are able to receive a profit, make investments, and produce goods and/or services. However, a for-profit entity has owners—those who hold the equity in the enterprise, such as stockholders of a corporation. The for-profit organization is operated for the benefit of its owners; the profits of the enterprise are passed through to them, perhaps as payments of dividends on shares of stock. A for-profit organization is *intended* to generate a profit for its owners. In the jargon of the tax law, when the owners of a for-profit organization transfer the profits from the organization to themselves, *private inurement* of net earnings occurs.

A nonprofit organization usually does not have any owners (equity holders), and it is not permitted to distribute its profits (net earnings)

54

to those who control and/or financially support it. (A few states allow nonprofit organizations to issue stock. This is done for control purposes only; the stock does not carry with it any dividend rights.) Private inurement is the substantive dividing line between nonprofit and for-profit organizations.

The private inurement doctrine is applicable to nearly all types of tax-exempt organizations. However, it is most pronounced for charitable organizations. By contrast, in a few types of nonprofit organizations—for example, employee benefit trusts, social clubs, and cemetery companies—private benefit is the exempt function.

PRIVATE INUREMENT

Charitable Organizations

The federal law of tax exemption for charitable organizations requires that each such entity be organized and operated so that "no part of . . . [its] net earnings . . . inures to the benefit of any private shareholder or individual." Literally, this means that the profits of a charitable organization may not be passed along to individuals in their private capacity, in the way that dividend payments are made to shareholders. In actual fact, the private inurement rule, as expanded and amplified by the IRS and the courts, today means much more.

The contemporary concept of private inurement is broad and wide-ranging. Recently, lawyers for the IRS advised that "[i]nurement is likely to arise where the beneficial benefit represents a transfer of the organization's financial resources to an individual solely by virtue of the individual's relationship with the organization, and without regard to accomplishing exempt purposes." That description is correct for today's private inurement doctrine, but it is a substantial embellishment of the original statutory rule.

The essence of the private inurement concept is to ensure that a charitable organization is serving public interests, *not* private interests. To be tax-exempt, an organization must establish that it is not organized and operated for the benefit of private interests—designated individuals, the creator of the entity or his or her family, shareholders of the organization, persons controlled (directly or indirectly) by private interests, or any persons having a personal and private interest in the activities of the organization.

One of the ways the law determines the presence of any proscribed private inurement is to look to the ultimate purpose of an organization.

If its basic purpose is to benefit individuals in their private capacity, then it cannot be tax-exempt as a charitable organization (and probably not as any other type of exempt organization), even though it may be performing exempt activities. Conversely, although the IRS officially believes the private inurement proscription is absolute, incidental benefits to private individuals could possibly not defeat tax exemption, as long as the organization otherwise qualifies for exempt status.

Is private inurement the same as commercial activities? Not necessarily. A charitable organization may usually engage in commercial activities in order to achieve a larger exempt purpose. However, the existence of a single commercial or otherwise nonexempt and substantial *purpose* will destroy or prevent the exemption.

The federal securities laws that govern business corporations target the notion of an *insider*—someone who has a special and close relationship with a corporation, frequently because he or she is a director, officer, and/or significant shareholder. The private inurement rules, using the term "private shareholder or individual," mirror the insider rule. They prohibit a transaction between a charitable organization and a person comparable to an insider, where the latter is able to cause the organization's net earnings to be turned to private purposes as the result of his or her control or influence. The IRS, in adopting this view, once observed that, as a general rule, "[a]n organization's trustees, officers, members, founders, or contributors may not, by reason of their position, acquire any of its funds." Stating its view another way, the IRS has rather starkly said that "[t]he prohibition of inurement, in its simplest terms, means that [with exceptions] a private shareholder or individual cannot pocket the organization's funds."

Private inurement involves two necessary components. The private individual (insider) to whom the benefit inures must have the ability to control or otherwise influence the actions of the charitable organization and must do so to cause the private benefit to come into existence. Second, the benefit must be intentionally conferred by the influenced organization and not be a permissible form of private inurement or a coincidental result.

The self-dealing rules that are applicable to private foundations represent a formal statement of the private inurement doctrine. (See Chapter 11.) An impermissible transaction must involve, in addition to the charitable entity (the foundation), *disqualified persons* (directors, trustees, officers, key employees, substantial contributors, their family members, and the family members of those whom they control).

People can receive private benefits in many ways, and private inurement can take many forms. Still, a charitable organization may incur ordinary and necessary operating expenditures without losing its tax-exempt status. It may pay compensation, rent, interest, and maintenance costs without penalty, because these expenses, even if paid to persons in their private capacity, further the organization's exempt purposes. The costs, however, must be justifiable and for reasonable amounts.

Compensation

The most common form of private inurement is excessive and unreasonable compensation. When a charitable organization pays an employee a salary, it is paying a portion of its earnings to an individual in his or her private capacity. However, payment of reasonable compensation is allowable; it is not private inurement. Compensation becomes private inurement when payment is excessive and unreasonable—and is made to an insider.

Many court cases have involved the payment of high compensation to the founder of an organization and/or the family members. Whether the compensation paid is reasonable is a question of fact, to be decided in the context of each case. Generally, under the law, allowable compensation is ascertained by comparing the compensation paid to individuals who have similar responsibilities and expertise in the same or comparable communities. The comparison is easier said than done; the key is the *reasonableness* of the compensation. The U.S. Tax Court once observed, "[t]he law places no duty on individuals operating charitable organizations to donate their services; they are entitled to reasonable compensation for their services."

Two aspects of compensation can make it unreasonable and excessive. One is the sheer amount of the compensation, in absolute terms. One federal court, in finding private inurement because of excessive compensation, characterized the salaries as being "substantial" amounts. Other courts tolerate "substantial" amounts of compensation, where the employees' services and skills warrant that level of payment. Some courts evidence a distinct bias when it comes to compensation paid by nonprofit organizations: they believe it should be lower than at for-profit organizations, even though all other material elements of the compensation are the same.

In many cases, it has been found that an insider was receiving high cash compensation in addition to other financial benefits from a charity (such as fees, commissions, and royalties), and that family members were also participating in the largess. Most of the cases denying tax exemption to religious organizations do so on the ground that the founders are engaging in private inurement transactions, including unwarranted levels of compensation.

The other aspect of compensation that can lead to private inurement is the manner in which the amount is calculated. The courts and the IRS may challenge compensation arrangements that are predicated on a percentage of gross receipts. Caselaw on this point is inconsistent and unclear, but, under a rule developed by the U.S. Tax Court, private inurement will not be found simply because a commission system is used; the important fact is still the reasonableness of the compensation actually paid. However, the Tax Court has found private inurement in a compensation arrangement based on a percentage of gross receipts, where no upper limit was placed on total compensation. In another instance, the Tax Court focused on the reasonableness of the percentage, not the reasonableness of the amount paid.

The special rules applying to self-dealing in private foundations may be used as a guide for determining whether private inurement exists. The rules allow compensation arrangements where the payments are reasonable and not excessive.

As a general proposition, then, a charitable organization may, without causing undue private inurement, pay reasonable compensation to its employees, suppliers, and consultants—even those who are its insiders. This compensation may be in the form of salaries, wages, and/or fees. It can also include benefits such as insurance, deferred compensation, and pension and retirement benefits. (See Chapter 10.)

Rents and Loans

A charitable organization generally may lease property and pay rent. However, the private inurement doctrine requires that the rental arrangement be beneficial and desirable to the organization, and that the rental payments be reasonable. (Inflated rental prices may well amount to a private benefit inuring to the lessor.) Loan arrangements between a private foundation and its disqualified persons are generally acts of self-dealing, and the rules that govern potential private inurement in other settings would apply here.

Rental arrangements and terms of a loan involving a charitable organization should be financially advantageous to the organization and in line with its exempt purposes. Where the charity is the borrower, the interest charges, amount of security, repayment period, terms of repayment, and other aspects of the loan must be reasonable. The scrutiny will heighten where an insider is borrowing from the charity. If a loan from a charity is not repaid on time, questions of private inurement will likely be raised. A federal court once observed that the "very existence of a private source of loan credit from [a charitable] organization's earnings may itself amount to inurement of benefit." Once again, the self-dealing rules will offer general guidance.

Some charitable organizations are called on to guarantee the debt of another entity, such as a related nonprofit or even a for-profit organization. The terms of such an arrangement must be carefully reviewed. If the loan guarantee does not advance exempt purposes or cannot be characterized as a reasonable investment, private inurement may be occurring.

Services

For charitable organizations, the interaction of the private inurement rules and the provision of services can be quite confusing. Many charitable organizations provide services in the ordinary advancement of their exempt functions. However, an organization cannot qualify as a charitable entity where its primary purpose is the provision of services to individuals in their private capacity. By contrast, individuals can be benefited by a charity where they constitute members of a charitable class (such as the poor, or students), or are considered merely instruments or means to a charitable objective, or are receiving private benefit that is merely incidental. (In this type of situation, where insiders are not involved, there may be "private benefit," which is not as objectionable as "private inurement.")

Some illustrations have occurred in caselaw:

- Generally, organizations operated to advance the arts are charitable; but a cooperative art gallery that exhibits and sells its members' works was held not to be a charitable entity because it was serving the private interests of its members.

- Quite frequently, the rendering of housing assistance for low-income families qualifies as a charitable undertaking; yet an organization that provides such assistance but gives preference for housing to employees of a particular organization was found to be advancing private, not charitable, interests.

- The operation of a private school can be a charitable program; but an organization that provides bus transportation for children attending a private school was held not to be tax-exempt because it was relieving the children's parents of their responsibility to transport their children to school.

- An organization primarily engaged in the testing of drugs for commercial pharmaceutical companies was ruled not to be engaged in scientific research but to be serving the private interests of the manufacturers.

- An association of professional nurses that operates a nurses' registry was ruled to be affording greater employment opportunities for its members and thus to be substantially operated for private ends.

Joint Ventures

Charitable organizations are increasingly involved in partnerships with individuals and/or other joint ventures with individuals or for-profit entities. Real estate ventures in which a charitable organization is the general partner in a limited partnership are common. Partnerships and similar vehicles are discussed in Chapter 16; the topic here is the IRS's concern about private inurement in joint ventures.

In a general partnership, all of the partners are subject to liability for the acts committed in the name of the partnership. In a limited partnership, which will have at least one general partner, the limited partners are essentially investors; their liability is confined to the extent of their investment. As investors, the limited partners expect to experience a return on their investment. Meanwhile, the general partner(s) in a limited partnership has the responsibility to operate the partnership in a successful manner—which includes seeing to it that the limited partners achieve an economic return that is worth the commitment of their capital.

In this structure and set of expectations, the IRS sees private inurement lurking. In its worst light, a limited partnership with a charitable organization at the helm can be construed as the running of a business (the partnership) for the benefit of private interests (the limited partners). This is rarely the case. A partnership (general or limited) is basically a financing entity—a means to an end. In this instance, a charitable organization is able to attract the funds of others for a legitimate purpose. Like the borrowing of money from a bank (where the charity pays interest), a charitable organization/general partner must pay the limited partners for its use of their money. But, because in the partnership structure the general partner is functioning in an active (not passive) manner, the IRS finds private benefit when the limited partners are paid but not when the bankers are paid.

When it went to litigation, the IRS lost every case. The position of the IRS has now evolved to this point: A charitable organization will lose its tax-exempt status if it participates as a general partner in a limited partnership, unless the purpose of the partnership is the advancement of charitable purposes. Even a charity that passes that test will forfeit tax exemption if it is not protected against the day-to-day duties of administering the partnership or if the payments to the limited partners are excessive.

There is much wrong with the IRS position, but it illustrates the contemporary application of the private inurement rules. Despite its ferocious stance against charitable organizations in partnerships, the IRS has yet (since losing the string of cases) to deny or revoke exempt status to a charitable organization that has ended up in a limited partnership as general partner. To date, the IRS has always found the partnership to be engaged in charitable purposes. Still, charitable organizations should be cautious when entering into any form of joint venture or partnership, in whatever capacity. They should avoid conferring private benefit on persons, or otherwise being used to generate unwarranted benefits to persons in their private capacities.

Social Welfare Organizations

Social welfare organizations, like most forms of tax-exempt organizations, cannot be operated primarily for private gain. The private inurement doctrine is not expressly applicable to these types of nonprofit entities, but the possible consequences are clear. For example, homeowners' associations may be exempt as social welfare organizations only if they are engaged in the promotion of the common good and general welfare of a community. If they operate for the benefit of a select group of individuals, they are not exempt.

A social welfare organization can use the criterion that it must not be operated primarily for the economic benefit or convenience of its members. Many cooperative entities fail to be social welfare organizations because, in the words of a federal court, they are operated "primarily to benefit the taxpayer's membership economically." A federal appellate court denied social welfare status to a mutual assistance organization established by a church because its policies and practices benefited a "select few"—its members—rather than a larger public.

As is the case with membership associations in general, the rendering of services to members does not necessarily bring a denial or loss of social welfare status. An organization may be able to qualify as a social welfare organization where its services are equally available to members and nonmembers.

As stated earlier in discussing charitable organizations, the private inurement rules for social welfare organizations are not the same as the restrictions on commercial practices. However, the federal tax law does expressly state that an exempt social welfare organization may not be organized or operated to carry on a business with the general public as though it were a for-profit entity. In addition, a social welfare organization (as well as a charitable organization) will lose or be denied tax-exempt status if a substantial part of its activities consists of the provision of commercial-type insurance.

Trade and Business Associations

The federal tax law governing the activities of tax-exempt trade, business, and professional associations (business leagues) expressly forbids inurement of the net earnings of these organizations to individuals in their private capacities. At first glance, this rule may seem somewhat anomalous, when the purpose of these associations is to promote the common business interests of the membership. Why would anyone join an association of this type, if the benefits it can offer its members are off-limits?

There is an important distinction between improving business conditions of a line of business (a business league's primary purpose; see Chapter 4) and performing services for members to the point where private inurement results. The federal tax law prohibits these types of associations from carrying on *business activities for profit*.

One tax rule applicable to business leagues is often misunderstood and ignored: A tax-exempt business league may not perform *particular* services for individual persons. In practice, this prohibition is enforced only where these services are the primary function of an association. It can be difficult, in a specific instance, to distinguish between performing particular services and engaging in activities directed to the improvement of business conditions.

An activity of a business league is exempt where the activity benefits the membership as a group, rather than in individual capacities. The benefit to the group occurs where the business league provides a product or service to its members for a fee, and the benefit is not directly proportional to the fee. One federal court stated, "the activities that serve the interests of individual . . . [members] according to what they pay produce individual benefits insufficient to fulfill the substantial relationship test, since those activities generally do not generate inherent group benefits that inure to the advantage of its members as members."

Labor and Other Organizations

Labor organizations, which frequently are unions, are much like business leagues: they operate to better the working conditions and economic opportunities of employees. Labor organizations are often membership groups that provide services to their members. The federal tax law forbids the net earnings of a labor organization from inuring to the benefit of persons in their private capacity.

The private inurement constraint also specifically applies to social clubs, agricultural and horticultural organizations, voluntary employees' beneficiary associations, certain teachers' retirement fund associations, veterans' organizations, shipowners' protection and indemnity associations, and homeowners' associations.

The distinctions between public and private benefit are evident in the law pertaining to other types of tax-exempt organizations. The net earnings of local associations of employees must be devoted to charitable purposes. The same "reverse inurement" rule applies to domestic fraternal societies, which are prohibited from paying life, sick, accident, or other benefits to their members.

In another twist on the prohibition of private benefits flowing from tax-exempt organizations, the law mandates that the economic benefits flowing out of employee benefit plans cannot discriminate in favor of highly compensated employees. This is particularly true with respect to voluntary employees' beneficiary associations and supplemental unemployment benefit trusts.

The federal tax law governing other exempt organizations simply states that they may not be operated "for profit." Cemetery companies and certain credit unions are subject to that general prohibition.

"Private Benefit" Tax-Exempt Organizations

Several types of tax-exempt organizations have, as their tax-exempt function, the provision of "private" benefits. These organizations serve to advance private ends; they do not transfer funds to individuals in their private capacity.

The most notable "private benefit" tax-exempt organizations provide economic benefits to employees, either during difficult personal times or at retirement. For example, the funds underlying retirement, pension, and profit-sharing plans are tax-exempt organizations. Other employee benefit organizations are: voluntary employees' beneficiary associations, which provide life, sick, accident, and other benefits to their members and dependents; supplemental unemployment benefit trusts, which provide unemployment compensation benefits to employees; group legal service organizations (that fund prepaid legal services for employees); Black Lung benefits trusts, which fund employer liabilities for pneumoconiosis under federal and state Black Lung benefits laws; and multi-employer pension plan trusts, which are designed.

to improve retirement income security under private multi-employer pension plans.

Other private benefit programs can be undertaken by tax-exempt fraternal and other organizations. For example, fraternal beneficiary societies that operate under the lodge system provide for the payment of life, sick, accident, and other benefits to their members and dependents, as do some veterans' organizations. Benevolent life insurance associations provide life insurance coverage to their members. Cemetery companies own and operate cemeteries for ultimate use by their members. Exempt credit unions provide financial services to their members, as do crop operations finance corporations. Farmers' cooperatives, shipowners' protection and indemnity associations, and homeowners' associations also function on behalf of their members.

The type of tax-exempt organization where private benefit is most blatant—permissibly—is the social club. The private inurement doctrine expressly applies, but exempt social clubs (country clubs, gourmet clubs, sports clubs, and so on) are organized and operated for the pleasure and recreation of their members. Nonprofit fraternities and sororities are usually classified as social clubs for federal tax purposes. A social club will lose its tax-exempt status if it makes its facilities unduly available to the general public.

The private inurement doctrine has several specific applications to social clubs. One emerges when an exempt club generates too much nonmember income and the membership gains a subsidy in the form of reduced dues and improved facilities. Or, a club with more than one class of member may attempt to have the dues payments of one class operate to subsidize the members of another class. In more conventional terms, private inurement can exist when a social club engages in undue dealings with its members, such as regular sales of liquor for consumption off the club's premises.

PRIVATE BENEFIT

The body of law that concerns "private benefit" is different from the law encompassed by private inurement. The relatively new private benefit doctrine, created largely by the courts, is more sweeping; it covers a wider range of activities. The private benefit rule can operate without the involvement of an insider.

The private benefit rule was recently illustrated by a case involving a nonprofit school. Individuals were trained there to become political campaign consultants, but the graduates of the school nearly always ended up working for candidates of the same political party. The school's instructional activities did not constitute political campaign activity (see Chapter 14), but the judge wanted to deny tax-exempt status. He ruled that the school could not be tax-exempt because it provided private benefits in the form of assistance to the political candidates by the school's alumni. (If this private benefit rule was applied literally, there could not be any tax-exempt schools.)

APPEARANCES

Occasionally, a nonprofit organization engages in activities that, to some, are "wrong" or "unethical." This description does not necessarily mean that the activities are illegal or contrary to tax-exempt status.

Consider, for example, a charge of "conflict of interest." This accusation is leveled at a person who is on both sides of a transaction, for example, a member of the board of directors of a nonprofit organization who provides consulting services to the organization for a fee. The term conflict of interest connotes wrongful activity; it is a derogatory phrase. However, it is often *not* a violation of law; rather, it is a state of affairs that looks suspicious and thus raises questions of "appearances." Some nonprofit organizations have conflict-of-interest policies that are designed to prevent even an appearance of wrongdoing. Conflicts of interest can be indications of private inurement or private benefit.

Other circumstances that may cause questions as to "appearances" are: having two or more members of the same family on the board or on the payroll of a nonprofit organization; luxurious travel and accommodations arranged for board members or staff; club memberships and other such perquisites for the officers of a nonprofit organization; and an array of taxable subsidiaries and joint ventures. A nonprofit organization can suffer at the hands of the media and in many other ways, if appearances suggest wrongdoing. The niceties of legal distinctions then invite only further chiding. The recent "scandal" involving United Way of America is an example. The organization has suffered nearly irreparable damage because of certain practices of its president, even though not a single law was broken.

As the federal law of tax-exempt organizations evolves, the private inurement/private benefit constraint is becoming more stringent. Entire classes of organizations have lost their tax exemption as the result of this evolutionary process. Homeowners' associations ceased being exempt social welfare organizations (although Congress stepped in and gave them their own exemption category). Veterans' organizations that provide benefits to their members and dependents were likewise extricated from the social welfare exemption (although, again, Congress intervened). So-called "self-interest" organizations, which provide sick and death benefits to members (such as individuals within a particular ethnic group) and their beneficiaries, are no longer exempt as social welfare organizations. (In this instance, Congress has let the IRS's policy decision stand.)

FOCUS: Campaign to Clean Up America

The Campaign to Clean Up America, as a charitable organization, is subject to the rule that its net earnings may not inure to the benefit of individuals in their private capacities. Because the CCUA is a public charity, the self-dealing rules do not apply; however, the concepts underlying these rules can often be used as helpful guides.

Application of the private inurement doctrine to the CCUA first requires an assessment of who its insiders are. The most likely insiders are founders, directors, and officers, and at the CCUA, the same individual may be serving in two or all three capacities. You, as the founder of the CCUA, and as a director and an officer (president) are obviously an insider. (In the parlance of the self-dealing rules, you are a disqualified person.) So, too, is your spouse, who is a director and officer (and may be a co-founder as well). Other directors and officers are insiders, and key employees and substantial contributors are potential insiders.

The other principal aspect of private inurement lies in the transactions, if any, between the CCUA and its insiders. You and the other directors and/or officers may function as employees and may be receiving a salary. To avoid private inurement, the compensation must be reasonable and not excessive. Because of the self-dealing taint of this type of compensatory arrangement, the IRS will likely give it more than passing scrutiny, so you and the other insiders would be wise to develop a substantive rationale for the salary amounts.

You happen to lease space to use as an office for your business. You decide to sublease space to the CCUA for its offices, at least until the organization has the wherewithal to locate in independent quarters. The CCUA can pay you rent without endangering its tax exemption, as long as the rental rate is reasonable. Again, the arrangement may well be subject to strict scrutiny, so you must be prepared to justify the normality of the rental rates.

You are contributing money to the CCUA, as are a few others, but it needs more funding now. You can lend money to the CCUA, at interest. However, with the private inurement doctrine in the picture, the interest rate must be reasonable, and you must be able to justify the interest rate selected.

The law theoretically tolerates rentals or loans from the CCUA, but these activities are not advisable for you or other insiders. If they are done, the charges must be reasonable. Moreover, the other terms of the arrangement (self-dealing) must be reasonable as well—the rental term and/or the borrowing term, and, in the case of the loan, the repayment terms and the security provided.

For the CCUA (and other public charities), because the self-dealing rules do not apply, there is no real limit on the types or number of its transactions with its insiders. However, there are limits as a matter of practicality. It is *possible* for the CCUA to lawfully employ every insider and each of his or her family members, but it would be imprudent, and your lawyer advises a minimization of that employment practice. He recites to you and the other directors a litany of court cases where tax exemption was lost or denied because the nonprofit organization involved was a nest of self-dealing and had incestuous employment practices. You decide to avoid that fate.

During the course of its existence, the CCUA will purchase goods and services, equipment, furniture, supplies, and the like. It will likely pay fees to consultants (such as lawyers, accountants, and fund-raisers, and, perhaps, investment counselors and management consultants). In these respects, the CCUA is no different than a for-profit organization. However, the private inurement constraint never goes away. When the consultants or vendors are insiders, the CCUA should always be in a position to justify both the relationship and the amounts paid. The law does not require "competitive bidding" on purchases and fee assignments, but, for nonprofit organizations, a good rule of thumb is to minimize, if not avoid, self-dealing transactions. Even if the transactions are legal, nothing can spoil a good fund-raising campaign more than adverse publicity about intrafamily business dealings.

For example, one of the programs of the CCUA is trash collection, using volunteers. To facilitate this program and at the same time to generate publicity about the organization, you decide that the

CCUA will purchase plastic trash bags, bearing its name and logo, for distribution and use by the volunteers. Your brother-in-law owns a company that manufactures lawn maintenance supplies, including trash bags, and the CCUA purchases the bags from his company. If the company gives the CCUA a discount, such as for purchasing in bulk, the acquisition of the bags from that particular company is not a transgression of the private inurement doctrine. But, if the bags are sold to the CCUA at a mark-up substantially in excess of the retail market price, private inurement could be occurring. Even if the purchase of the bags was for a fair price (or at a discount), the launching of the CCUA, its programs, and its fund-raising effort could be hindered. Members' or volunteers' gossip might reach an enterprising reporter, and the organization could face an accusation of being manipulated for private gain.

The absence of private gain is what separates the CCUA and other nonprofit organizations from for-profit businesses. Charitable and similar organizations are expected to serve the *public,* not private individuals. If the CCUA wishes to further an activity that would best be housed in a for-profit entity, it should explore the establishment of a for-profit subsidiary. (See Chapter 15.)

CHAPTER SIX

Tax Exemption: The Art of Application

Under the federal income tax system, every element of gross income received—whether by a corporate entity or an individual—is subject to taxation, unless an express statutory provision exempts from tax either that form of income or that type of person.

Many types of nonprofit organizations are eligible for exemption from the federal income tax. (See Chapter 4.) However, the exemption is not automatic merely because an organization has not been set up and operated as a for-profit organization. Organizations become tax-exempt when they meet the requirements of the particular statutory provision that allows the tax-exempt status.

RECOGNITION OF TAX-EXEMPT STATUS

Whether a nonprofit organization is entitled to tax exemption, initially or on a continuing basis, is a matter of law. The U.S. Congress defines the categories of organizations that are eligible for tax exemption, and it is up to Congress to determine whether an exemption from tax should be continued, in whole or in part. Except for state and local governments, no entities have a constitutional right to a ta exemption.

The IRS does not "grant" tax-exempt status. (See Myth 7 in Chapter 3.) Congress grants it, under sections of the Internal Revenue Code that it has enacted. The function of the IRS is to *recognize* tax exemption.

When an organization applies to the IRS for a ruling or determination on its tax-exempt status, it is requesting the IRS to recognize a tax exemption that already exists (assuming the organization qualifies). It is not asking the IRS to grant tax exemption. After review, the IRS may determine that an organization is no longer entitled to tax-exempt status and may revoke its prior recognition of exempt status.

Most nonprofit organizations that are eligible for a tax exemption do not need to have their exemption recognized by the IRS. When should a nonprofit organization seek an IRS determination? Management personnel must decide, taking into account their own degree of confidence in the organization's eligibility for the exemption and the costs associated with the application process. Most organizations in this position elect to pursue recognition of tax-exempt status.

Charitable organizations and employee benefit organizations must file (successfully) with the IRS for recognition of their exemption. Entities such as social welfare organizations, labor organizations, trade and professional associations, social clubs, and veterans' organizations need not file an application for recognition of tax-exempt status.

A request for recognition of tax exemption generally is commenced by filing a form, entitled "Application for Recognition of Exemption." Charitable organizations file Form 1023; most other organizations file Form 1024. (In rare instances, neither form is used; the filing is done by letter.)

The IRS can revoke recognition of exemption for good cause (such as a change in the law), but an organization that has been recognized by the IRS as being tax-exempt can rely on that determination as long as there are no substantial changes in its character, purposes, or methods of operation. If material changes occur, the organization should notify the IRS and may have to undergo a reevaluation of its exempt status.

The Application Procedure

The IRS has specific procedures by which a ruling or determination letter may be issued to an organization that is filing for recognition of its tax-exempt status. The organization must file an application with the office of the key district director of the IRS in or closest to the district in which the principal place of business or principal office of the organization is located. The determination of exemption will be issued by that district director's office unless the application presents a matter of some controversy or involves an unresolved or novel point of law. In that case, the application will be sent for resolution to the National Office of the IRS in Washington, D.C.

Organizations should allow at least three months for the processing of an application for recognition of tax exemption. There is a procedure for expedited consideration in extreme cases, but the IRS is reluctant to consider applications out of the order in which they are received.

A favorable ruling or determination will be issued, as long as the application and supporting documents establish that the organization meets the particular statutory requirements. The application must include a statement describing the organization's purposes, copies of its governing instruments (such as, in the case of a corporation, its articles of incorporation and bylaws), and either a financial statement or a proposed multi-year budget.

The application filed by a charitable organization must also include a summary of the sources of its financial support, its fund-raising program, the composition of its governing body (usually a board of directors), its relationship with other organizations (if any), the nature of its services or products and the basis for any charges for them, and its membership (if any).

The IRS is generally free to seek and obtain other information it deems necessary for a determination or ruling, and it frequently does so. The ability of the IRS to pursue additional information is not unlimited, however, and the courts have held that recognition of exemption must be granted once an organization makes the requisite "threshold showing."

If the application is not complete, the IRS will return the application and all supporting documents to the organization and instruct it to file again, by submitting a complete application.

The proper preparation of an application for recognition of exemption involves far more than merely filling in the blanks of a government form. The process is similar to the preparation of a prospectus in conformance with the federal securities laws requirements, and every statement made in the application should be carefully considered. The prime objective should be to be accurate; all material facts must be fully and fairly disclosed. Determining which facts are material requires careful judgment.

The phrasing of the answers to questions in the application can be extremely significant. The exercise is more one of "art" than "science." Whoever prepares the form should be able to anticipate any concerns the contents of the application may cause, see that the application is drawn properly, and yet minimize if not completely avoid conflict with the IRS. Organizations that are entitled to a particular tax exemption have often been denied recognition of tax-exempt status because poor or wrong wording in their applications enabled the IRS to build a case against their exemption.

Preparing an application for recognition of exemption is a useful exercise. It forces an organization to think through what it wants to do, how its activities will be financially supported, and other aspects of its organization and operation. Frequently, the language developed in preparing the application can be useful in grant applications and fundraising appeals. Sometimes, preparation of the application causes an organization to focus on significant aspects of its organization and operation that it would otherwise ignore.

Preparation of an application is even more important for charitable organizations. The information filed with the IRS is used to make three sets of determinations: whether the organization will be recognized as tax-exempt, whether it will be eligible to receive deductible charitable contributions (and sometimes to what extent), and whether the organization will be a public charity or a private foundation.

A nonprofit organization does not need to retain the services of a lawyer or other professional for preparation of an application for recognition of exemption (see Myth 15 in Chapter 3). However, because of the complexities involved, it is a good idea to have a professional who understands the process (see Myth 16) review the documents before they are filed. In many instances, a lawyer is involved during the entire process of preparing the governing instruments.

An application for recognition of exemption should be regarded as an important legal document and prepared accordingly. Throughout an organization's existence, this document will be subject to review. A nonprofit organization is required to keep a copy of this application, along with supporting documents and related correspondence, available for scrutiny by anyone during regular business hours.

A nonprofit organization seeking recognition of its tax-exempt status has the burden of proving that it satisfies all of the requirements of the particular exemption provision. If the application process is not initially successful, the organization has certain appeals rights within the IRS. If the organization fails to successfully navigate the administrative process, there are opportunities to pursue the matter in federal court.

The Application Itself

This section provides some guidance for preparing an application for recognition of tax exemption. (The next section shows some sample answers, using the facts involving the Campaign to Clean Up America.) Because it is more complex, Form 1023 will be used for analysis rather than Form 1024. It is useful to have a copy of Form 1023 available while reading the rest of this chapter.

Form 1023 comes in a packet. The packet includes instructions for preparation of the form, the form itself (in duplicate), and some copies of Form 872-C (discussed later in the chapter). Only one copy of Form 1023 need be filed with the IRS; the other copy may be used in drafting the application.

The application will require some attachments. These should be identified and keyed into the form as Exhibit A, Exhibit B, and so on. Some answers will be longer than the space provided on the form. These can be treated as attachments.

Part I. Part I of Form 1023 requests certain basic information about the organization, such as its name, address, and date of formation. Every nonprofit organization must have an "employer identification number" (even if there are no employees). The number is obtained by filing Form SS-4 (see Chapter 2). Form SS-4 may be filed as soon as the organization is formed and organized or it may be filed with Form 1023. Thus, question 2 should be answered by inserting the number or the statement "Form SS-4 attached," as the case may be.

The contact person (question 4) may be someone directly involved with the organization, such as an officer or director, or an independent representative of the organization, such as a lawyer or accountant. If such a representative is being used, he or she must be granted a power of attorney, which is filed on Form 2848 and attached to the application.

The organization must state the month in which its annual accounting period ends (question 5). The determination of a fiscal year should be given some thought; most organizations prefer the calendar year (in which case, the answer is December). Whatever period is selected, the organization should be certain that the same period is stated on Form SS-4 and used when compiling its multi-year budget (Part III).

The date of formation must be recorded (question 6). If the organization is incorporated, this date will be the date the state agency issued the certificate of incorporation. This date is significant in relation to the 15-month rule (see Part II).

The application requires the organization to select up to three "activity codes" that best describe or most accurately identify its purposes, activities, and other operations. These code numbers are found on the back of the Form 1023 package. The numbers are used for all types of exempt organizations, so they should be selected with caution. Some codes are inappropriate for some organizations. For example, a nonprofit organization seeking recognition as a charitable entity would be ill-advised to select code number 483 ("support, oppose, or rate political candidates").

Part II. Part II of Form 1023 requires an applicant organization to identify its "type." As discussed in Chapter 2, the organization must be one of three types: nonprofit corporation, trust, or unincorporated association.

If a corporation, the attachments will be the articles of incorporation and bylaws (and any amendments to them), and the certificates of incorporation and amendments (if any) issued by the state. If a trust, the attachments will be the trust document(s). If an unincorporated association, the attachments will be the constitution and bylaws. As an example, if the entity is an unincorporated association, the constitution can be attached as Exhibit A and the bylaws as Exhibit B.

These attachments must be submitted as "conformed" copies. Each of the documents must be accompanied by a certification from an appropriate individual (usually an officer or director) that the copy is a true, correct, and complete copy of the original, and that the individual is authorized to make the certification. This does not mean, in the case of a corporation, sending in the "certified" copy of the articles of incorporation.

Part III.   For most organizations, Part III of Form 1023 will be the most important portion of the application. It can also be the most difficult to prepare and the most sensitive, in terms of potential trouble with the IRS.

The organization must identify, in order of size, its sources of financial support (question 1). The answers will be something like the following: contributions from the general public, other contributions, grants, dues, other exempt function (fee-for-service) revenue, and investment income. Whatever sources of support are identified here, the organization should be careful to be consistent when preparing the multi-year budget and selecting the non-private-foundation status, if any. (See later discussion.)

The organization must describe its actual and planned fund-raising program (question 2), summarizing its actual use of, or plans to use, selective mailings, fund-raising committees, professional fund-raisers, and the like. Again, the organization should be certain to coordinate its discussion of financial support with that of its fund-raising plans. There are some questions in Form 1023 that can be answered in any reasonable way (that is, there is no "right" or "wrong" answer), and this is one of them. Thus, the organization can describe a very detailed fund-raising program or it can state that it has yet to develop a fund-raising program. If the organization has developed material for the solicitation of contributions or dues, it should attach copies (perhaps as Exhibit C).

The organization must provide a narrative of its purposes and activities (question 3)—perhaps the most important single portion of the form. Usually, this is an essay that describes the organization's programs. It should be carefully written. Good practice is to open with a description of the organization's purposes and follow with one or more paragraphs summarizing its program activities. This response should be as full as is reasonable and may occupy more space than is provided. The response can be prepared as a separate submission (perhaps as Exhibit D).

This segment of the form can generate many questions from the IRS, once the application is filed. Moreover, some activities can generate additional questions to be answered elsewhere on the application. Organizations preparing the application often overlook Part VIII, entitled "Required Schedules for Special Activities." If an applicant organization engages in, or is planning to engage in, one or more of these special activities, the appropriate schedule(s) must be filed as part of the application.

Regarding follow-up questions, the IRS tends to use form sets of questions. Two types of activities, scholarships and research, are detailed here, to illustrate the questions and information that will have to be dealt with. If the applicant organization is to have a *scholarship program*, here are the typical questions it will have to answer (unless answered in Part VIII, Schedule 2):

- Describe the class of eligibles, or potential recipients, of the organization's grants.

- Indicate whether there are any restrictions or limitations on who may make application for a scholarship or whom the organization will consider as possible grantees.

- Who makes the selection of eventual recipients from the class of eligibles? If these people are related to the organization, give complete details.

- List and describe all criteria used by the selection committee in selecting recipients from the class of eligibles.

- Will any grants be made to spouses, children, descendants, spouses of children or of descendants, or other persons disqualified in relationship to the organization, its directors or officers?

- Describe how the scholarship program is publicized to ensure that all eligible individuals are reasonably likely to be informed of the availability of the scholarship aid.

- Will all grants be limited to students attending qualified educational institutions?

- Will the organization provide aid to students both as grants and as loans?

- If loans are to be made, describe the interest rates (if any) applicable to any loans to be given, how such interest rates are determined, and the terms of repayment of the loans.
- Explain the follow-up procedures in place to ensure that all scholarship funds will be used for the stated purposes.
- Explain the procedures that will be followed if a misuse of funds is discovered.
- Will funds be paid to the individual students or will they be paid directly to the school the students will be attending?
- When did the organization begin giving scholarship aid?
- How many scholarships have been given?
- Provide a list of all grant recipients together with an indication of how much money was received by each recipient.

If the applicant organization is to have a research program, here are the questions it will likely have to answer:

- Describe the nature of the research engaged in or contemplated.
- Describe research projects completed or presently being engaged in.
- How and by whom are research projects determined and selected?
- Does the organization have or is it contemplating having contract or sponsored research? If so, submit the names of past sponsors or grantors, the terms of the contract or grant, and copies of any executed contracts or grants.
- Summarize the disposition made or to be made of the results of the research, including whether preference has been or will be given to any organization or individual, either as to results or timing of the release of results.
- Who will retain ownership or control of any patents, copyrights, processes, or formulas resulting from the research?
- Submit copies of publications or other media showing reports of the research activities.
- If the organization is engaged in medical research, is the research performed in connection with a hospital?

The names and addresses of the organization's officers and directors must be provided, along with the amount (if any) of their annual compensation (question 4). All compensation must be included, not just the fee for serving as an officer or a director (or trustee). For example, an individual may simultaneously be a director, officer, and employee. Whatever the compensation is, it must be reasonable (see Chapter 5). Usually, there is insufficient room on the form to provide this information. It can be submitted on a separate attachment (perhaps as Exhibit E).

The balance of question 4 is self-explanatory. (In question 4d, the term "disqualified person" is discussed; see Chapter 5.)

Question 5 can be very important for some organizations. As a general rule, it does not matter whether the charitable organization has a special relationship with, or is controlled by, another organization. For example, some charitable organizations are controlled by other types of tax-exempt organizations, such as social welfare organizations or trade associations (see Chapter 4), or are controlled by for-profit corporations, such as corporation-related foundations. This question usually has no "right" or "wrong" answer. If the organization has an interlocking directorate, it is good practice to refer to the provision in the governing instruments that describes the overlap of directors.

Some caution may be required when responding on whether the organization is an "outgrowth" of another. A typical problem arises where the applicant organization is a corporation and the other organization is an unincorporated organization and has been operating as a charitable entity, without recognition of tax-exempt status.

Question 6 can relate to the facts in question 5. Beyond the control exercised administratively, some organizations are financially accountable to others. For example, the recipient of a grant may be required to periodically report on the progress of the funded project to the grantee.

Question 7a is self-explanatory. Often, a new organization will simply answer that it does not have any assets at this time. Question 7b is somewhat perplexing: regarding an organization's tax exemption as a charitable entity, it does not make the slightest difference whether the applicant organization does or does not have, or plans to have, an endowment fund.

Question 8 is intended to identify situations where private inurement may be taking the form of a siphoning-off of the organization's funds, by means of a management contract. There is nothing inherently wrong with a management arrangement, and the organization should not be concerned about disclosure of the terms of a bona fide arrangement.

Question 9a brings the applicant organization into a sensitive area. A charitable organization can appropriately charge a fee for its "benefits, services, or products." However, the IRS is on the lookout for commercial practices, so the focus is on *how the charges are determined.* The answer will largely be governed by the particular facts, but a response that the charges "are set to return a profit" would be a mistake. The organization might say, if it is true, that the charges are determined so as to recover actual costs. Alternatively, the answer may be that the charges are ascertained on the basis of cost.

Question 9b and question 10 are self-explanatory. However, question 10 relates to organizations that have a true membership, not merely arrangements where the concept of a "membership" is used as a fundraising technique.

Question 11 is self-explanatory, but the applicant organization must be careful in formulating the response. (See Chapters 13 and 14.)

Question 12 is another instance where the answer does not affect tax-exempt status.

Question 13 can be of no importance or it can be of extreme importance, depending on the circumstances. The basic "15-month rule" is that the recognition of exemption will be retroactive to the date of formation of the organization, if the application is filed with the IRS within 15 months from the end of the month in which the organization was established. (This is why the date inserted in response to question 6 of Part I can be of importance.) For example, if the organization is created on January 15, 1993, and the application for recognition of exemption is filed before April 30, 1994, the recognition of exemption (if granted) will be retroactive to January 15, 1993, regardless of when the determination is made by the IRS. If the application is filed on or after May 1, 1994, the recognition of exemption is effective only as of the date the application was received by the IRS.

As for tax-exempt status, the 15-month rule may not be of any particular importance because the organization can qualify as a tax-exempt social welfare organization until the date of its classification as a charitable organization. (Remember, social welfare organizations *do not* have to have a ruling recognizing their exempt status.) However, this alleviation of the tax-exemption problem does not help with the organization's posture as a charitable donee (or, if applicable, as a nonprivate foundation). Donors making gifts during the interim period will, upon audit, find their charitable deductions disallowed. Private foundations making grants during the interim period may be subject to taxation for failure to exercise "expenditure responsibility." (See Chapter 11.) Thus, an organization desiring to be recognized as a charitable organization from the outset must file a completed application for recognition of tax exemption prior to the expiration of the 15-month period.

If it files within 15 months, the applicant organization can answer "yes" to question 13a. If not, an exception may be available or the organization may be eligible for special relief (question 13c and d). Otherwise, the organization must agree that the determination of exemption will only have prospective effect (question 13e).

Part IV.   Part IV of Form 1023 is the smallest part but the answers can have very large consequences. This is where the public charity/private foundation rules come into play. (See Chapter 11.)

If the applicant charitable organization is a private foundation, the completion of Part IV is generally simple; the answer to question 1 is "yes." If the organization is seeking classification as a private operating foundation, it should so indicate in response to question 2 and then complete Part VII.

However, if the applicant organization believes it can avoid private foundation status, it must select either a "definitive" ruling or an "advance" ruling. For new charitable organizations that are seeking to be classified as publicly supported entities, an advance ruling (selected by responding to question 3b) is the correct choice. They lack the financial history to demonstrate actual public support, which is required before a publicly supported organization can receive a definitive ruling. If the applicant believes it will be supported principally by gifts and grants, it should check the first box of question 3b. The second box of question 3b is for organizations that are expecting support in the form of a blend of gifts, grants, and exempt function income. (See Chapter 11.)

Either type of publicly supported organization must demonstrate its initial qualification for nonprivate foundation status by convincing the IRS that it will receive the requisite extent of public support. This is done by submitting (in what would be, in our sequence, Exhibit F) a proposed budget. This budget should summarize contemplated types of revenue (such as gifts, grants, exempt function revenue, and investment income) and types of expenses (such as expenditures for programs, compensation, occupancy, telephones, travel, postage, and fundraising) for each of four years. For this purpose, a year is a period consisting of at least eight months. (For new organizations, this budget is submitted in lieu of the financial statements reflected in Part V.) The four-year period is the "advance ruling period."

If an organization's first fiscal year is shorter than eight months, it must meet the applicable public support test for the next four full fiscal years. The advance ruling period for this organization would consist of the full four-year period plus the initial "short" fiscal year. Some organizations can obtain a definitive ruling after meeting the public support test for their first full fiscal year.

In designing the budget, the four years involved are the fiscal years of the organization. The applicant organization should be certain that the fiscal year used to develop the budget is the same period referred to in the response to question 5 of Part I. The applicant should also be certain that the types of revenue stated in the budget correspond to the types of revenue summarized in the response to question 1 of Part III.

The advance ruling pertains only to the applicant organization's status as a publicly supported entity; it is not an advance ruling on its tax-exempt status or charitable donee status. The advance ruling period is probationary or conditional as to "public" status. Once the advance ruling period expires and the organization has in fact received adequate public support during the four-year period, that fact will be reported to the IRS. A definitive ruling that the organization is a publicly supported charity will then be issued by the IRS. The advance ruling is conditional; the definitive ruling is permanent (unless upset by a subsequent loss of qualification or change in the law).

A publicly supported charitable organization must, during and after the expiration of the advance ruling period (on an ongoing basis), continue to show that it qualifies as a publicly supported charity (assuming it wants to retain that status). This is done by reporting the financial support information as part of the annual information return (see Chapter 7), using a matrix like the one in section B of Part VI.

It does not matter which type of publicly supported organization the charitable entity is at any point in its existence; the principal objective is to qualify, at any one time, under one category or another. Thus, an organization can "drift" from one classification of publicly supported organization to another throughout its duration. A charitable organization can, without harm, select one category of publicly supported organization when it completes Part IV and only satisfy the requirements of the other category as of the close of the advance ruling period.

As discussed in Chapter 11, the two categories of publicly supported organizations are sometimes referred to as *donative publicly supported charities* and *service provider publicly supported charities*. A charitable organization can, at any time in its existence, qualify as one or both of these types of public charities without concern. It does not matter which category the organization complies with as of the end of any year, nor does it matter which category the organization initially selected (and to which the IRS agreed).

The IRS, private foundations, and major donors do not care why the organization is publicly supported—they simply want to have the assurance that it is.

If an organization selects a category of publicly supported charitable organization when it prepares Part IV, and then finds that it has not met either set of requirements for publicly supported status at the close of the advance ruling period, it will be categorized as a private foundation, unless it can demonstrate that it is eligible for otherwise avoiding private foundation status. This can be done if the organization qualifies as an entity such as a church, school, hospital, or supporting organization (see below).

If the organization is classified as a private foundation following the close of its advance ruling period, it will have to pay the excise tax on its net investment income (see Chapter 11) for each of the years in the advance ruling period (and thereafter). For the IRS to be able to assess a tax retroactively for four years, the taxpayer must agree to waive the running of the statute of limitations, which otherwise would preclude the IRS from reaching that far back. The waiver is granted by the execution of Form 872-C (in duplicate), which is part of the Form 1023 package.

An applicant organization that qualifies as a church, school, hospital, supporting organization, or the like, is eligible to receive a definitive ruling at the outset. Its financial support is not the factor used in classifying it as a "public" entity. Instead, its public status derives from what it does programmatically.

An organization can receive a definitive ruling that it is publicly supported if it has been in existence at least two years and received the requisite public support during those years. An organization in this situation would submit a completed Part V for each of these years. It would also complete section B of Part VI.

An organization that seeks to be categorized as a supporting organization (see Chapter 11) must complete section C of Part VI.

Every organization that is requesting a definitive ruling must evidence its selection of non-private-foundation status by completing section A of Part VI. This section graphically displays the various options open to a charitable organization that desires to avoid private foundation status.

Other Parts. Parts V through VIII of Form 1023 have been discussed in the course of describing Part IV. Together, these parts of the form, if properly completed, amount to a rather complete portrait of the applicant organization. It is important to devote proper time and thought to the preparation of the form. It is a public document and, during the course of the organization's existence, copies may be requested by prospective donors or grantors, or representatives of the media.

A ruling from a governmental agency is only as good as the facts on which it is based. If the material facts of a charitable organization change, the determination letter granting recognition of tax-exempt status may become void. It will then be necessary to contact the IRS and arrange for review, to ensure ongoing tax-exempt status.

FOCUS: Campaign to Clean Up America

The Campaign to Clean Up America, desiring to be a charitable and publicly supported organization, must complete and file Form 1023. The following answers to selected questions in Form 1023 illustrate the form and content of these answers for any applicant organization. Questions that require particularly fact-specific answers have not been included.

Part I, Question 7

The appropriate activity codes for the Campaign to Clean Up America are 354 (preservation of scenic beauty), 125 (giving information or opinion), and 402 (activities aimed at combating community deterioration).

Part III, Question 1

The CCUA would answer question 1 of Part III as follows:

The sources of financial support of the Campaign to Clean Up America will be, in order of size, (1) contributions from the general public, (2) grants from private foundations, (3) other contributions and grants, (4) incidental exempt function revenue, (5) incidental unrelated income, and (6) miscellaneous investment income.

Part III, Question 2

The CCUA would answer question 2 of Part III as follows:

The fund-raising program of the Campaign to Clean Up America is in the process of formulation. The Campaign will commence its fund-raising program with selective mailings and other attempts to reach the general public (such as brochures, flyers, and newspaper advertisements). The Campaign will endeavor to secure gifts of money and property, including charitable bequests. The Campaign will soon commence a planned giving program and will likely, in the future, begin a capital campaign. The Campaign is in the process of retaining the services of a professional fund-raising consultant but an agreement has not been executed as yet. A copy of the first fund-raising letter that has been developed is attached as Exhibit C.

Part III, Question 3

The CCUA would answer question 3 of Part III as follows:

As the name of the organization indicates, the purpose of the Campaign to Clean Up America is to rid the cities, towns, suburbs, and other areas of the United States of trash, debris, and other litter. It is the vision of those who have formed the organization that the beauty of the landscapes of this country should not be tarnished, or hidden, by accumulations of garbage and other trash.

It is the Campaign's belief that much of the solution to the nation's trash problem lies in individuals' attitudes and mind-sets. An area that is clean is less likely to be trashed than one that is already littered. A community where its occupants are sensitized to the litter accumulation problem is less likely to be full of trash than the one where its occupants have subconsciously repressed the ugly sights. A community whose members are willing to rid the area of trash, and keep it that way, will be a far more beautiful place to live and work, and be proud of, than one that is constantly strewn with litter.

Therefore, the focus of the Campaign will always be on the prevention of littering and the pick-up of litter where it is found. As to the latter, the Campaign will, on a community-by-community basis, organize teams of volunteers who will pick up trash so as to keep their community clean and scenic. It will supply these teams with the equipment necessary to achieve this end, including rakes, shovels, gloves, trash bags, and safety signs to alert traffic that Clean Up America teams are at work in their community. If funding permits, the Campaign will provide members of these teams with "Clean Up America" tee-shirts, to both stimulate spirit in their volunteer work and advertise the program of the Campaign.

The Campaign will provide these teams with information as to organizational techniques, safety matters, and ideas for coordinating their efforts with local governmental officials. This latter aspect will be of importance in organizing means of trash disposal. The Campaign will also provide the teams with practical guidelines on matters such as trespassing, personal safety, and similar aspects that involve considerations of law.

The Campaign will endeavor to prevent littering from occurring in the first instance through public education programs. These will consist of the distribution of literature, media advertising, and community meetings. The public education aspect of the Campaign's program will be intertwined with its fund-raising program. Essentially, the public education component of the Campaign's efforts will be directed to ways to sensitize individuals to the problem of litter accumulation, in the hope that they will not litter, be moved to dispose of litter caused by others, and join a Campaign volunteer team to make and keep their community trash-free.

It is the belief of the Campaign that a community that is physically attractive (litter-free) is a community that will have other desirable attributes that contribute to a better way of life for its members.

The Campaign will undoubtedly engage in some attempts to influence legislation, mostly at the local level, such as laws to toughen the fines for littering and to force trucks to travel with their loads covered. However, any such activities will be insubstantial in relation to total activities.

The Campaign may engage in some activities that may constitute unrelated business. For example, the Campaign may sell trash bags (bearing its name and an antilitter message) to the general public. Again, any unrelated business activities will be insubstantial in relation to total activities.

Part III, Question 7b

The CCUA would answer question 7b of Part III as follows:

The Campaign to Clean Up America intends to hold some of the contributions it receives in an endowment fund, to provide a source of stable funding for its programs.

Part III, Question 10

The CCUA would answer question 10 of Part III "no." However, in the future, it may formally organize community groups, perhaps in the nature of chapters, that would be members of the corporation. Still, such a development is so speculative at this point that there is no need to reference it in the application. But if the CCUA became a membership corporation, it would have to amend its articles of incorporation and bylaws accordingly, and notify the IRS of the development, because the change would be a material one in its character and method of operation.

At the same time, the CCUA can use the "membership" concept in its fund-raising, without being a formal membership corporation and without having to answer "yes" to question 10 and complete the balance of the answer. For example, the CCUA can have, without creating true memberships, recognition levels for donors, such as "founding members," "sustaining members," and "associate members."

Part III, Question 11

The CCUA would answer "yes" to question 11 of Part III and then simply cross-refer to the answer to question 3 of Part III. It would not, however, file Form 5768. (See Chapter 13.)

Part IV

The CCUA would answer "no" to question 1 of Part IV. It would also check the first box in question 3b and enclose with its Form 1023 two executed copies of Form 872-C.

Part V

The CCUA would not file any financial statement in Part V. Instead, it would provide a four-year budget, showing its financial support and its anticipated expenditures.

Remainder of Form 1023

Given the facts, the CCUA does not have to complete Parts V through VIII. Other organizations filing straightforward applications for recognition of tax exemption for a charitable organization may also be able to utilize only the first four pages of the form.

The attachments to Form 1023 can be as important—if not more important—as the contents of the form itself, particularly if the statement of activities (the response to question 3 of Part III) is submitted as a separate exhibit. A review of the attachments to accompany Form 1023, submitted on behalf of the CCUA, serves as a basic checklist for all of these submissions:

- Form SS-4 (application for an identification number)
- Form 2848 (power of attorney)
- Form 8718 (user fee form)
- A check in payment of the user fee
- Conformed copy of organizing document (e.g., articles of incorporation)
- Conformed copy of rules of operation (e.g., bylaws)
- Form 872-C (in duplicate)
- Other attachments, such as copies of solicitations for financial support (question 2, Part III), statement of activities (question

3, Part III), list of directors and officers (question 4, Part III), copies of any assignments of income or assets (question 4e, Part III), any management agreement (question 8, Part III), any schedule of membership fees and dues (question 10a, Part III), any descriptive literature for prospective members (question 10b, Part III), and any documents or other attachments that may be required in responding to the questions in Part VIII.

- A cover letter to the IRS, stating exactly what is being requested. If expedited consideration of the application is being requested, this is the place to include that statement. It is also good practice to include a request for an administrative hearing in the event the IRS decides to (initially at least) rule adversely with respect to the organization.

GROUP EXEMPTION

An underutilized procedure allows a charitable (and other) organization to be tax-exempt without having to file an application for recognition of tax exemption. This procedure is tax exemption on a "group" basis.

For the procedure to be available, there must be a "group," which must consist of a "central" (or parent) organization and at least one "subordinate" (or affiliated) organization. An affiliated organization is a chapter, local, post, or like entity that is affiliated with and subject to the general supervision or control of a central organization—usually a state, regional, or national organization. (The term "affiliated" is not defined in this context but usually entails a mix of funding and decision making.) In this way, an organization is recognized as exempt by reason of its relationship with the parent organization, in addition to its own qualifying activities.

The group exemption requires the parent organization to evaluate, responsibly and independently, the tax-exempt status of its subordinate organizations, using applicable organizational and operational tests. The parent organization must annually certify to the IRS the specific organizations that are part of the group. Private foundations and foreign organizations may not be included in these groups.

A central organization may be involved in more than one group exemption arrangement; for example, a charitable parent organization may have both charitable and social welfare organization affiliates. Or, a central organization may be subordinate to another central organization; a state organization that has subordinate units may be affiliated with a national organization. All of the subordinate organizations in the group must have the same category of tax-exempt status, but the tax-exempt status of the central organization may be different from that of the subordinates.

EXEMPTIONS FROM FILING

A few charitable organizations are exempted from filing an application for recognition of exemption with the IRS. These entities are considered tax-exempt as charitable organizations, even though they do not file a Form 1023:

- A church, an interchurch organization, a local unit of a church, a convention or association of churches, or an integrated auxiliary of a church
- An organization that is not a private foundation (see Chapter 11) and normally has gross receipts of not more than $5,000 in each tax year
- An organization that is a subordinate organization covered by a group exemption, but only if the central organization timely submits a notice covering the subordinates

CHAPTER SEVEN

Tax Exemption: Not a Paperwork Exemption

Nonprofit organizations have not, for the most part, escaped the burdens of governmental regulation—the returns, reports, and other paperwork demanded by federal, state, and some local governments. Tax exemption may mean that an organization does not have to file a tax return. Instead, it will probably have to file an information return, which can be even more complex than a tax return. One set of reporting obligations has been discussed in Chapter 6—those in connection with the process of applying for recognition of tax-exempt status.

This chapter reviews the current basic reporting requirements for most nonprofit organizations. This summary covers only the basics, particularly when it comes to state and local requirements. Some reporting requirements are unique to certain types of nonprofit organizations. Other nonprofit organizations (churches are the best example) may be exempt from one or more reporting requirements that most others have to face.

Some nonprofit organizations have to comply with reporting requirements that are not directly imposed by government. For example, a nonprofit organization that receives a grant usually owes a periodic report to the grantor. A nonprofit organization that is under a group exemption (see Chapter 6) may report annually to the central organization, for the purpose of preparing combined information returns. A nonprofit organization that reports to one or more of the "voluntary watchdog agencies" can expect at least annual scrutiny.

INFORMATION RETURN

Nearly all nonprofit organizations that are tax-exempt under federal law are required to file an annual information return with the IRS. For most organizations, this annual information return is Form 990. Smaller organizations (those with year-end gross receipts of less than $100,000 and total assets of less than $250,000) file a short form—Form 990EZ (another example of IRS humor). Other organizations file the following forms:

- Private foundations: Form 990-PF
- Black Lung benefit trusts: Form 990-BL
- Cooperatives (certain types): Form 990-C
- Religious and apostolic organizations: Form 1065 (the partnership return)

Not all nonprofit organizations are freed from filing an annual tax return. Political organizations file Form 1120-POL and homeowners' associations file Form 1120-H. Nonprofit corporations that are not tax-exempt file the regular corporate tax return, Form 1120. Trusts that do not file Form 990 generally file Form 1041.

Annual Returns

The general annual information return for tax-exempt organizations (Form 990) must show the organization's items of "support and revenue" (gifts, grants, dues, program service revenue, other public support, revenue from the sales of assets, rents, and investment income). According to the form's instructions, the term "gifts" does not include the value of donated services or items such as the free use of materials, equipment, or facilities. The return differentiates between "direct" support—amounts received from individuals, corporations, trusts, estates, foundations, and other tax-exempt organizations—and "indirect" support—amounts received from federated fund-raising agencies and similar fund-raising organizations. "Program service revenue" is derived from the performance of services that are related to the organization's tax-exempt purposes: tuition received by a school, patient fees paid to a hospital, or revenue from admissions to a conference or from sales of publications.

Unrelated income and related expenses must be reflected on the annual information return as well as on the unrelated income tax return.

The return also must reflect disbursements (grants awarded, compensation, employee benefits, professional fund-raising fees, legal and accounting fees, occupancy, travel, conferences, and supplies). Expenses must be categorized by function: program services, management/general and administrative, and fund-raising (see Chapter 9). Expenses that relate to more than one functional category may be allocated on a reasonable basis. The four largest program services (measured by the total expenses incurred) and their related expenses must be identified.

The return must include a balance sheet showing assets, liabilities, and net worth. The directors' and officers' names, addresses, time expended, and compensation must be listed.

The return includes a list of questions about the organization's activities. Among them are:

- Has the organization engaged in any activities not previously reported to the IRS?

- Have any changes been made in the organizing or governing documents and not previously reported to the IRS?

- Was there a liquidation, dissolution, termination, or substantial contraction during the year?

- Is the organization related to any other tax-exempt or nonexempt organization?

- Did the organization receive donated services or the use of materials, equipment, or facilities at no charge or at substantially less than fair rental value?

The annual information return filed by a charitable organization must include the following information (in Schedule A of Form 990):

- The compensation of the five highest paid employees

- The total number of other employees paid over $30,000

- The compensation of the five persons who received the highest payment for professional services

- The total number of others receiving over $30,000 for professional services

- A description of any legislative or political campaign activities (see Chapters 13 and 14)

- An explanation of any acts of self-dealing between the organization and its directors and officers (see Chapter 11)

- The reason for the organization's non-private-foundation status and, if applicable, details as to the extent of its public support (see Chapter 11)
- If a school, certain information concerning policies that may involve discrimination
- Information concerning legislative activities if the organization has elected to come within the special lobbying rules for public charities (see Chapter 13)
- Information on direct or indirect transfers to, and other direct or indirect transactions and relationships with, tax-exempt organizations other than charitable ones (such as lobbying and political campaign entities)

The organization is required to provide its address, identification number, accounting method, and group exemption number (if applicable), as well as the federal tax law provision describing its tax exemption.

The annual information return for private foundations (Form 990-PF) must include:

- An itemized statement of the foundation's support, expenses, assets, and liabilities
- A report of capital gains and losses
- A calculation of the excise tax on net investment income
- An information statement concerning any legislative or political campaign activities
- An information statement concerning any acts of self-dealing, mandatory payout, excess business holdings, jeopardy investments, or taxable expenditures
- A list of all directors, officers, highly paid employees, and contractors
- A list of the five persons who received the highest payment for professional services
- A computation of the minimum investment return and distributable amount
- An itemized list of all grants made or approved, showing the amount of each grant, the name and address of each recipient, any relationship between a grant recipient and the foundation's managers or substantial contributors, and a concise statement of the purpose of each grant

- The address of the principal office of the foundation and (if different) of the place where its books and records are maintained
- The names and addresses of the foundation's managers who are substantial contributors or who own 10 percent or more of the stock of any corporation of which the foundation owns 10 percent or more, or corresponding interests in partnerships or other entities

A private foundation must divulge, on Form 990-PF, a schedule of relevant statistical information regarding its principal direct charitable activities and program-related investments: organizations and other beneficiaries served, conferences convened, or research papers produced. The foundation must also provide information demonstrating conformance with the public inspection requirements, including a copy of the newspaper notice.

Fund-Raising Aspects

Form 990 is an integral part of the federal government's participation in the regulation of fund-raising for charitable purposes. Some aspects of this regulation warrant mention here.

Form 990 gives particular attention to "special fund-raising events and activities." In computing "total revenue" (but not, as discussed below, "gross receipts"), an organization need use only net income from these events and activities.

Fund-raising events and activities include dinners, dances, carnivals, raffles, bingo games, and door-to-door sales of merchandise. These undertakings are not exempt functions but they are engaged in solely or primarily to raise funds for the organization's programs. The organization is offering goods or services of more than nominal value in return for a payment that is higher than the direct cost of the goods or services provided. The payment is not a deductible gift (if only "nominal value" is involved, the payment is a deductible gift, the receipts are reported elsewhere on the return as contributions, and the undertaking is not a "special fund-raising event or activity"). If, in the course of a fund-raising event or activity, a purchaser pays more than the value of the goods or services furnished, the excess is a contribution (and reported as such) and the amount paid that is equal to the value of the goods or services is reported as gross revenue from the event or activity.

An organization must attach to the return a schedule describing and providing financial detail for the three largest (as measured by gross receipts) special events conducted. Summary information must be provided for the other events.

Some or all of the dollar limitations applicable to Form 990 when filed with the IRS may not apply when using the form to satisfy state or local filing requirements. Examples of federal-law dollar limitations that do not meet some state requirements are the $25,000 gross receipts minimum, which identifies an obligation to file with the IRS (see the next section, "Exceptions"); the short reporting format for organizations that report total revenue of $25,000 or less (also in the next section); and the $30,000 minimum for listing professional fees in Schedule A of Form 990 (see the previous discussion).

Exceptions

Form 990 must be filed by nearly all tax-exempt organizations whose annual gross receipts are normally in excess of $25,000. Organizations with less gross receipts should file only the identification portion of the return. This entails no more than giving the IRS the organization's name and address, and an indication, by marking a box on the first page of the return, that its gross receipts are under the $25,000 threshold. (Technically, this filing is not required; but if it is not made, the IRS does not know whether the organization is not filing because it does not have to or because it is avoiding the requirement.) All private foundations *must file* Form 990-PF.

The $25,000 filing threshold is frequently misunderstood. Generally, an organization's annual gross receipts are the total amount it received during its annual accounting period, without subtraction of any costs or expenses. However, the form allows an organization, in computing its "total revenue," to net certain income items and related expenses: receipts (and associated expenses) from rents, revenue from assets sales, revenue from special fund-raising events, and certain other gross sales. An organization's "gross receipts" can be more than $25,000, even though the "total revenue" shown on the return is less than $25,000. To add to the confusion, "normally" here means a three-year average. An organization is not necessarily excused from filing an information return in any year in which its gross receipts for the year are less than $25,000. In fact, depending on its age and its particular circumstances, an organization can have more than $25,000 in gross receipts in a year and be excused from filing an information return. According to the rules, an organization's gross receipts are considered to be $25,000 or less if the organization is:

- Up to one year old and has received, or holds donors' pledges for, $37,500 or less during its first tax year
- Between one and three years old and has averaged $30,000 or less in gross receipts during each of its first two tax years

- Three or more years old and has averaged $25,000 or less in gross receipts for the immediately preceding three tax years (including the year for which the return would be filed)

The requirement to file an annual information return does not apply to:

- A church (including an interchurch organization of local units of a church)
- An integrated auxiliary of a church
- A convention or association of churches
- A financing, fund management, or retirement insurance program management organization functioning on behalf of the foregoing organizations
- Certain other entities affiliated with a church or convention or association of churches
- State institutions
- Certain schools and mission societies
- Organizations that normally receive less than $25,000 annually

Just because an organization is exempt from filing an annual information return does not always mean a return should not be filed. Preparation of the return may be a good discipline for keeping the organization's financial records up to standards, and a rehearsal for when gross receipts go over the filing threshold and a return becomes mandatory. In addition, filing the return starts the statute of limitations running—a protection against audits for years long passed.

If an organization's total revenue is $25,000 or less and its gross receipts are normally more than $25,000, it must (unless excepted) file Form 990 but need not complete all items on the form. A box on the first page of the return should be marked to indicate this filing status.

PUBLICITY AND PENALTIES

Failure to file the information return in a timely way, without reasonable cause or an exception, can give rise to a $10-per-day penalty. The organization must pay for each day the failure continues, up to a maximum of $5,000. An additional penalty can be imposed, at the same rate and up to the same maximum, on the individual(s) responsible for the failure to file, without reasonable cause. Other fines and imprisonment can be imposed for willfully failing to file returns or for filing fraudulent returns and statements with the IRS.

A tax-exempt organization must make its three most recent annual information returns available to anyone who wishes to inspect them at its principal office during regular business hours. (This requirement does not cause disclosure of the names or addresses of donors.) If an organization regularly maintains one or more regional or district offices where at least three people are employed, this inspection requirement applies to each office. The penalty for failure to provide copies of these three annual information returns for inspection is $10 per day, in the absence of reasonable cause. The maximum penalty per return is $5,000.

A copy of a private foundation's annual return must be made available to anyone for inspection at its principal office during regular business hours. Notice of the availability of the return must be published in a newspaper that has general circulation in the county in which the principal office of the foundation is located. Failure to properly publicize the availability of the annual return can result in the same sanction as the failure to file it.

Forms 990 and 990-PF are also available for public inspection and copying at the IRS. However, the IRS is not permitted to disclose certain portions of the returns and attachments, such as the list of contributors required to accompany Form 990. A request for inspection of a return must be in writing and must include the name and address of the organization that filed it. A request to inspect a return should indicate the type (number) of the return and the year(s) involved. The request should be sent to the District Director (Attention: Disclosure Officer) of the district in which the person making the request desires to inspect the return. For an inspection at the IRS National Office in Washington, DC, the request must be sent to the Commissioner of Internal Revenue, Attention: Freedom of Information Reading Room, 1111 Constitution Avenue, NW, Washington, DC 20224.

There is still another dimension to the filing of annual information returns. Organizations that are eligible to receive tax-deductible contributions are listed in an IRS publication titled *Cumulative List of Organizations Described in Section 170(c) of the Internal Revenue Code* (Publication 78). This list, which the IRS periodically supplements, is frequently relied on by donors and their advisers, when they are planning charitable giving. An organization may be removed from this listing if IRS records show that the organization failed, without good cause, to file Form 990 or to advise the IRS that it was not required to file. (Even if this happens, contributions to the organization remain deductible.)

The annual information return embodies the *functional method of accounting* for the reporting of expenses. This accounting method requires the identification, line by line, of expenses (including program expenses, such as publications and conferences, and professional expenses, such as the fees paid to lawyers and accountants), and the allocation of expenses by function or category—"program service," "management and general," and "fund-raising." (The law also requires an allocation of any expenses for legislative activities.) Organizations must identify their sources of program-service revenue, and they have the option of distinguishing between revenue that is restricted and unrestricted.

The annual information return is now also used to elicit and make available information about a charitable organization's fund-raising program and results.

Form 990 is due on or before the 15th day of the fifth month following the close of the tax year. Thus, the information return for an organization with a fiscal year the same as the calendar year should be filed by May 15 of each year.

UNRELATED INCOME TAX RETURNS

A tax-exempt organization with unrelated business taxable income (see Chapter 12) must file—in addition to an annual information return—a tax return, Form 990-T. On this return, the source or sources of unrelated income, and accompanying expenses, are reported, and any tax due is computed. The first $1,000 of annual net unrelated income is exempt from taxation.

Form 990-T also contains special schedules concerning rental income, unrelated debt-financed income, investment income of social clubs and certain other tax-exempt organizations, and income from controlled organizations.

This return is also due on or before the 15th day of the fifth month following the close of the organization's tax year.

For failure to file this tax return in a timely manner, additional tax may be imposed.

MATERIAL CHANGES

A nonprofit organization that has been recognized by the IRS as a tax-exempt organization must report to the IRS any material changes in its purposes, character, or methods of operation. This requirement enables the IRS to determine whether the change or changes may lead to revocation or alteration of the entity's tax-exempt status. A determination by the IRS that an organization is exempt is like a ruling by any other government agency—the ruling is only as valid as the facts on which it is based. If the facts materially change, the ruling may change as well.

The key word here is *materially*. An example of a material change would be a substantial alteration in the organization's statement of purpose, a major new program undertaking, or a significant structural change (such as the creation of a membership). Identifying a material change often involves a judgment, perhaps best made with the advice of a lawyer or accountant. If in doubt, the organization can send the information to the IRS. It is not always necessary to request a review of the original ruling; it may be enough to simply submit the changes and not ask for anything. In any event, all changes (such as amendments to by-laws or alterations in program activities) are to be reported to the IRS as part of the preparation and filing of the annual information return. The government should get the changes sooner or later—it is just a question of when.

DONEE RETURNS

In many instances, a charitable organization that sells, exchanges, or otherwise disposes of gift property within two years after the date of receipt of the property must file an information return with the IRS (Form 8282).

The basic purpose of this return is to enable the IRS to compare a charity's selling price of property with the value claimed by the donor in computing a charitable contribution deduction. This filing requirement is part of a package of rules concerning the need for appraisals of gift property and other aspects of the charitable deduction substantiation (including proof-of-value) rules. (See Chapter 8.)

STATE ANNUAL REPORTS

Most states require organizations created under their laws and/or operating in their jurisdictions to file annual reports with the state's appropriate governmental agency. This requirement is usually applicable to nonprofit organizations. These corporate annual reports, filed most frequently with the state's secretary of state, are not tax returns. In some states, these reports are due whether the entity is formally a corporation or not.

Some states have additional filing requirements for charitable trusts. This type of filing is usually made with the office of the state's attorney general. States may also require information and/or tax returns similar to federal Forms 990 and 990-T.

This is an area of the law where it is difficult to generalize. Each organization must, on its own or with professional assistance, determine what reports and returns may be required by the state, county, and/or other governmental jurisdiction in which it is located.

The filing requirements may be even more complex, if a nonprofit organization operates in more than one state.

An organization is a "domestic" organization to the state in which it is formed. In all other states, the organization is a "foreign" entity. The domestic organization may have reporting obligations under the law of the home state. However, the organization may also have reporting obligations under the law of the states to which it is a foreign organization "doing business" in those states. The concept of "doing business" is not particularly definitive, but it includes the maintenance of an office.

An organization that is doing business in a state other than the domestic state must first obtain from that jurisdiction a certificate of authority to conduct operations. The organization will have to name a registered agent in that state and probably will have to file an annual report there.

A nonprofit organization that has multistate operations will likely have a registered agent and file an annual report in each state in which it is operational. These requirements are in addition to those that may be required under the states' charitable solicitation acts.

CHARITABLE SOLICITATION ACTS

Many states are heavily into the practice of regulating fund-raising by charitable organizations by means of the enforcement of charitable solicitation acts. Some counties and cities are involved in this process as well.

Annual reporting is a mainstay of charitable fund-raising regulation. A charitable organization that solicits contributions is generally required to file a report with every state in which it seeks funds. (A similar reporting requirement is applicable to professional fund-raisers and professional solicitors.) As noted in Chapter 9, a charitable organization that is raising funds throughout the country is expected to file reports with about 45 states, not to mention the counties and towns that want reports as well.

Worse, a few states treat the process of raising funds for charitable purposes as being a form of "doing business" in the state. These states insist that the charity, in addition to complying with the states' charitable solicitation acts, obtain permission to do business there. The charity must then appoint a registered agent in each state and thereafter begin filing annual reports as a foreign corporation. If all states were to take this position, a charitable organization engaging in fund-raising in each of the states would have to register and report under 45 charitable solicitation acts and 51 (including the District of Columbia) nonprofit corporation acts!

OTHER REPORTING

Depending on state law, a nonprofit organization may have to report to a state on its exemption from or compliance with state income, sales, and/or property (tangible or intangible, personal or real) taxation.

If a nonprofit organization is an employer, it must file all of the federal and state forms concerning payment of compensation. Pertinent federal forms include Form W-2 (wage and tax statement), Form W-3 (transmittal of income and tax statements), Form W-2P (statement for recipients of annuities or pensions), Form 1096 (annual summary and transmittal of federal information returns), Form 940 (employer's annual federal unemployment tax return), Form 941 (employer's quarterly federal tax return, used to report the withholding of federal income taxes and social security taxes), and Form 5500, 5500-C, or 5500-R (reporting on employee benefit plans).

A nonprofit organization generally must file an information return (Form 1099) with the IRS when paying a person (other than an employee) more than $600 a year. Charitable organizations that make payments to individuals for information about the commission of crimes do not have to file Form 1099 for these payments.

FOCUS: Campaign to Clean Up America

The Campaign to Clean Up America fully expects to annually receive gross receipts in excess of $25,000, so it will be obligated to prepare and file with the IRS an annual information return (Form 990). The CCUA will be a publicly supported charitable organization, not a private foundation, so it will not be filing the annual return for foundations (Form 990-PF). There are no present plans to have unrelated business income, so there is no current obligation to file a tax return (Form 990-T).

The CCUA will be soliciting contributions throughout the United States, so it will be registering with each state that has a charitable solicitation act. In some of these states, the CCUA will have to obtain a certificate of authority to do business as a foreign corporation. However, at present, the CCUA does not intend to actually do business in any other state.

The state in which the CCUA is organized (Michigan) has an annual report requirement, which the CCUA will be obligated to fulfill.

At this time, the CCUA has no employees. The federal and state reporting requirements associated with a payroll are therefore not applicable for now. The CCUA will be using consultants (a lawyer, an accountant, and a fund-raising professional). The compensation paid to them will have to be annually reported to the IRS (Form 1099).

CHAPTER EIGHT

The Basic Charitable Giving Rules

The basic concept of the federal income tax deduction for a charitable contribution is this: corporate taxpayers and individual taxpayers who itemize their deductions (for individuals, those who file a "long form") can deduct on their annual tax return, within certain limits, an amount equivalent to the amount contributed or to the value of a contribution to a "qualified donee." A *charitable contribution* for income tax purposes is a gift to or for the use of one or more qualified donees.

Deductions for charitable gifts are also allowed under the federal gift tax and estate tax law. Donors and the charitable organizations they support commonly expect gifts to be in the form of outright transfers of money or, occasionally, property. For both parties (the donor and the donee), a gift is usually a unilateral transaction, in a financial sense: the donor parts with the contribution and the charity acquires it. The advantages to the donor are confined to the resulting charitable deduction and the emotional enhancement derived from making the gift.

Another type of charitable giving, referred to as *planned giving* or *deferred giving*, provides far greater financial and tax advantages to the donor. This type of giving is discussed in Chapter 17.

TYPES OF CHARITABLE GIVING

There are three categories of charitable giving: *impulse giving*, *interest giving*, and *integrated giving*. Each provides some form of emotional and/or financial satisfaction to the donor.

101

Impulse Giving

Impulse giving is just that—the donor is responding on impulse to an appeal for a charitable gift. The gift is made in immediate response to a compelling plea (for example, children ravaged by war, hunger, or disease; suffering animals; or an impending cure for a deadly disease). A direct-mail, television, radio, telephone, door-to-door, or street corner solicitation usually invites the response.

An impulse gift almost always is cash and usually is a relatively small amount. The donor may not have donated previously to the organization, probably does not intend to become involved with the organization's programs or administration, and has likely not thought about any subsequent gifts. The gift may have been prompted by the receipt of a premium (a magazine, a discount, or a token gift) and an accompanying appeal letter or other literature. Many impulse gifts are not particularly important as charitable contribution deductions because of the amounts involved. If the donor does not itemize deductions or if the donee is not a charitable entity, the deduction is not even available.

Interest Giving

A donor's ongoing and authentic involvement in a charitable organization's program will result in interest giving. Interest donors usually have some unique relationship with the charitable organization—it is the donor's church, synagogue, or other religious institution; the school, college, or university from which he or she graduated; the hospital serving his or her family or community; or a charitable organization with programs that have some special appeal to the donor's personal beliefs, background, or current interests.

Interest giving is usually done on a periodic basis (for example, weekly in church or annually in response to a yearly fund effort). Compared to an impulse gift, the typical amount of an interest gift is higher, and there is a greater possibility that the gift will consist of property— probably securities or real estate.

Integrated Giving

Integrated giving is the most sophisticated form of charitable giving. Unlike the other two categories of giving, the gift is deliberately planned as part of the donor's overall financial and tax affairs and/or his or her estate. An integrated gift is most often from a donor who has a substantial relationship with the charitable organization. A large contribution is involved. The integrated gift is less likely to involve outright gifts of cash or property than gifts utilizing trusts, contracts, and/or wills. The charitable deduction is of major importance to this type of contributor, is a reason for the donation, and is an integral part of the transaction.

ACTUAL PRACTICE

In actual practice, the lines of demarcation among the three categories of charitable giving are often blurry. The somewhat arbitrary labels are not meant to suggest that an impulse donor lacks an authentic interest in the recipient charity or that an integrated donor is motivated solely by personal financial advantages. One category of charitable gift can lead to another: impulse giving can evolve into interest giving, or interest giving can give rise to integrated giving.

A good fund-raising professional can bring about a progression in donors' giving. Any development (fund-raising) program worthy of that name is aimed toward upgrading a donor from an impulse donor to an interest donor, and perhaps to an integrated donor. For example, a direct-mail program may result in a donor's first gift (as part of a donor acquisition effort). The organization is generally interested in the donor's regular giving, that is, becoming an interest donor (as part of a donor renewal effort). Many planned giving programs (integrated gift programs) are built on the conversion of interest donors to integrated donors.

These are the economic advantages resulting from a charitable gift:

- A federal, state, and/or local tax deduction for the charitable contribution
- A way of avoiding capital gains taxation
- A creation of or an increase in cash flow
- An improved tax treatment of income
- Free professional tax and investment services
- An opportunity to transfer property between the generations of a family
- Receipt of benefits (usually services) from the charitable donee

For an impulse donor, none of these advantages may be involved, although the charitable deduction may be a possibility. For an interest donor, the charitable deduction is usually a significant amount, and avoiding capital gains tax may be important. The interest donor may receive a premium (such as a magazine, discount, or token gift in return). Only an integrated donor realizes all of the economic advantages—plus the satisfaction of making a major gift to a favorite charitable organization.

WHEN IS A GIFT A GIFT?

In books and articles on nonprofit organizations, much time and attention are devoted to charitable giving.

The federal tax law on charitable giving is contained in the Internal Revenue Code (IRC) and in the interpretations of the IRC, Treasury Department and IRS regulations, and IRS public and private rulings. The IRC is rather specific on some components of the law of charitable giving—qualification of charitable donees, percentage limitations on deductibility of donations made in one year, gifts of particular types of property (such as inventory and works of art), and eligibility of various planned giving vehicles.

Despite the extent and detail of the IRC, there is a glaring omission in the rules concerning charitable giving. Oddly, this omission exists at the threshold: the law is very scarce regarding the definition of the word *gift*. This omission is highly significant because there must be a *gift* in order to have a *charitable gift*.

A fundamental requirement of the charitable contribution deduction is that the cash or property transferred to a charitable donee must be transferred as a *gift*. Just because cash is paid (or property is transferred) to a charity does not necessarily mean that the payment (or transfer) is a gift. When a university's tuition, a hospital's health-care fee, or an association's dues are paid, there is no gift and thus no charitable deduction for the payment.

Most of the law on what constitutes a gift has been generated by the federal courts. The IRC and the tax regulations are essentially silent on the subject. Basically, a "gift" has two elements: it involves a transfer that is *voluntary* and is motivated by something other than "consideration" (something being received in return for a payment). Where payments are made to receive something in exchange (education, health care, and so on), the transaction is more in the nature of a purchase. The law places more emphasis on what is received than on the payment given. The income tax regulations state that a transfer is not a contribution when made "with a reasonable expectation of financial return commensurate with the amount of the transfer." A single transaction can be partially a gift and partially a purchase; when a charity is the payee, only the gift portion is deductible.

Years ago, the U.S. Supreme Court observed that a gift is a transfer motivated by "detached or disinterested generosity." The Court has also characterized a gift as a transfer stimulated "out of affection, respect, admiration, charity, or like impulses." (This is the factor frequently referred to as "donative intent.") One federal court of appeals described the issue of a gift more starkly: "[a] particularly confused issue of federal taxation." The existing IRC structure on this subject, said this appellate court, is "cryptic," and "neither Congress nor the courts have offered any very satisfactory definition" of the terms "gift" and "contribution."

These concepts have been revisited many times in recent years. One trouble spot has been the availability of a charitable deduction for the transfer of money to a college or university, when the transferor is then granted preferential access to good seating at the institution's athletic events. The IRS has refused to regard these payments as gifts, arguing that the payment results in receipt of a "substantial benefit." (The IRS concedes that the portion of a payment that is in excess of the value of the benefits received in return can be a gift.) The IRS struggled with this issue in the early 1980s, when it was popular for homes to be auctioned, with the benefits accruing to a charitable organization. In one ruling, the IRS said that those who purchase tickets from a charity are not making gifts. Various tax shelter programs involving gifts of artwork and donors' use of premiums and other items of property in response to their contributions have recently come under fire.

The IRS, for years, has been advising the charitable community that, when a "donor" receives some benefit or privilege in return for a payment to charity, the payment may not, in whole or in part, constitute a deductible charitable gift. The IRS's position is that charitable organizations must advise individuals and corporations when a payment is not deductible or is only partially deductible, but the requirement lacks any sanctions. For example, suppose a charity sponsors a dinner as a fund-raising event, and charges $75 dollars for a ticket. Each patron receives a dinner priced at $50 (its fair market value). The charity is supposed to advise the purchasers of the tickets that the deductible gift is $25, not $75.

As part of passage of the Revenue Act of 1987, Congress passed a law requiring noncharitable organizations that solicit gifts to disclose in their fund-raising literature that the contributions are not deductible. (See Chapter 9.) The report of the House Committee on Ways and Means, which accompanied the Committee's version of the tax legislation, contained a discussion of the nondeductibility of payments to charitable organizations. The Committee wrote that it "is concerned that some charitable organizations may not make sufficient disclosure, in soliciting donations, membership dues, payments for admissions or merchandise, or other support, of the extent (if any) to which the payors may be entitled to charitable deductions for such payments."

The Committee's discussion focused on "memberships" in a charitable entity, typically a museum or library, where the "members" receive benefits of some monetary value, such as free admission to events when others are charged, merchandise discounts, and free subscriptions. The Committee cautioned that some or all of these membership payments are not deductible as charitable contributions.

The Committee's analysis also referenced payments to a charity that are not deductible charitable gifts at all, such as the sale of raffle tickets and the auctioning of property or services. (However, those who donate property to be used by a charity in an auction are entitled to a charitable deduction, within the limits described below.) This legislative history states that the portion of the winning bid at a charity auction that is in excess of the fair market value of the item or service received may be deductible. The Committee noted that some charities wrongfully imply that all of these payments are fully deductible, while "many other charities carefully and correctly advise their supporters of the long-standing tax rules governing the deductibility of payments made to a charitable organization in return for, or with the expectation of, a financial or economic benefit to the payor."

The Committee wrote that it "anticipates" that the IRS "will monitor the extent to which taxpayers are being furnished accurate and sufficient information by charitable organizations as to the nondeductibility of payments to such organizations where benefits or privileges are received in return, so that such taxpayers can correctly compute their Federal income tax liability." The Committee expected the charitable community to do its part. Groups representing the community were to further "educate their members as to the applicable tax rules and provide guidance as to how charities can provide appropriate information to their supporters in this regard."

The Ways and Means Committee fired its warning shot; five years later, it decided that the charitable community was unable to voluntarily provide the requisite disclosure to donors. In 1992, Congress included as part of major tax legislation a requirement that charitable organizations disclose the nondeductibility (as charitable gifts) of payments to them. (Some payments of this nature are deductible as business expenses.) The legislation was vetoed (for other reasons), but the provision may well reappear in subsequent tax legislation. In the meantime, the IRS is writing "donor recognition" guidelines, which will have a major impact on the nondeductibility (as charitable gifts) of a variety of payments.

How is it that the statutory law can be so explicit on the consequences in tax law of making a charitable gift, yet be so skimpy in defining the threshold word *gift?*

QUALIFIED DONEES

Qualified donees are charitable organizations (including educational, religious, and scientific entities), certain fraternal organizations, certain cemetary companies, and most veterans' organizations. (These and other types of tax-exempt organizations are described in Chapter 4.) Contributions to both private and public charities are deductible, but the law favors gifts to public charities.

Federal, state, and local governmental bodies are, under the tax law, charitable donees. However, other law may preclude a governmental entity from accepting charitable gifts. In many jurisdictions, a charitable organization can be established to solicit deductible contributions for and make grants to governmental bodies. This is a common technique for public schools, colleges, universities, and hospitals.

An otherwise nonqualifying organization may be allowed to receive a deductible charitable gift, where the gift property is used for charitable purposes or received by an agent for a charitable organization. An example of the former is a gift to a trade association that is earmarked for a charitable fund within the association. An example of a receiving agent would be a title-holding corporation that operates a property for charitable purposes.

GIFT PROPERTIES

Aside from the eligibility of the gift recipient, the other basic element in determining whether a charitable contribution is deductible is the nature of the property given. Basically, the distinctions are between outright giving and planned giving, and between gifts of cash and gifts of property. In many instances, the tax law differentiates between personal property and real property, and tangible property and intangible property (stocks and bonds). The value of a qualified charitable contribution of an item of property often is its fair market value.

The federal income tax treatment of gifts of property is dependent on whether the property is capital gain property. The tax law makes a distinction between *long-term capital gain* and *short-term capital gain* (although generally a net gain of either type is taxed as ordinary income). Property that is neither long-term capital gain property nor short-term capital gain property is *ordinary income property*. These three terms are based on the tax classification of the type of revenue that would be generated upon sale of the property. Short-term capital gain property is generally treated the same as ordinary income property. Therefore, the actual distinction is between capital gain property (really long-term capital gain property) and ordinary income property.

Capital gain property is a capital asset that has appreciated in value and, if sold, would give rise to long-term capital gain. To result in long-term capital gain, property must be held for a specified period, generally 12 months. (For property acquired after June 22, 1984, and before January 1, 1988, the long-term capital gain holding period is 6 months.) Most forms of capital gain property are stocks, bonds, and real estate.

The charitable deduction for capital gain property is often equal to its fair market value or at least is computed using that value. Gifts of ordinary income property generally produce a deduction equivalent to the donor's cost basis in the property. The law provides exceptions to this "basis-only rule"; an example is a gift by a corporation out of its inventory.

PERCENTAGE LIMITATIONS

The amount of charitable contributions that can be deducted for a particular tax year is limited to a certain percentage, which for individuals is related to the donor's *contribution base*—essentially, the individual's adjusted gross income. There are five percentage limitations. They are dependent on several factors, principally the nature of the charitable recipient and the nature of the property donated. The examples used here assume an individual donor has an annual contribution base (adjusted gross income) of $100,000.

The first three limitations apply to gifts to public charities and private operating foundations.

First, there is a percentage limitation of 50 percent of the donor's contribution base for contributions of cash and ordinary income property. A donor may, in any one year, make deductible gifts up to a total of $50,000. If an individual makes contributions that exceed the 50 percent limitation, the excess generally may be carried forward and deducted in 1 to 5 subsequent years. Thus, if a donor gave $60,000 to public charities in year 1 (and made no other charitable gifts), he or she would be entitled to a deduction of $50,000 in year 1 and $10,000 in year 2.

The second percentage limitation is 30 percent of the donor's contribution base for gifts of capital gain property. A donor may, in any one year, contribute up to $30,000 in qualifying stocks, bonds, real estate, and like property, and receive a charitable deduction for that amount. Any excess (more than 30 percent) is subject to the carryforward rule. If a donor gave $50,000 in capital gain property in year 1 (and made no other charitable gifts that year), he or she would be entitled to a charitable contribution deduction of $30,000 in year 1 and $20,000 in year 2.

A donor who makes gifts of cash and capital gain property to public charities (and/or private operating foundations) in any one year generally must use a blend of these percentage limitations. For example, if a donor in year 1 gives $50,000 in cash and $30,000 in appreciated capital gain property to a public charity, his or her charitable deduction in year 1 is $30,000 of capital gain property and $20,000 of cash (to keep the deduction within the overall 50 percent ceiling); the other $30,000 of cash is carried forward to year 2 (or years 2 through 5, depending on the donor's circumstances).

The third percentage limitation allows a donor of capital gain property to use the 50 percent limitation, instead of the 30 percent limitation, where the amount of the contribution is reduced by all of the unrealized appreciation in the value of the property. This election is usually made by donors who want a larger deduction in the year of the gift for a property that has not appreciated in value to a great extent. As discussed later in the chapter, this election can be useful in avoiding a problem with the alternative minimum tax.

The fourth and fifth percentage limitations apply to gifts to private foundations and certain other charitable donees (other than public charities and private operating foundations). These donees are generally veterans' and fraternal organizations.

Under the fourth percentage limitation, contributions of cash and ordinary income property to private foundations and other entities may not exceed 30 percent of the individual donor's contribution base. The carryover rules apply to this type of gift. If a donor gives $50,000 in cash to one or more private foundations in year 1, his or her charitable deduction for that year (assuming no other charitable gifts) is $30,000, with the balance of $20,000 carried forward into subsequent years.

The carryover rules blend with the first three percentage limitations. For example, if in year 1 a donor gave $65,000 to charity, of which $25,000 went to a public charity and $40,000 to a private foundation, his or her charitable deduction for that year would be $50,000: $30,000 to the private foundation and $20,000 to the public charity. The remaining $10,000 of the gift to the foundation and the remaining $5,000 of the gift to the public charity would be carried forward into year 2.

The fifth percentage limitation is 20 percent of the contribution base for gifts of capital gain property to private foundations and other charitable donees, up to a maximum of $20,000. There is no carryforward for any excess deduction. For example, if a donor gives appreciated securities, having a value of $30,000, to a private foundation in year 1, his or her charitable deduction for year 1 (assuming no other charitable gifts) is $20,000; the remaining $10,000 would never be deductible. In this situation, a wise donor would elect to contribute $20,000 of the securities in year 1 and postpone the gift of the remaining $10,000 in securities until year 2. Or, if the value of the stock may substantially decline and an immediate charitable deduction is of prime concern, the donor could in year 1 donate $20,000 of the securities to the private foundation and $10,000 of the securities to a public charity.

Deductible charitable contributions by corporations in any tax year may not exceed 10 percent of pretax net income. Excess amounts may be carried forward and deducted in subsequent years (up to 5 years). For gifts by corporations, the federal tax laws do not differentiate between gifts to public charities and private foundations. As an illustration, a corporation that grosses $1 million in a year and incurs $900,000 in expenses in that year (not including charitable gifts) may generally contribute to charity and deduct in that year an amount up to $10,000 (10 percent of $100,000); in computing its taxes, this corporation would report taxable income of $90,000. If the corporation instead gave $20,000 in that year, the numbers would stay the same, except that the corporation would have a $10,000 charitable contribution carryforward.

A corporation on the accrual method of accounting can elect to treat a contribution as having been made in a tax year if it is actually donated during the first 2¹/₂ months of the following year. Corporate gifts of property are generally subject to the deduction reduction rules, discussed next.

DEDUCTION REDUCTION RULES

A donor (individual or corporate) who makes a gift of *ordinary income property* to any charity (public or private) must confine the charitable deduction to the amount of the cost basis of the property. The deduction is not based on the fair market value of the property; it must be reduced by the amount that would have been gain (ordinary income) if the property had been sold. As an example, if a donor gave to a charity an item of ordinary income property having a value of $1,000 for which he or she paid $600, the charitable deduction would be $600.

Any donor who makes a gift of *capital gain property* to a public charity generally can compute the charitable deduction using the property's fair market value at the time of the gift, regardless of the cost basis and with no taxation of the appreciation (the capital gain inherent in the property). However, suppose a donor makes a gift of capital gain tangible personal property (e.g., a work of art) to a public charity and the gift's use by the donee is unrelated to its tax-exempt purposes. The donor must reduce the deduction by all of the long-term capital gain that would have been recognized had the donor sold the property at its fair market value as of the date of contribution.

Generally, a donor who makes a gift of capital gain property to a private foundation must reduce the amount of the otherwise allowable deduction by all of the appreciation element in the gift property. However, an individual is allowed full fair market value for a contribution to a private foundation of certain publicly traded stock, if the gift is made before 1995.

"TWICE BASIS" DEDUCTIONS

As a general rule, when a corporation makes a charitable gift of property from its inventory, the resulting charitable deduction cannot exceed an amount equal to the donor's cost basis in the donated property. In most instances, this basis amount is rather small, being equal to the cost of producing the property. However, under certain circumstances, corporate donors can receive a greater charitable deduction for gifts out of their inventory. Where the tests are satisfied, the deduction can be equal to cost basis plus one-half of the appreciated value of the property. The deduction may not, in any event, exceed an amount equal to twice the property's cost basis.

Five special requirements have to be met for this twice-basis charitable deduction to be available:

- The donated property must be used by the charitable donee for a related use.

- The donated property must be used solely for the care of the ill, the needy, or infants.

- The property may not be transferred by the donee in exchange for money, other property, or services.

- The donor must receive a written statement from the donee representing that the use and disposition of the donated property will be in conformance with these rules.

- Where the donated property is subject to regulation under the Federal Food, Drug, and Cosmetic Act, the property must fully satisfy the Act's requirements on the date of transfer and for the previous 180 days.

For these rules to apply, the donee must be a public charity; that is, it cannot be a private foundation or a private operating foundation. An "S corporation"—the tax status of many small businesses—cannot utilize these rules.

ALTERNATIVE MINIMUM TAX

The alternative minimum tax is intended to cause an individual or corporate taxpayer to pay some tax, no matter how sophisticated his, her, or its financial affairs are structured from a tax point of view. The alternative minimum tax is a flat tax of 21 percent, payable on the economic value of a variety of "tax preference items," less certain adjustments. This tax is to be paid when it is greater than the regular income tax.

In 1986, Congress decided to lower overall tax rates and absorb the resulting revenue losses by taxing the wealthy and corporations, and by eliminating many deductions, credits, and the like. In this environment, the alternative minimum tax was toughened.

One of the tax preference items used to construct the alternative minimum income tax base is an amount equal to the appreciation in value of contributed long-term capital gain property, to the extent it is included in the allowable charitable contribution deduction for regular income tax purposes. This is the *appreciated property charitable deduction.* For example, a donor gave $100,000 in appreciated securities to a public charity in a tax year and claimed an income tax deduction in that amount. The donor made no other charitable gifts that year. The securities had a cost basis of $10,000, so the donor has a tax preference item for alternative minimum tax purposes of $90,000.

However, this tax preference rule cannot be applied where the contributed appreciated property, normally subject to a 30 percent limitation, is the subject of the elective 50 percent limitation.

When computing the alternative minimum tax, these are the steps an individual taxpayer must take:

- Compute the regular income tax. In the process, determine the presence (if any) of the 13 tax preference items.
- Determine the adjusted gross income.
- Identify the (six) deductions that are allowed in computing the alternative minimum tax, and subtract them from the adjusted gross income.
- Combine this amount and the total of the tax preference items. The sum is the total "gross minimum taxable income."
- Determine the "net minimum taxable income" by subtracting the alternative minimum tax exemption from the gross minimum taxable income. This exemption ($40,000 for joint taxpayers and $30,000 for single taxpayers) is phased out at 25 cents per dollar, once gross minimum taxable income exceeds $150,000 for couples and $112,500 for singles. The exemption disappears for married

couples with adjusted gross income of $310,000 and for singles with adjusted gross income of $232,500.

- Multiply the net minimum taxable income by the 21 percent rate, to arrive at the alternative minimum tax.

Congress is aware that its action in creating the appreciated property charitable deduction tax preference was a mistake. It attempted to somewhat ameliorate its error by creating an exception for gifts to charity of tangible personal property during the period January 1, 1991, through June 30, 1992. As part of the 1992 tax legislation, Congress proposed to permanently repeal the rule. The legislation was vetoed, but the proposal is likely to appear as part of the Clinton Administration's tax package.

The alternative minimum tax will not trouble most donors of appreciated property; usually it involves a donor with a large income and highly appreciated gift property. Where other tax preference items may be involved, some mitigating factors are present. A 1986 tax law revision eliminated some tax preference items that would otherwise trigger the alternative minimum tax.

There are three important things a taxpayer can do to eliminate the alternative minimum tax when making charitable gifts:

- Stage the gifts (such as shares of stock) to avoid even the threat of the alternative minimum tax.
- Make remainder interest gifts instead of outright gifts (see Chapter 17).
- Use the 50 percent limitation election (for basis-only gifts) rather than the 30 percent limitation in computing the charitable contribution deduction for the year.

PARTIAL INTEREST GIFTS

Most charitable gifts are of all ownership of a property: the donor parts with all right, title, and interest in the property. A gift of a *partial interest* is also possible—a contribution of less than a donor's entire interest in the property.

As a general rule, charitable deductions for gifts of partial interests in property, including the right to use property, are denied. The exceptions, which are many, are: gifts made in trust form (using a so-called "split-interest trust"); gifts of an outright remainder interest in a personal residence or farm; gifts of an undivided portion of one's entire interest in a property; gifts of a lease on, option to purchase, or easement with respect to real property granted in perpetuity to a public charity exclusively for conservation purposes; and a remainder interest in real property granted to a public charity exclusively for conservation purposes.

Contributions of income interests in property in trust are basically confined to the use of charitable lead trusts. Aside from a charitable gift annuity and gifts of remainder interests, there is no charitable deduction for a contribution of a remainder interest in property unless it is in trust and is one of three types: a charitable remainder annuity trust, a charitable remainder unitrust, or a pooled income fund. (The concept of "partial interest" gifts, more popularly known as "planned giving," is the subject of Chapter 17.)

Defective charitable split-interest trusts may be reformed to preserve the charitable deduction where certain requirements are satisfied.

GIFTS OF INSURANCE

One underutilized type of charitable giving involves life insurance. To secure an income tax deduction, the gift must include all rights of ownership in a life insurance policy. Thus, an individual can donate a fully paid-up life insurance policy to a charitable organization and deduct (for income tax purposes) its value. Or, an individual can acquire a life insurance policy, give it to a charity, pay the premiums, and receive a charitable deduction for each premium payment made.

For the donation of an insurance policy to be valid, the charitable organization must be able to demonstrate that it has an insurable interest in the life of the donor of the policy. From an income tax deduction standpoint, it is not enough for a donor to simply name a charitable organization as a beneficiary of a life insurance policy. There is *no income tax charitable contribution deduction* for this philanthropic act. However, although the life insurance proceeds become part of the donor's estate, there will be an offsetting estate tax charitable deduction.

APPRAISAL RULES

The law contains requirements relating to proof, when charitable deductions for contributions of property are claimed by an individual, a closely held corporation, a personal service corporation, a partnership, or an S corporation. These requirements, when applicable, must be complied with if the deduction is to be allowed.

The requirements apply to contributions of property (other than money and publicly traded securities) if the aggregate claimed or reported value of the property (and all similar items of property for which deductions for charitable contributions are claimed or reported by the same donor for the same tax year, whether or not donated to the same donee) is in excess of $5,000. The phrase "similar items of property" means property of the same generic category or type, including stamps, coins, lithographs, paintings, books, nonpublicly traded stock, land, or buildings.

For each gift of this type, the donor must obtain a "qualified appraisal" and attach an "appraisal summary" to the return on which the deduction is claimed. For a gift of nonpublicly traded stock, the claimed value of which does not exceed $10,000 but is greater than $5,000, the donor does not have to obtain a qualified appraisal but must attach a partially completed appraisal summary form to the tax or information return on which the deduction is claimed.

A *qualified appraisal* is an appraisal made no more than 60 days prior to the date of the contribution of the appraised property. The appraisal must be prepared, signed, and dated by a "qualified appraiser" and cannot involve a prohibited type of appraisal fee.

Certain information must be included in the qualified appraisal:

- A sufficiently detailed description of the property
- The physical condition of the property (in the case of tangible property)
- The date (or expected date) of contribution
- The terms of any agreement or understanding concerning the use or disposition of the property
- The name, address, and social security number of the qualified appraiser
- The qualifications of the qualified appraiser
- A statement that the appraisal was prepared for tax purposes
- The date or dates on which the property was valued
- The appraised fair market value of the property on the date (or expected date) of contribution
- The method of valuation used to determine the fair market value
- The specific basis for the valuation
- A description of the fee arrangement between the donor and the appraiser

The qualified appraisal must be received by the donor before the due date (including extensions) of the return on which the deduction for the contributed property is first claimed. If a deduction is first claimed on an amended return, the appraisal must be received before the date on which the return is filed.

One qualified appraisal for a group of similar items of property contributed in the same tax year is acceptable, as long as the appraisal includes all of the required information for each item. If a group of items has an aggregate value appraised at $100 or less, the appraiser may select these items for a group description rather than a specific description of each item.

The appraisal summary must be on IRS Form 8283, signed and dated by the donee and qualified appraiser (or appraisers), and attached to the tax return on which the donor is first claiming or reporting the deduction for the appraised property. The signature by the donee does not represent concurrence in the appraised value of the contributed property.

Certain information must be included in the appraisal summary:

- The name and taxpayer identification number of the donor
- A sufficient description of the property
- A summary of the physical condition of the property (in the case of tangible property)
- The manner and date of acquisition of the property
- The basis of the property
- The name, address, and taxpayer identification number of the donee
- The date the donee received the property
- The name, address, and taxpayer identification number of the qualified appraiser (or appraisers)
- The appraised fair market value of the property on the date of contribution
- A declaration by the qualified appraiser

The rules pertaining to separate versus group appraisals apply to appraisal summaries. A donor who contributes similar items of property to more than one charitable donee must attach a separate appraisal summary for each donee.

If the donor is a partnership or S corporation, it must provide a copy of the appraisal summary to every partner or shareholder who is allocated a share in the deduction for a charitable contribution of property described in the appraisal summary. The partner or shareholder must attach the appraisal summary to his or her tax return.

The *qualified appraiser* declares on the appraisal summary that he or she holds himself or herself out to the public as an appraiser; because of the competencies described in the appraisal, he or she is qualified to make appraisals of the type of property being valued; and that he or she understands that a false or fraudulent overstatement of the value of the property described in the qualified appraisal or appraisal summary may subject the appraiser to a civil penalty for aiding and abetting an understatement of tax liability, and consequently the appraiser may have appraisals disregarded.

An individual is not a qualified appraiser if the donor had knowledge of facts that would cause a reasonable person to expect the appraiser to falsely overstate the value of the donated property. The donor, donee, or certain other related persons cannot be a qualified appraiser of the property involved in the transaction. (In formulating these rules, the government did not include in the criteria certain professional standards or the establishment of a registry of qualified appraisers.) More than one appraiser may appraise donated property, as long as each appraiser complies with the requirements.

Generally, no part of the fee arrangement for a qualified appraisal can be based on a percentage (or set of percentages) of the appraised value of the property. If a fee arrangement is based in any way on the amount of the appraised value of the property that is allowed as a charitable deduction, it is treated as a fee based on a percentage of the appraised value of the property. (In certain circumstances, this rule does not apply to appraisal fees paid to a generally recognized association that regulates appraisers.)

RECORD-KEEPING RULES

A corporate or individual donor must keep some record of contributions of money to charity—preferably, canceled checks or receipts. Alternately, the record must be "written" and "reliable," showing the name of the donee, the date of the contribution, and the amount of the contribution.

A letter or other written communication from the recipient charity acknowledging receipt of the contribution, and showing the date and amount of the contribution, constitutes a "receipt." A donor has the burden of establishing the "reliability" of a written record other than a check or receipt. Factors indicating that such other written evidence of the contribution is "reliable" include the contemporaneous nature of the writing, the regularity of the donor's record-keeping procedures, and—in the case of a "small amount"—any other written evidence from the charity that would not otherwise constitute a "receipt" (such as an emblem or a "donor" button).

For contributions of property other than money, a corporate or individual donor must obtain a receipt from the charitable donee and a reliable written record of specified information about the donated property. The receipt must include the name of the donee, the date and location of the contribution, and a detailed description of the property (including its value). A receipt is not required where the gift is made in circumstances where it is impractical to obtain a receipt, such as when a donor drops off used clothing at a charity's receiving site after business hours.

A donor of property that has appreciated in value must maintain a "reliable written record" of the following specified information for each item of property:

- The name and address of the charitable donee
- The date and location of the contribution
- A detailed description of the property (including the value of the property) and, in the case of securities, the name of the issuing company, the type of security, and whether it is regularly traded on a stock exchange or in an over-the-counter market
- The fair market value of the property at the time of the gift, the method utilized in determining the value, and a copy of the report signed by the appraiser
- The cost or other basis of the property if it is "ordinary income property" or other type of property where the deduction must be reduced by the gain
- Where the gift is of a "remainder interest" or an "income interest" (see Chapter 17), the total amount claimed as a deduction for the year because of the gift, and the amount claimed as a deduction in any prior year or years for gifts of other interests in the property
- The terms of any agreement or understanding concerning the use or disposition of the property—any restriction on the charity's right to use or dispose of the property, a retention or conveyance of the right to the income from the donated property, or an earmarking of the property for a particular use

Additional rules apply to charitable gifts of property other than money for which the donor claims a deduction in excess of $500. The donor is required to maintain additional records showing how the property was acquired and the property's cost or other basis, if it was held for less than 6 months prior to the date of gift. For property held for 6 months or more preceding the date of contribution, the cost or other basis information should be submitted by the donor if it is available.

REPORTING RULES

If a charitable organization donee sells or otherwise disposes of gift property within two years after receipt of the property, it generally must file an information return (Form 8282) with the IRS. Copies of this information return must be provided to the donor and retained by the donee.

This information return must include the name, address, and tax-payer identification number of the donor and the donee; a detailed description of the property; the date of the contribution; the amount received on the disposition; and the date of the disposition.

A donee that receives from a corporation a charitable contribution valued in excess of $5,000 generally does not have to file a donee information return.

FOCUS: Campaign to Clean Up America

The Campaign to Clean Up America, as a "qualified donee," desires to be financially supported largely by charitable contributions. At the outset, these gifts are likely to be cash, in relatively small amounts. However, as the organization grows and its programs take hold in communities, larger gifts of cash should result, as well as gifts of property. The CCUA will be embarking on a gift solicitation program, relying at the beginning principally on a direct-mail effort and per-haps a telemarketing program.

The CCUA is in the process of preparing literature generally de-scribing the deductibility of contributions of cash and property. For the larger gifts, the CCUA will generally advise donors about the ap-praisal, substantiation, and record-keeping requirements.

The CCUA hopes to receive gifts from corporations out of their inventory (such as trash bags and trash collection equipment) and will be developing the requisite documentation to support the de-ductibility of those gifts.

The CCUA will be looking for ways to integrate its general chari-table giving program with its planned giving program. (See Chap-ter 17.) Its fund-raising activities will be fully registered with the pertinent states.

CHAPTER NINE

Charity under Siege: The Regulation of Fund-Raising

Those who manage and advise nonprofit organizations are often unaware of all of the law—federal, state, and local—that is applicable to the organizations and the individuals involved.

Nowhere are the gaps in knowledge more pronounced than in the field of fund-raising regulation. The sheer magnitude of state governments' regulation of charitable gift solicitation is substantially unimagined, even unknown. The role of the federal government when it comes to the regulation of some aspects of nonprofit organizations' functions is the best kept secret. Governmental regulation of fund-raising is becoming so pervasive and onerous, and yet so misunderstood and even ignored despite its rapid growth, that it is next to impossible to place this body of law in some meaningful context. This most widespread and sidestepped aspect of governmental regulation is growing to the point where it is threatening the very meaning of philanthropy itself.

FUND-RAISING REGULATION AT THE STATE LEVEL

Most governmental regulation of fund-raising has been at the state level. Forty-five states have "charitable solicitation acts" (laws or statutes on fund-raising). Many counties, cities, and towns compound the process with similar ordinances. As discussed later in the chapter, the federal government is rapidly becoming more involved in the regulation of fund-raising for charity.

The scope of the laws on fund-raising is grossly misunderstood. Most fund-raising charitable organizations know that they must comply with the charitable solicitation act (if any) of the state in which they are principally located. However, they may not know that these laws frequently mandate compliance by professional fund-raisers, commercial co-venturers, and others who assist in fund-raising endeavors, or that they are expected to adhere to the law in *each state* in which they are soliciting funds. A charitable organization that is fund-raising in all the states must—under a strict legal interpretation—be in compliance annually with the laws of 45 of these states. In addition, those who aid charities in their fund-raising programs must comply with these laws. Administrators of county and city ordinances on fund-raising usually expect the nationwide charities to comply with them as well.

What does "compliance" with these laws mean? Compliance varies from state to state, but essentially it means that a charity must obtain permission from the appropriate regulatory authorities before a fund-raising effort can begin. The permission is usually termed a "permit" or "license," acquired as the result of filing a "registration." Most states also require a filing fee, a bond, and the registration of professional fund-raisers and others who will assist in the effort. The registration is usually updated by filing annually a report on the fund-raising program, including financial information.

This process would be amply difficult if the registration and reporting requirements were uniform. The staff time and expense required to obtain, maintain, and disseminate the information throughout the states can be enormous. But there is very little uniformity. Charities must constantly face differing registration and reporting forms, accounting methods, due dates, enforcement attitudes, and other substantial twists in the states' regulations.

It is not possible to give a brief summary of the states' charitable solicitation acts. Instead, a prototype solicitation statute, developed under the auspices of the National Association of Attorneys General, is summarized here, to provide insight on the scope of some of the fund-raising laws. The prototype will be referred to as "the model law."

Definitions

The model law opens with a series of definitions. A fund-raising professional is termed a *fund-raising counsel,* "a person who for compensation plans, manages, advises, consults, or prepares material for, or with respect to, the solicitation in this state of contributions for a charitable organization, but who does not solicit contributions and who does not employ, procure, or engage any compensated person to solicit contributions." A bona fide salaried officer, employee, or volunteer of a charitable organization is not a fund-raising counsel, nor are lawyers, investment counselors, or bankers.

A paid solicitor is "a person who for compensation performs for a charitable organization any service in connection with which contributions are, or will be, solicited in this state by such compensated person or by any compensated person he employs, procures, or engages, directly or indirectly, to solicit." There is an exclusion from this definition for officers, employees, and volunteers of charitable organizations.

Other terms defined in this package are *charitable organization, solicit, solicitation, charitable purpose, contribution, commercial co-venturer,* and *charitable sales promotion.*

Regulation of Charitable Organizations

The model law is generally in conformance with the pre-existing regulatory approach in this field.

Every charitable organization (unless exempt) desiring to solicit contributions in the state must, in advance, file a "registration statement" with the appropriate state agency. This requirement applies whether the charity is to solicit on its own behalf, or have funds solicited for it by another organization, or be the recipient of gifts generated through the services of a commercial co-venturer or paid solicitor.

If the organization is in compliance, the state issues a certificate of registration, and the solicitation can proceed. The statement must be filed in every year in which the charitable organization is soliciting in the state. A registration fee is levied.

A charitable organization is also required to file an annual financial report. However, an organization with gross support and revenue not exceeding a certain amount (the specific amount may vary in each state) is excused from filing an annual financial report. The financial information may be provided by submitting a copy of the annual information return filed with the IRS. (See Chapter 7.) Where the gross support and revenue of a charitable organization exceeds a certain amount (again, it may vary), the organization must submit audited financial statements.

Churches, other religious organizations, and charitable organizations closely affiliated with them are exempt from the registration requirements. Also exempt are organizations that engage in small annual solicitations—that is, they do not receive gifts in excess of a certain amount or do not receive gifts from more than 10 persons—but only if all of their functions (including fund-raising) are carried on by persons who are not paid for their services.

Every charitable organization engaged in a solicitation in the state must disclose, at the point of solicitation, its name, address, telephone number, a "full and fair" description of the charitable program that is the subject of the campaign, and the fact that a financial statement is available upon request. Where the services of a paid solicitor are utilized, additional disclosures at the point of solicitation are required, as described below.

Regulation of Fund-Raising Counsel

The model law differentiates between fund-raising counsel "who at any time has custody of contributions from a solicitation" and fund-raising counsel who does not. A fund-raising counsel who has custody of contributions is required to register with the state, post a bond, and comply with an accounting requirement and a "presolicitation contract" filing requirement.

It is unusual for fund-raising counsel to have any access to the gifts made to a charitable organization. These individuals are consultants who are paid a fee for their advice in structuring a fund-raising program. Even professional fund-raisers, who are not primarily consultants because they have some active role in the solicitation, rarely have access to contributions. Those who do are frequently referred to as "paid solicitors." (See the next section.)

The registration is annual, for a fee. The application contains such information as the state may require. The bond amount is not specified in the model law. Within 90 days following the completion of a solicitation campaign, and on the anniversary of the commencement of a campaign longer than one year, the fund-raising counsel must account in writing to the charitable organization for all income received and expenses paid.

Every contract between a charitable organization and a fund-raising counsel must be in writing. The fund-raising counsel must file it prior to performing any material services. From the contract, the state regulator must be able to identify the services the fund-raising counsel is to provide.

A fund-raising counsel who does not have custody of contributions is required to comply only with the presolicitation contract filing requirement.

Regulation of Paid Solicitors

A paid solicitor is required to register annually with the state prior to any activity—using an application containing the information the state may require—and to pay a fee (unspecified). At that time, the solicitor must post a bond (in an unspecified amount).

Prior to a solicitation campaign, the paid solicitor must file with the state a copy of its contract with the charitable organization. In addition, the paid solicitor must file with the state a "solicitation notice." This notice must include a "copy of the contract . . . , the projected dates when soliciting will commence and terminate, the location and telephone number from where the solicitation will be conducted, the name and residence address of each person responsible for directing and supervising the conduct of the campaign, a statement as to whether the paid solicitor will at any time have custody of contributions, and a full and fair description of the charitable program for which the solicitation campaign is being carried out."

Every contract between a paid solicitor and a charitable organization must be in writing and must "clearly state the respective obligations" of the parties. The contract must state a fixed percentage of the gross revenue (or a reasonable estimate of it) from the solicitation campaign, which is the amount the charitable organization will receive. The stated minimum percentage may not include the expenses of the solicitation paid by the charity.

The model law imposes a "point-of-solicitation" requirement, for which paid solicitors are responsible. Under this rule, before an oral request or within a written request for a contribution, the potential donor must be told that the solicitor is a paid solicitor and that the charitable organization will receive a percentage of gross receipts as stated in the contract. The disclosures must be "clear" and "conspicuous." In an oral solicitation (such as by telephone), a written receipt must be sent to each contributor within five days of the gift, and it must include a clear and conspicuous disclosure of the point-of-solicitation items.

Within 90 days after the completion of a solicitation campaign, and on the anniversary of the start of a solicitation campaign longer than one year, the paid solicitor is required to file with the state a financial report for the campaign.

A paid solicitor is required to maintain certain information during each solicitation campaign and for at least three years afterward—the name and address of each contributor, the date and amount of each contribution, the name and residence of each employee or other person involved in the solicitation, and all expenses incurred in the course of the solicitation campaign.

All monies collected by a paid solicitor must be deposited in a bank account in a timely manner and the account must be in the name of the charitable organization involved. The charitable organization must have sole control over withdrawals from the account.

Special rules are applicable to situations where paid solicitors represent that tickets to an event will be donated for use by other persons. These rules include limitations on solicitations for donated tickets and record-keeping requirements.

Regulation of Commercial Co-Venturing

Every charitable sales promotion must be the subject of a written contract, when a charitable organization hires a commercial co-venturer. A copy of the contract must be filed with the state at least 10 days prior to the start of the promotion.

The model law defines a "commercial co-venturer" as a "person who for profit is regularly and primarily engaged in trade or commerce other than in connection with soliciting for charitable organizations or purposes and who conducts a charitable sales promotion." A *charitable sales promotion* is defined as "an advertising or sales campaign, conducted by a commercial co-venturer, which represents that the purchase or use of goods or services offered by the commercial co-venturer will benefit, in whole or in part, a charitable organization or purpose."

The charitable sales promotion contract must include a statement of the goods or services to be offered to the public, the geographic area where the promotion will occur, the starting and concluding dates of the promotion, the manner in which the name of the charitable organization will be used (including the representation to be made to the public as to the amount or percent per unit of goods and services purchased or used that will benefit the charitable organization), a provision for a final accounting on a per-unit basis by the commercial co-venturer to the charitable organization, and the date by when and the manner in which the benefit will be conferred on the charitable organization.

The commercial co-venturer is required to disclose in each advertisement for the charitable sales promotion the amount per unit of goods or services purchased or used that will benefit the charitable organization or purpose. This amount may be expressed as a dollar amount or percentage.

The final accounting must be retained by the commercial co-venturer for three years and be made available to the state upon request.

Commercial co-venturers (or charitable sales promotions) are becoming quite common in the United States. Often, a merchant will offer to pay a portion of proceeds from the sales of certain products (or services), during a stated period, to a charitable organization. For example, the management of a fast-food restaurant may advertise that, over the coming weekend, five cents from the sale of every cheeseburger will be contributed to a named charity. This is done both to encourage sales and to benefit a charity (thus the term "co-venture").

Other Provisions

The model law provides that all documents required to be filed (principally registration statements, applications, and contracts) are matters of public record.

True records must be maintained by every charitable organization, fund-raising counsel, commercial co-venturer, and paid solicitor required to register. These records, which must be retained for at least three years, must be available to the state authorities for inspection.

The model law authorizes the state to enter into reciprocal agreements with other states or the federal government for the purpose of exchanging or receiving information filed by a charitable organization in another state, instead of requiring the organization to file under the particular state's law.

The state agency is authorized to conduct investigations and enjoin solicitations. Certain civil penalties can be imposed for failure to adhere to the law. Under various circumstances, a registration can be revoked, canceled, or suspended.

CONSTITUTIONAL LAW CONSIDERATIONS

Fund-raising regulation for charitable organizations is more than the states' charitable solicitation acts and the rules governing the deductibility of charitable gifts. This aspect of the law also involves fundamental principles of constitutional law.

First, there is the doctrine of free speech, protected at the federal level by the First Amendment and at the state level by the Fourteenth Amendment. There are two forms of free speech: "pure" free speech, which may be regulated by the state by only the narrowest of means, and "commercial" free speech, which may be regulated by the state by any means that is "reasonable." Fund-raising by charitable organizations is a form of pure free speech.

The courts have held that, although government has legitimate interests in regulating this field, it may not do so by broad and arbitrary classifications. As the Supreme Court has written, government can regulate charitable fund-raising but "must do so by narrowly drawn regulations designed to serve those interests without unnecessarily interfering with First Amendment freedoms." The Court observed in another context: "Broad prophylactic rules in the area of free expression are suspect. Precision of regulation must be the touchstone . . . ."

One of the most significant clashes between governmental police power to regulate for the benefit of its citizens and rights of free speech involves the application of percentage limitations on fund-raising costs as a basis for determining whether a charity may lawfully solicit funds in a jurisdiction. Many aspects of this head-on conflict were resolved in 1980, when the Supreme Court held that a municipal ordinance was unconstitutionally overbroad and in violation of free speech. The ordinance had prohibited solicitation by charitable organizations that expend more than 25 percent of their receipts for fund-raising and administrative expenses (known as an absolute percentage limitation). Subsequently, the Court addressed the so-called "rebuttable percentage limitation" (fund-raising expenses in excess of a percentage are presumed to be unreasonable, with the charity given the opportunity to rebut the presumption) and found that it too was contrary to charities' rights of free speech. These free speech rights also apply when charities obtain outside fund-raising assistance.

Both the absolute percentage limitation and the rebuttable percentage limitation can initiate another constitutional law violation: denial of due process. Laws regulating the fund-raising activities of charitable organizations must afford due process rights to persons subject to the laws, as prescribed in the Fifth and Fourteenth Amendments to the U.S. Constitution.

A charitable solicitation act must be in conformance with the guarantee of equal protection of the laws provided by the Fourteenth Amendment. This means that such an act may not discriminate in its classification of organizations. An equal protection argument can be raised because of exceptions from the coverage provided in a charitable fund-raising regulation law.

A cardinal doctrine of administrative law is that a governmental agency may issue regulations. However, it must do so in the context of a policy established by a legislative body that has fixed standards for the guidance of the agency in the performance of its functions. A charitable solicitation act may run afoul of this doctrine (born of the separation-of-powers principle) where the executive regulatory agency is granted such a wide range of discretionary authority that it is exercising legislative power.

THE STATES' POLICE POWER

How is it that the states can regulate this field the way they do, often crossing state lines (via radio and television) and involving the federal system (by using the mails)? The answer lies in the "police power" that every state and municipality inherently possesses.

Its police power enables a state or political subdivision to regulate— within the bounds of constitutional law principles—the conduct of its citizens and others, in order to protect the safety, health, and welfare of its people. A state can enact and enforce a charitable solicitation act in the exercise of its police power. It can require a charity planning on fund-raising in the jurisdiction to register with the appropriate regulatory authority and to render periodic reports on the results of the solicitation.

The rationale is that charitable solicitations may be reasonably regulated in order to protect the public from deceit, fraud, unreasonable annoyance, or the unscrupulous obtaining of money under a pretense that the money is being collected for a charitable purpose. The laws that regulate charitable solicitations are by no means constitutionally deficient; they are, instead, utilizations of the states' police power. At the same time, these laws, like all legislation, must conform to certain basic legal standards or face challenges in the courts.

FEDERAL REGULATION OF FUND-RAISING

We saw in Chapter 3 (Myth 12) how the federal government is becoming greatly involved in the process of regulating fund-raising for charitable purposes. Although the regulation of fund-raising was once the province of the states, it is now also being conducted at the federal level, largely through the tax law. (Agencies such as the U.S. Postal Service and the Federal Election Commission may also be involved.) Too often, federal involvement in this area of law is ignored or, worse, unknown.

Fund-Raising Disclosure

Congress specifically brought the IRS into fund-raising regulation when it legislated certain fund-raising disclosure rules. These rules are not presently applicable to charitable organizations, but legislative history strongly hints that this type of law may soon be extended to them. The activities drawing legislative fire are those that secure from individuals payments that are not gifts (such as dues, or payments made for raffle tickets or at auctions) under circumstances where the payors think that the payments are gifts and try to deduct them as charitable contributions. (Legislation against these payments was part of the major tax bill passed by Congress in 1992 but vetoed by then-President George Bush.) The fund-raising disclosure rules apply to all other types of tax-exempt organizations, including political organizations (see Chapter 4), unless the organizations have annual gross receipts that are normally no more than $100,000.

Under these rules, each fund-raising solicitation by or on behalf of a noncharitable organization must contain an express statement, in a "conspicuous and easily recognizable format," that gifts to it are not deductible as charitable contributions for federal income tax purposes. A fund-raising solicitation is any solicitation of gifts made in written or printed form, by television or radio, or by telephone. (There is an exclusion for letters or calls that are not part of a coordinated fund-raising campaign soliciting more than 10 persons during a calendar year.) Despite the clear reference in the statute to "contributions and gifts," the IRS interprets this rule as requiring disclosure when any tax-exempt organization (other than a charity) seeks funds, even dues from members.

Failure to satisfy this disclosure requirement can result in a penalty of $1,000 per day (maximum of $10,000 per year), unless a reasonable cause justifies an exception. For an "intentional disregard" of these rules, the penalty for the day on which the offense occurred is the greater of $1,000 or 50 percent of the aggregate cost of the solicitations that took place on that day—and the $10,000 limitation is denied. For penalty purposes, the IRS counts the days on which the solicitation was telecast, broadcast, mailed, otherwise distributed, or telephoned.

Exemption Application Process

To be tax-exempt as charitable entities and to be charitable donees, organizations are required to secure a letter to that effect from the IRS. The application process requires the organization to reveal some information about itself. As discussed in Chapter 6, the application requires details on the applicant's fund-raising program (Form 1023, Part III, response to questions 1 and 2), and on its fund-raising costs (in the financial statements or the proposed budgets submitted with the application).

Reporting Requirements

Few people realize how much regulation the federal government exercises through the reporting obligations it has imposed on charitable organizations. (These are discussed in Chapter 7.)

The annual information return (Form 990) requires charitable organizations to use the functional method of accounting to report their expenses (Part III of the return). This accounting method requires not only the identification, line by line, of expenses but also an allocation of expenses by function—program services, management and general, and fund-raising.

To comply with the requirements of the functional method of accounting, organizations must maintain detailed records on their fund-raising (and other) expenses; the fund-raising component of each line-item expenditure must be separately identified and reported. Because of this separate identification, some indirect fund-raising costs may be revealed, which, when combined with direct fund-raising expenses, result in considerably higher total outlays for fund-raising. This amount could have adverse repercussions for the organization's status under state charitable solicitation acts, particularly those that seek to place limits on allowable fund-raising expenses. Other pertinent accounting issues are raised: What basis is to be used in making these allocations among functions? Will the state regulators accept reports containing the allocations as being in compliance with the states' reporting requirements?

The instructions accompanying the return define the term *fund-raising expense* as "all expenses, including allocable overhead costs, incurred in: (a) publicizing and conducting fund-raising campaigns; (b) soliciting bequests, grants from foundations or other organizations, or government grants . . . ; (c) participating in federated fund-raising campaigns; (d) preparing and distributing fund-raising manuals, instructions, and other materials; and (e) conducting special fund-raising events that generate contributions . . . ." The IRS does not differentiate, when using the term *professional fund-raiser*, between fund-raising counsel and solicitors. It defines the phrase *professional fund-raising fees* to mean "the organization's fees to outside fund-raisers for solicitation campaigns they conducted, or for providing consulting services in connection with a solicitation of contributions by the organization itself."

At least four other areas of disclosure pertaining to fund-raising are mandated by the annual information return:

- Organizations must separately identify their sources of "program service revenue."

- Organizations have the option of distinguishing between the reporting of revenue that is restricted and revenue that is unrestricted.

- Organizations must report their receipts from and expenses of "[s]pecial fund-raising events and activities," separating the information for each type of event. Typically, these events include dinners, dances, carnivals, raffles, bingo games, and door-to-door sales of merchandise.

- Organizations must fulfill the IRS requirements on unrelated income. (See the next section and Chapter 12.)

Regarding special fund-raising events, the IRS observes in the return's instructions that "[i]n themselves, these activities only incidentally accomplish an exempt purpose" and that "[t]heir sole or primary purpose is to raise funds (other than contributions) to finance the organization's exempt activities. . . . This is done by offering goods or services of more than nominal value (compared to the price charged) in return for a payment higher than the direct cost of the goods or services provided." An activity that generates only contributions (such as a direct-mail campaign) is not a "special fund-raising event." That description applies to events that generate both contributions and revenue, such as when a purchaser pays more than the value of the goods or services furnished.

The contents of the annual information return pertain to how the federal government and the state regulatory agencies share the regulation of fund-raising for charity. These levels of government are coordinating their respective roles. The IRS has taken a significant step toward implementation of this process by stating, in its summary of its adoption of the present return, that "[s]tates are encouraged to use this return as the basic form satisfying State reporting requirements" and "[a]ny additional information needed by a particular State could be provided by that State's own supplemental schedules and by requiring every filer to complete all parts of Form 990 to be filed with the State." More states than ever before use Form 990 for compliance with the states' charitable solicitation acts; for some reason, the IRS wants to know the states in which the return is filed and expects the organizations to report that information.

The instructions accompanying the annual information return suggest that fund-raising is a form of "doing business" and therefore requires separate registration under the states' nonprofit corporation acts.

Unrelated Income Rules

One of the ways in which the IRS is regulating the charitable fund-raising process is through the unrelated income rules. These rules are the subject of Chapter 12 and will be only briefly described here.

It would be a substantial understatement to say that charitable organizations do *not* regard their fund-raising activities as unrelated business endeavors. Yet the fund-raising practices of charities and the unrelated business rules have been enduring a precarious relationship for years. The IRS is more frequently using the unrelated income rules to characterize the receipts from certain fund-raising activities as unrelated income.

Many fund-raising practices do possess all of the technical characteristics of an unrelated business. Reviewing the basic criteria for unrelated income taxation, some fund-raising activities are indeed trades or businesses, regularly carried on, and not efforts that are substantially related to the performance of tax-exempt functions. Applying some of the tests often used these days by the IRS and the courts, there is no question that some fund-raising endeavors have a commercial counterpart and are being undertaken in competition with that counterpart and with the objective of realizing a profit. Some fund-raising activities are sheltered by law from consideration as businesses—for example, an activity in which substantially all of the work is performed for the organization by volunteers; or one that is carried on primarily for the convenience of the organization's members, students, patients, officers, or employees; or one that consists of the sale of merchandise, substantially all of which has been received by the organization as gifts.

As the functional accounting method's rules indicate, the law regards program activities and fund-raising activities as separate matters. Even a simple undertaking like a car wash or a bake sale is an unrelated business. It is saved from taxation only because it is not regularly carried on or is conducted wholly by volunteers. Some fund-raising activities—the mailing of greeting cards, charitable sales promotions, affinity card programs, and "membership" arrangements—are currently undergoing close scrutiny by the IRS, the courts, and/or Congress. The IRS is examining charities' practices of providing donors with substantial "recognition" for their gifts, and charity-sponsored gambling.

These rules may go beyond the question of unrelated income and may raise issues pertaining to eligibility for tax-exempt status. Fund-raising charitable groups are facing a new wave of regulation, and their tax exemption or taxation of income is the federal government's leverage.

Lobbying Restrictions

The Treasury Department and the IRS have written regulations that define the term *fund-raising costs* and spell out rules by which to distinguish those costs from (that is, allocate them between) the expenses of administration and program. These regulations were drawn as part of the effort to state the rules governing elective lobbying restrictions for public charities. (See Chapter 13.)

Under these lobbying rules, certain percentages are applied to the organizations' outlays for program expenditures but not most fund-raising expenditures. An organization seeking to comply with these rules must distinguish between its fund-raising expenses and its other costs. The amounts against which these percentages are applied are called *exempt purpose expenditures*. But exempt purpose expenditures do not include amounts paid or incurred to or for (1) a separate fund-raising unit of the organization, or an affiliated organization's fund-raising unit, or (2) one or more other organizations, if the amounts are paid or incurred primarily for fund-raising.

To adhere to these rules, an electing public charity must determine its direct and indirect fund-raising costs, assuming that it understands the scope of the term *fund-raising* in this context.

Public Charity Classifications

A charitable organization is classified as either a *public* or a *private* charity. (See Chapter 11.) One of the ways to avoid private foundation status is to be a publicly supported organization, and one of the ways to be a publicly supported organization is to qualify as a *donative* charity. An organization can achieve that classification by meeting a *facts-and-circumstances* test, where the amount of public support normally received by the organization may be as low as 10 percent of its total support.

A variety of criteria may be utilized to demonstrate compliance with this test. One criterion is the extent to which the charitable organization is attracting public support: Can the organization demonstrate an active and ongoing fund-raising program? The tax regulations state that an entity may satisfy this aspect of the test "if it maintains a continuous and bona fide program for solicitation of funds from the general public, community, or membership group involved, or if it carries on activities designed to attract support from governmental units or other [publicly supported] organizations . . . ."

The IRS may monitor the extent of a charitable organization's fund-raising efforts, to ascertain whether the organization qualifies as an entity other than a private foundation.

Other Aspects of Federal Regulation

Federal tax law prohibits a private educational institution from qualifying as a charitable entity if it has racially discriminatory policies. Under IRS guidelines, schools must adhere to an assortment of record-keeping requirements. Every private school must maintain, for at least three years, copies of all materials used by or on behalf of it to solicit contributions. Failure to maintain or to produce the required reports and information creates a presumption that the school has failed to comply with the guidelines and thus has a racially discriminatory policy toward its students. Loss or denial of tax-exempt status could result.

FOCUS: Campaign to Clean Up America

The Campaign to Clean Up America intends to solicit funds in nearly all of the states, principally by mail. The CCUA will register in Michigan, the state in which the fund-raising will originate. Before the fund-raising begins, someone representing CCUA must review the laws of every state in which a gift solicitation will occur, determine which states require registration, obtain the necessary forms, and secure the appropriate registrations (licenses). You, as president of the CCUA, realize that this will be a very time-consuming and expensive process because of the enormous variety and sheer amount of questions that must be answered. The expense will come in diverted staff time, registration fees, bond premiums, and perhaps accounting and legal fees. The CCUA's lawyer advises that the organization has no real choice; it must comply with these state laws.

The CCUA will likely use the services of a professional fund-raiser; its first project will be to develop and implement a direct-mail fund-raising program. (There are no plans to hire a professional solicitor.) The lawyer for CCUA reminds you to coordinate the organization's state registrations with those of the professional fund-raiser.

This fund-raising activity will principally involve outlays that are not exempt purpose expenditures under the federal tax lobbying rules. If the CCUA elects under the expenditure test (see Chapter 13), these fund-raising expenses cannot be counted in the base against which the various percentages are applied. The CCUA does not intend to engage in any gift solicitation practices that would constitute an unrelated business.

CHAPTER TEN

Compensating the Nonprofit Employee

Nonprofit organizations almost always have employees, just as their for-profit counterparts usually do. (A growing practice is to have the nonprofit organization administered by a professional management firm.) Employees are compensated, whether they work for a nonprofit or for-profit employer.

There is a tendency in our society to expect employees of nonprofit organizations to work for levels and types of compensation that are less than those paid to employees of for-profit organizations. Somehow, the nonprofit characteristics of the organization become transferred to the "nonprofit" employee. At times, the description may be correct, given the budgetary constraints of some nonprofit organizations. In other cases, a nonprofit mentality persists: the employees feel they must accept low compensation. Some employees choose to work for low-paying nonprofit organizations because they are dedicated to the organizations' programs. Other nonprofit organization employees are better compensated than their for-profit counterparts. However, many employees of nonprofit organizations are simply undercompensated.

A 1987 study supported some of these conclusions. The analysis concluded that those who work for nonprofit organizations (expected to be 9.3 million in 1995) "display few characteristics that set them off from other service workers." Overall, the study found that workers in the nonprofit sector earn less than four-fifths of the salaries of their for-profit counterparts. The exceptions were in a number of services, such as health and social services, and research and development. The researchers questioned any conclusion that "lower pay is acceptable to nonprofit employees because of a variety of intrinsic job benefits that nonprofit employees receive."

Many nonprofit organizations, particularly the larger ones (universities, hospitals, major charities, and trade associations), require sophisticated and talented employees. Because these individuals are not likely to want to be "nonprofit" employees, nonprofit and for-profit organizations compete for the same pool of talented persons. This competition extends not only to salaries but also to benefits and retirement programs.

Whatever the compensation—salaries, bonuses, commissions, benefits, and/or retirement arrangements—most nonprofit organizations are constrained by the private inurement doctrine. (See Chapter 5.) This means that, for an employer to be tax-exempt, all compensation, no matter how it is determined or what form it takes, must be "reasonable."

CURRENT COMPENSATION

A nonprofit organization may pay a salary or wage. This is a form of "current" compensation (as opposed to "deferred" compensation, discussed in a later section). Generally speaking, the payments must be "reasonable," largely using community standards and taking into account the comparable services being rendered. (In a sense, the same rule applies to for-profit employers: to be deductible as a business expense, cash compensation must be "ordinary and necessary.") Reasonable current compensation includes appropriate salary increases based on merit and cost-of-living adjustments.

At private foundations, unreasonable (excessive) compensation is a form of self-dealing that can lead to penalty taxes. (These legal issues may have to be tempered by outside "appearances": a form of compensation may in fact be "reasonable" and perfectly "legal," and still draw public criticism as being "excessive." The United Way of America "scandal" illustrated this reaction.)

Nonprofit organizations are allowed to pay "reasonable" bonuses. A bonus is likely to be more closely scrutinized than regular current compensation. As *additional* compensation, it is more likely to be excessive compensation (and therefore a form of inurement of net earnings). The sensitivity is increased where a bonus is paid to an "insider" at a nonprofit organization.

In many respects, commissions are subject to the same rules as bonuses: both are forms of incentive compensation. However, commissions and other forms of percentage-based compensation can result in heightened inquiry. By nature, they are computed using percentages and, to the IRS, they get close to the concept of private inurement. The IRS will carefully scrutinize compensation programs of nonprofit organizations that have incentive features whereby compensation is a function of revenues received, is guaranteed, or is otherwise outside the boundaries of conventional arrangements. For example, the IRS is particularly concerned about some hospitals' recruitment programs to attract physicians and about colleges' and universities' incentives for their coaches, which are designed to stimulate success on the athletic fields.

The IRS has developed the following criteria for assessing compensation arrangements based on a percentage of a tax-exempt organization's gross revenues:

- Was the compensation actually paid reasonable?
- Was the agreement completely negotiated at arm's length?
- Did the service provider participate in or have any control over the conduct of the organization?
- Did the "contingent" payments serve a "real discernible business purpose" of the exempt organization (that is, independent of any purpose to benefit the service provider)?
- Was the amount of compensation dependent on the accomplishment of the objectives of the compensatory arrangement?
- Did the actual operating results reveal any evidence of abuse or unwarranted benefits to the service provider?
- Was there a "ceiling or reasonable maximum limit" in the compensation agreement to avoid a "windfall benefit" to the service provider based on factors that "had no direct relationship to the level of services provided"?

All forms of current compensation paid by tax-exempt organizations are subject to the rule of reasonableness, and the tax exemption of the employer is on the line.

BENEFITS

Federal tax law and other legislation does not prohibit the payment of benefits by nonprofit organizations. A "benefit" basically is a form of noncash compensation to the employee, although it may well entail a cash outlay by the employer. Any benefit (or benefit package) must be reasonable, to preserve the tax exemption of the employer.

Typically, an employer will pay for benefits such as health insurance, major medical insurance, disability insurance, and, perhaps, travel insurance. Nonprofit organizations can pay for one or more of these benefits without tax law difficulties.

Other common benefits paid (either directly or by reimbursement) by employers are entertainment costs, costs of operating an automobile, moving expenses, costs of attending conventions and/or educational seminars, parking fees, club memberships, and certain professional fees (such as physicians' charges for annual physicals, financial planners' fees, and stress management expenses).

Many types of benefits are taxable to employees. Benefits that are not taxable are often termed "working condition" benefits or "no-additional-cost services." For example, a nonprofit organization can provide insurance coverage for its officers and directors who are employees, to protect against their personal liability for acts done (or not done) while in the service of the organization. The value of the insurance is not taxed to the employees. Indeed, under new rules developed by the IRS, the value of this type of insurance is not taxable to volunteers.

Some types of benefits are likely to cause problems for the tax-exempt organizations that pay them. Payment of moving expenses, continuing education expenses, and perhaps automobile operating and parking expenses may not attract too much investigation. However, a nonprofit organization will be suspect, in the eyes of legislators and regulators (and perhaps the general public), if its employees are granted country club memberships, financial planning services, or an entertainment allowance. Golden parachutes are not frequent in the nonprofit world.

DEFERRED COMPENSATION

It is becoming common for nonprofit organizations to provide "deferred compensation" to their employees. Colleges, universities, and hospitals have paved the way in this area. Yet, many tax and other issues are resulting from this practice. As with current compensation, deferred compensation is subject to the rule of reasonableness.

Deferred compensation embraces retirement plans and profit-sharing plans. (Yes, a nonprofit organization can maintain a profit-sharing plan; the words "excess of revenue over expenses" are used instead of "profit.") These plans are usually subject to the law laid down by the Employee Retirement Income Security Act (ERISA), amended from time to time, and related Internal Revenue Code (IRC) provisions.

Deferred compensation plans are divided into qualified and nonqualified plans.

Qualified Plans

To be qualified, a plan must satisfy a variety of tax law requirements as to coverage, contributions, other funding, vesting, nondiscrimination, and distributions.

For for-profit organizations, it is desirable for a plan to be qualified, to enable employer contributions to the plan to be deductible as business expenses. This feature is not relevant to tax-exempt organizations. Other advantages of a qualified plan are: the income and capital gains from the assets underlying the plan are not subject to the federal income tax, in that they are held in a tax-exempt trust (see Chapter 4); and employees are usually not taxed until the benefits of the plans are actually received.

Qualified plans are either *defined benefit* plans or *defined contribution* plans (also referred to as *individual account* plans). A pension plan may fall into either category.

Defined Benefit Plans. A defined benefit plan is established and maintained by an employer primarily to provide systematically for the payment of a definite and determinable benefit to the employees over a period of years (usually life) following retirement. Retirement benefits under a defined benefit plan are measured by and based on various factors, such as years of service rendered and compensation earned by the employee. The determination of the amount of benefits and the contributions made to the plan are not dependent on the profits of the employer. Under a defined benefit plan, the benefits are established in advance according to a formula, and the employer contributions are determined, within federal tax law limits, by an actuary using a variety of interest and mortality factors.

Defined Contribution Plans. A defined contribution plan provides an individual account for each participant and bases benefits solely on the amount allocated to the participant's account. Adjustments are made for investment gains or losses and for forfeitures allocated to the account.

This type of plan defines the amount of contribution to be added to each participant's account. This may be done in one of two ways: by directly defining the amount the employer will contribute on behalf of each employee or by leaving to the employer's discretion the amount of contribution but defining the method of allocation. The individual accounts are adjusted, at least annually, to reflect investment gains and losses.

Ordinarily, the total plan assets are completely allocated to the individual accounts. If a participant terminates his or her employment before becoming vested, the account balance is forfeited and is either applied to reduce future employer contributions or allocated to accounts of other participants. When a participant becomes eligible to receive a benefit, his or her benefit equals the amount that can be provided by the account balance. The benefit may be paid as a lump-sum distribution, a series of installments, or an annuity for the lifetime of the participant or for the joint lifetimes of the participant and other beneficiary.

Where periodic contributions are set aside according to a predetermined formula, the plan is referred to as a "money purchase pension plan." Contributions are generally expressed as a percentage of covered payroll, and the rate may vary with the employee's age at entry into the plan. A "target benefit plan" is a money purchase plan that sets a targeted benefit amount to be met by actuarily determined contributions. Special antidiscrimination rules apply to target benefit plans.

A *profit-sharing* plan, another type of defined contribution plan, is established and maintained by an employer to provide for participation in profits by employees or their beneficiaries. The plan must have a definite, predetermined formula for allocating among the participants the contributions made under the plan. It must clearly state whether the funds accumulated under the plan will be distributed after a fixed number of years, or the attainment of a stated age, or upon the prior occurrence of some event, such as layoff, illness, disability, retirement, death, or severance of employment. A plan cannot qualify as a profit-sharing plan unless the employer's contributions are contingent on the existence of the necessary profits. A profit-sharing plan may have, but is not required to have, a definite, predetermined formula for computing the amount of annual employer contributions.

Other defined contribution plans (some of which are profit-sharing plans) include stock bonus plans, employee stock ownership plans, thrift plans, simplified employee pension plans (which can be a form of individual retirement accounts), and so-called cash or deferred arrangements.

THE FUNDING MECHANISM

The usual method of funding a pension or profit-sharing plan is through a tax-exempt trust. A "trusteed" plan uses a trust to receive and invest the funds contributed under the plan and to distribute the benefits to participants and/or their beneficiaries. For a trust forming part of a pension, profit-sharing, or similar plan to be a qualified trust, the law requires that the following conditions must be met:

- The trust must be created or organized in the United States and must be maintained at all times as a U.S. domestic trust

- The trust must be part of a pension, profit-sharing, or similar plan established by the employer for the exclusive benefit of the employees and/or their beneficiaries

- The trust must be formed or made available for the purpose of distributing to employees and/or their beneficiaries the corpus and income of the fund accumulated by the trust in accordance with the plan

- All liabilities to employees and their beneficiaries must be satisfied before any part of the trust's corpus or income can be used for, or diverted to, purposes other than the exclusive benefit of employees and/or their beneficiaries

- The trust must be part of a plan that benefits a nondiscriminatory classification of employees under applicable IRS guidelines and provides nondiscriminatory benefits

- If the trust is part of a pension plan, the plan must provide that forfeitures cannot be applied to increase the benefit of any participant

Instead of using a trust, an organization can obtain the tax advantages of a qualified plan through an "annuity plan," under which contributions are used to purchase retirement annuities directly from an insurance company. An annuity contract is treated as a qualified trust if it would, except for the fact that it is not a trust, satisfy all the requirements for qualification. The person holding the annuity is then treated as if he or she was the trustee.

A segregated asset account of a life insurance company can be used to invest assets of a qualified pension, profit-sharing, or annuity plan. Insurance companies establish special funds to hold plan investments; trusts are not required.

Another form of nontrusteed plan uses a custodial account. The employer arranges with a bank or other qualified institution to act as custodian of the plan funds placed in the account. Although a custodial account is not a trust, a qualifying custodial account is treated for tax purposes as a qualified trust.

Nonqualified Plans

Nonqualified plans are used as means to provide supplemental benefits and/or to avoid the technical requirements imposed on qualified plans. However, the advantages of nonqualified plans for many employers (particularly for-profit ones) have been substantially eroded by recently enacted laws. The employer's deduction is deferred until the amount attributable to the contribution is includable in the employees' income. Yet, nonqualified plans are of great importance to nonprofit employers.

The federal tax consequences of nonqualified plans vary, depending on whether a plan is funded or unfunded. Where a plan is funded, contributions by an employer to a nonexempt employees' trust are includable in an employee's gross income in the first tax year in which the employee's rights in the trust are transferable. The contributions are not subject to any substantial risk of forfeiture. Unfunded plans are contractual promises to pay, but the employer is not setting aside any dollars into an annuity contract or trust. The tax consequences to an employee under an unfunded arrangement are determined by application of the doctrines of constructive receipt or economic benefit (by which the moneys are taxed as soon as the employee is entitled to them).

Funds in these plans can be deemed taxable to employees and accessible by creditors of the employer.

"457 Plans"

Congress, in 1986, extended rules for the provision of nonqualified unfunded deferred compensation to employees of nonprofit organizations. The programs covered by these rules are called "457 plans" (named after the section of the Internal Revenue Code that authorizes them). Prior to 1986, 457 plans were available only to employees of state and local governments.

Compliance with the rules for 457 plans enables employees to defer the taxation of income; otherwise, the deferred amount is immediately taxable. These plans are "unfunded"; the deferred amounts (and the resulting earnings) remain the property of the employer and are subject to the creditors of the employer.

In a 457 plan, the most compensation that can be deferred in a year is the lesser of $7,500 or one-third of the employee's or other participant's gross income. Under certain circumstances, catch-up deferrals are permitted, up to $15,000 annually. Distributions cannot be made before the earlier of the discontinuance of employment or the occurrence of an unforeseeable emergency. Distributions payable upon death must be paid within 15 years or within the life expectancy of a surviving spouse.

The law requires that 457 plans satisfy certain minimum distribution requirements and imposes a penalty excise tax equal to 50 percent of the amount that should have been distributed. For lifetime distributions, at least two-thirds of the total amount payable must be paid during the life expectancy of the participant. Any amount not distributed during the life of the participant must be distributed at death at least as rapidly as required by the method that was used during the participant's life. If distributions do not begin until after the participant's death, the entire amount payable must be paid during a period that does not exceed 15 years or, if the beneficiary is the surviving spouse, the life expectancy of that spouse.

Amounts in a 457 plan cannot be rolled over (that is, transferred without taxation) to a qualified plan or to an individual retirement account. However, a transfer from one 457 plan to another will not trigger a tax.

"403(b) Plans"

Another form of deferred compensation used by nonprofit organizations is the tax-sheltered (or tax-deferred) annuity. This is an annuity paid out of a "403(b) plan" (again, a plan named after the section of the IRC that authorizes it). A tax-sheltered annuity is treated as a defined contribution plan.

Tax-sheltered annuity programs are available only to employees of charitable (including educational and religious) organizations and employees of public educational institutions. Essentially, amounts are contributed by an employer toward the purchase of an annuity contract for an employee. As long as the amounts do not exceed the "exclusion allowance" (see below) for the tax year of the employee, the law says that the employee is not required to include the amounts in gross income for that tax year. These "plans" are usually funded through an individual annuity contract purchased by the employee, or a group annuity contract held by the employer. A separate account is maintained for each participant. As an alternative, funding may be through a custodial account arrangement.

Contributions to a 403(b) plan—usually made through salary reductions—are excluded from the employees' taxable income. Certain limitations apply. Generally, elective (employee) contributions may not exceed $9,500 annually. The funds held under these programs are generally permitted to appreciate without any tax obligation.

The exclusion allowance for a year is:

$$\frac{\begin{array}{c}\text{20 percent of an employee's}\\ \text{includable compensation}\end{array} \times \begin{array}{c}\text{Employee's years of service as}\\ \text{of the close of the taxable year}\end{array}}{\begin{array}{c}\text{Aggregate amount contributed by the employer and}\\ \text{excludable from the employee's gross income during prior years}\end{array}}$$

The minimum exclusion allowance is the lesser of $3,000 or the employee's includable compensation. All of an eligible employee's includable compensation may be contributed to a 403(b) plan on an excludable basis, up to $3,000.

Tax-sheltered annuity plans are generally subject to minimal federal law regulation. However, various provisions of ERISA are applicable, as are many of the nondiscrimination, distribution, and other limitations (including restrictions on loans) of qualified plans.

Distributions from a 403(b) plan are generally taxed in the same way as are periodic distributions from qualified plans.

CONCLUSION

Most nonprofit organization employers offer their employees some type of payment arrangements beyond basic current compensation. The type and extent of the plan(s) and the benefits provided are subject to many factors, including the budgetary constraints on the employer. As competition for talent escalates between for-profit and nonprofit employers, the costs to the nonprofit employers go up, as does the intricacy of the law. (The law currently prevents one form of competition over benefits: tax-exempt organizations may not maintain the qualified cash or deferral arrangements known as "401(k) plans"; this restriction is likely to be eliminated soon.)

The law in this field has become quite complex. Congress has repeatedly visited the subject in recent years. The enactment of ERISA in 1974 brought a vast amount of new statutory law on the subject, for nonprofit and for-profit employers alike. In 1986, Congress extended the 457 plan rules to nonprofit employment and made it clear that tax-exempt organizations can maintain qualified profit-sharing plans. Congress, Treasury, and the IRS will assuredly add more law in this field in the coming years. Much of it will be directly applicable to nonprofit organizations.

It is difficult these days for a nonprofit organization of any appreciable size to *not* pay somewhat reasonable salaries and offer a wide range of current and retirement benefits. For-profit employers take some solace in the fact that the costs of these benefits are tax-deductible, but that feature is useless to a nonprofit organization (except in the unrelated business context). Successful nonprofit organizations know that these benefit programs must be maintained, if only to attract and retain competent employees.

FOCUS: Campaign to Clean Up America

Being a new organization, the Campaign to Clean Up America is not in a position to maintain a large payroll or to promise large salaries, an array of benefits, a profit-sharing plan, and a retirement plan.

However, the CCUA will have employees and they will be fairly paid as resources allow. In time, and assuming reasonable growth, benefits will be added: health insurance, sick and vacation leave, cost-of-living adjustments, merit increases, and perhaps bonuses.

As the CCUA matures, a retirement program will be installed— either a traditional tax-sheltered annuity (403(b)) program or, depending on developments in the law and cash flow, a deferred compensation (457) plan.

PART THREE

Tax-Exempt Organizations Can Be Taxable . . . and So Can Their Managers

CHAPTER ELEVEN

Be Public, Not Private

One of the great myths about tax-exempt organizations is that they are not taxable. (See Chapter 3, Myth 5.) The truth is, they *can be taxable*. In some situations, they may be subject to heavy taxation. Moreover, the individuals involved—founders, officers, or directors—can be personally taxable. Of all types of tax-exempt organizations, the degree of taxation is most stringent for private foundations.

WHAT IS A "PRIVATE FOUNDATION"?

The term *private foundation,* used generically in the nonprofit organization community for decades, was not defined in the Internal Revenue Code until 1969. At that time, Congress was on an antifoundation rampage, legislating against foundations in every way it could think of. Congress wanted to be certain that each charitable organization that was not clearly "public" (as explained below) would be treated as a private foundation; it wanted that term to be as all-encompassing as possible. Indeed, in its search for a way to cast a superwide net, it could not write a definition of the term "private foundation." Instead, it wrote a definition of what a private foundation *is not.*

Under the federal tax law, every charitable organization—every church, university, hospital, or local community group—is presumed to be a private foundation. Each charitable organization must either rebut that presumption (and become public) or exist as a private foundation.

Despite the intricacies of the tax law, the concept of a *private foundation* is simple. A true private foundation has three fundamental characteristics:

- Its financial support came from one source, usually an individual, family, or company
- Its annual expenditures are funded out of earnings from investment assets, rather than from an ongoing flow of contributions (in this way, a private foundation is much the same as an endowment fund)
- It makes grants to other organizations for charitable purposes, rather than operate its own programs

A hybrid entity called a *private operating foundation* (a blend between a private foundation and a public charity) conducts its own programs but has most of the other features of a private foundation.

There is no advantage to private foundation status. These are some of the disadvantages:

- A need to comply with a battery of onerous rules, such as prohibitions on self-dealing, insufficient grants for charitable purposes, excess business holdings, jeopardizing (highly speculative) investments, and certain types of grants
- A tax on net investment income
- Extensive reporting responsibilities
- Narrow limitations on gift deductibility
- The reality that private foundations are highly unlikely to make grants to other private foundations

The word "private," as used here, means funding comes from a single source. "Private" has nothing to do with the composition of an organization's board of directors or trustees. There is a fairly widespread belief that an advantage to private foundation status is an ability to function "in private," that is, without scrutiny from outsiders. Quite the opposite is often true.

A lawyer or other professional helping a new charitable organization through the tax law maze can provide no greater service than steering the organization away from private foundation status.

AVOIDING PRIVATE FOUNDATION STATUS

Three types of charitable organizations are not private foundations and thus are *public charities:* the "institutions" of the charitable world, the "publicly supported" charities, and the supporting organizations. To avoid being a "private" charity, an organization must demonstrate "public" involvement, "public" financial support, or an operating relationship with a "public" organization.

Institutions

Federal tax law identifies certain institutions within the philanthropic sector that are exempted from the private foundation rules and taxes:

- Churches, or conventions or associations of churches
- Operating educational institutions, such as universities, colleges, and schools
- Operating health care providers (including hospitals) and certain medical research organizations
- Governmental units, whether federal or state

Publicly Supported Organizations

One of the chief characteristics of a private foundation is that it is or was funded from one source. One way for an organization to be a public charity is to draw its funding from many sources (the public). An organization is not a "private foundation" if it is publicly supported.

There are two types of publicly supported organizations. The law has not assigned either of them a name, so we will call them *donative* charities and *service-provider* charities. These classifications are flawed—most publicly supported charities receive a blend of gifts, grants, and fee-for-service revenue (as well as investment income)—but they will serve to identify the two types of charities.

Donative Charities. A donative charity is one that "normally" receives a "substantial part" of its support from one or more governmental units in the form of grants, and/or from direct or indirect contributions from the "general public."

Most donative organizations derive at least one-third of their financial support (the "support ratio") from eligible governmental and/or public sources. Except for new entities, the "normal" time span for measuring the organization's support is its four most recent fiscal years (the "support computation period").

Public support comes from individuals, trusts, corporations, or other legal entities. The total amount of contributions from any one donor during the support computation period is not to exceed 2 percent of the organization's total support received during that period. The 2 percent limitation generally does not apply to support received from other donative organizations or from governmental units. All support from these two sources is public support.

Donors who have a defined relationship to one another (such as husband and wife) must share a single 2 percent limitation. Multiple contributions from any one source are aggregated over the support computation period.

When it is identifying income from its support ratio, an organization cannot include amounts received from the exercise or performance of its tax-exempt functions. However, an organization will not meet the "support ratio test" if it receives almost all of its support from its related activities and only an insignificant amount from governmental units and/or the general public.

An organization's lawyer or accountant should be consulted on whether the support ratio test requirements have been met. A formula fraction called a "support fraction" will be applied by the professional, using the organization's specific revenues in each category.

Service-Provider Charities.
A service-provider charitable organization normally receives more than one-third of its support from gifts and grants, membership fees, and/or gross receipts from the performance of exempt functions. Amounts that are eligible are derived from so-called "permitted sources": governmental agencies, the three basic types of institutions (churches, educational institutions, and health care/medical research entities), donative charities, and persons who are not "disqualified persons" (described below).

To qualify as a service-provider charitable organization, no more than one-third of the organization's support can come from investment income.

Both the donative organization rules and the service-provider organization rules measure support over the most recent four years, and both utilize a one-third support fraction.

However, there are some major differences. Exempt function revenue can count as public support for the service-provider organization, but only to the extent that the revenue from any one source does not exceed the greater of $5,000 or 1 percent of the organization's support for the year involved.

The rules limit gifts and grants to service-provider charitable organizations. Public support cannot come from "disqualified persons": an organization's directors and officers, members of their families, or any "person" or "substantial contributor" (whether an individual, trust, estate, corporation, or other entity) who contributes or bequeaths an aggregate amount of more than $5,000, where that amount is more than 2 percent of the total contributions and bequests received by the organization.

Supporting Organizations

The final category of charitable organization that is *not* a private foundation is the *supporting organization*, an entity that is related, structurally or operationally, to one or more institutions or publicly supported organizations. (For simplicity, these institutions and publicly supported organizations will be referred to collectively as "public charities.") A supporting organization must be organized, and at all times operated, within an active relationship with one or more public charities.

The relationship must be one of three types; as outlined below, the interaction is different for each type:

Supporting Organization Relationship	Effect
Operated, supervised, or controlled by public charity(ies)	Substantial direction of policies, programs, and activities by the public charity(ies); similar to parent–subsidiary corporation relationship
Supervised or controlled in connection with public charity(ies)	Common supervision or control by the persons heading both the supporting organization and the public charity(ies); similar to "brother–sister" relationship
Operated in connection with public charity(ies)	Supporting organization responsive to and significantly involved in operation of public charity(ies)

A supporting organization may not be controlled directly or indirectly by one or more disqualified persons.

Most supported organizations are charitable entities, but it is possible to structure a relationship where the supported organization is a tax-exempt social welfare, agricultural, labor, or trade or professional organization.

Special Rules for New Organizations

Some charitable organizations will be able to avoid private foundation classification because they are institutions or supporting organizations. Others are able to demonstrate that they are publicly supported.

A newly created organization has no financial history as proof of public support. For these newcomers, the IRS will give a classification on the basis of a proposed budget.

Where an organization's non-private-foundation status is based on a classification linked to what it is programmatically (for example, a church, university, college, school, hospital, or supporting organization), the IRS will issue a "definitive ruling." However, where the non-private-foundation classification depends on the organization's prospective ability to function as a publicly supported organization (that is, one of the institutions, a donative charitable organization, or a service-provider charitable organization), the IRS will issue an "advance ruling," which protects the organization from private foundation status during an "advance ruling period." The advance ruling period is the organization's first four fiscal years. If the startup year is shorter than eight months, it is not counted as a full year.

Planning Considerations

A charitable organization that is trying to avoid classification as a private foundation will need to do some solid financial planning, especially if the goal is to be a publicly supported organization.

For organizations that desire to be regarded as publicly supported (essentially the donative and service-provider charities), the matter is somewhat more complicated than for institutions or organizations that intend to be classified as supporting organizations. Also, the planning may be different for the advance ruling period than for the period following.

An organization that can expect to receive nearly all of its support in the form of many relatively small gifts will have no trouble in achieving either donative or service-provider status. An organization that is essentially dues-based will be a service-provider, although not a donative entity. An organization that anticipates receiving most of its financial support as exempt function revenue must look to the category of service-provider (rather than donative) organization, for relief from the private foundation rules. The reverse is probably true for an organization that is relying largely on government grants (not contracts) for support; it will look to the donative organization category.

Many organizations, during their formative years, rely on just a few sources of financial support (for example, one or more private foundations and/or makers of large gifts). For these entities, compliance with either the donative organization rules or the service-provider organization rules—particularly during the advance ruling period—can be difficult (if not impossible). Under the service-provider organization rules, because their sources of support are likely to be "substantial contributors," none of their support is eligible for treatment as public support. The outcome will be more favorable where the donative organization rules are applied: at least the amount received from each of these sources up to the 2 percent threshold can count as public support.

Compliance with either the donative organization rules or the service-provider organization rules at any time (including as of the close of the advance ruling period) is all that is required. An organization is not locked in to one set of these rules or the other.

SOME ADDITIONAL OPTIONS

A charitable organization may not be able to satisfy the requirements of the rules pertaining to institutions, publicly supported (donative or service-provider) organizations, or supporting organizations. There still remain alternatives to private foundation status, or ways to alleviate some of the stringencies of the private foundation rules.

"Facts and Circumstances" Test

Some organizations generically are not private foundations, yet they come within the broad reach of that term under the federal tax law. These organizations include museums, libraries, and other entities that have substantial endowment funds. Some of these organizations may be able to gain non-private-foundation status by means of the "facts and circumstances" test.

To meet this test, an organization must demonstrate that:

- The total amount of public support it receives is at least 10 percent of its total support
- It has a continuous and bona fide program for the solicitation of funds from the general public, governmental units, and/or other public charities
- It has other attributes of a "public" organization

Among its other attributes, an organization might cite the composition of its governing board (showing how it is representative of the general public), the extent to which its facilities or programs are publicly available, its membership dues rates, and how its activities are likely to appeal to persons having some broad common interest or purpose.

The higher the percentage of public support, the easier the burden of establishing the publicly supported nature of the organization through the other factors.

Bifurcation

An organization that is, or might be classified by the IRS as, a private foundation can avoid that consequence by bifurcating (splitting) into two entities. Each of the two organizations may be able to qualify as a nonfoundation, where they could not do so if combined.

An organization may have within it a function that, if separately evaluated, would qualify as an institution, a donative publicly supported organization, or a service-provider publicly supported organization. This function could be spun off into a separate organization and qualified as a public entity. The original organization, with its remaining activities, could then become qualified as a supporting organization with respect to its offspring. In this way, one private organization becomes two public organizations.

For example, suppose an individual established a private foundation for educational purposes. Over time, the foundation begins providing direct instruction to students. The board of trustees would like the foundation to remain in existence. The trustees convert the direct-instruction part of the foundation into an operating educational institution—a school with a board of educators and community leaders. That organization gains classification as a public charity—one of the institutions. The remaining part of the foundation, with the original board of trustees, is converted into a supporting organization for the school. The "foundation" board remains in place but the organization itself is now public in nature.

Private Operating Foundation

The major program activity of a private foundation is the making of grants. The more a charitable organization engages in programs itself (rather than funding those of others), the greater the likelihood that it will be classified as something other than a private foundation.

Because of this distinction between grant making and program administration, a hybrid entity has evolved, one that has some of the characteristics of a private foundation and some of those of a public charity. It is called the *private operating foundation,* and it devotes most of its earnings and much of its assets directly for the conduct of its charitable, educational, or similar purposes.

To be a private operating foundation, the organization must meet an "income" test. Annually, it must expend directly, for the active conduct of its exempt activities, an amount equal to substantially all of the lesser of its adjusted net income or its "minimum investment return." "Substantially all" means at least 85 percent. The minimum investment return is equal to 5 percent of the foundation's assets that are not used for charitable purposes. For example, to pass this test, an organization with $100,000 of investment (noncharitable) assets (such as securities) would have to expend at least $4,250 (85 percent × 5 percent × $100,000) for that year, unless an amount equal to 85 percent of its adjusted net income is less than $4,250, in which case it would have to timely expend the actual income amount.

To qualify as an operating foundation, an organization must satisfy at least one of the three other tests:

- The "assets" test—at least 65 percent of its assets must be devoted directly to the active conduct of its charitable activities
- The "endowment" test—the organization must normally expend its funds directly for the active conduct of its charitable activities in an amount equal to at least two-thirds of its minimum investment return ($2/3 \times 5 = 3^1/3$)
- The "support" test—at least 85 percent of its support (other than investment income) must be normally received from the general public and/or at least five tax-exempt organizations (that are not disqualified persons); no more than 25 percent of its support can be derived from any one exempt organization; and no more than one-half of its support can be normally received from gross investment income

Because of these rules, a private operating foundation is not subject to the minimum payout requirement imposed on "standard" private foundations. Contributions to a private operating foundation are deductible to the full extent permitted for gifts to public charities (see Chapter 8). That is, the percentage limitations that restrict the deductibility of contributions to "standard" private foundations do not apply to gifts to private operating foundations.

EXEMPT OPERATING FOUNDATIONS

Not content with the complexity introduced with the hybrid form of private foundation known as the operating foundation, Congress created a hybrid of a hybrid. This one is known as the *exempt operating foundation*. "Exempt" here does not mean exempt from federal income taxes (which foundations generally are anyway).

Exempt operating foundations are presumably otherwise private operating foundations, but they enjoy two characteristics that the others do not have:

- Grants to them are exempt from the expenditure responsibility requirements otherwise imposed on grantor foundations
- They do not have to pay the tax imposed on foundations' net investment income

To be an exempt operating foundation, an organization must (in addition to satisfying the requirements to be a private operating foundation) meet three tests:

- It must have been publicly supported (under the donative charity or service-provider charity rules) for at least 10 years or have qualified as an operating foundation as of January 1, 1983
- It must have a board of directors that, during the year involved, consisted of individuals at least 75 percent of whom are not so-called "disqualified individuals" and was broadly representative of the general public (presumably, using the facts and circumstances test)
- It must not have an officer who is a disqualified individual at any time during the year involved

To be an exempt operating foundation, an organization must have a ruling from the IRS to that effect. However, one of the anomalies of the law in this area is that an organization that is able to qualify as an exempt operating foundation often is also able to qualify under the facts and circumstances test—and thereby avoid all of the private foundation rules!

FACING THE INEVITABLE

If it fails to comply with any of the rules discussed so far in this chapter, a charitable organization will be classified as a *private foundation.* It becomes subject to a battery of stringent requirements that are not applicable to any other type of tax-exempt organization, charitable or otherwise.

Facts and/or the law can change. An organization may, later in its existence, shift from a private foundation to a private operating foundation (or perhaps to an exempt operating foundation). Or, a private foundation can terminate its private foundation status and become a public charity.

The point is that the private/public status of a charitable organization can be changed at any time. The same is true for nonprivate foundations, which can change the nature of their public charity status at any time, if the facts warrant. For example, a donative charity can switch to being a service-provider charity (or vice versa) very easily, and a supporting organization can convert itself into a publicly supported charity (or vice versa).

THE ONEROUS RULES

For some pages now, we have been talking about a battery of stringent and onerous rules imposed by law on private foundations. What makes these rules worth avoiding?

Taking them in no particular order, these rules:

- Concern "self-dealing"
- Force a minimum payout (grant-making) amount
- Limit the extent of holdings of businesses
- Pertain to the nature of investments
- Concern the nature and scope of programs
- Impose a tax on net investment income
- Make it quite unlikely that one private foundation will make a grant to another private foundation
- Force more detailed annual reporting
- Make charitable giving to private foundations less attractive

The term *self-dealing* means a transaction that occurs between, directly or indirectly, a private foundation and a disqualified person. Generally, self-dealing transactions include sale or exchange of property; lease of property; lending of money or other extension of credit; furnishing of goods, services, or facilities; payment of unreasonable compensation; and transfer to, or use by or for the benefit of, disqualified persons of the income or assets of a private foundation. There are many exceptions to the self-dealing rules.

A private foundation must annually expend for charitable purposes an amount equal to 5 percent of the value of its investment assets. This *distributable amount* is determined by calculating the foundation's "minimum investment return." If a private foundation does not achieve at least a 5 percent return on its principal, it must use part of its assets to satisfy this minimum payout requirement. The amounts expended must constitute "qualifying distributions," which essentially are grants for charitable purposes (including "set-asides") and reasonable administrative expenditures. The onerous rules thus require valuation of the investment assets (which do not include assets used for charitable purposes).

Generally, a private foundation and its disqualified persons may not have combined holdings of more than 20 percent of a business enterprise. The rule applies to voting stock in a corporation, units in a partnership, and other forms of holdings in a business venture. Holdings are termed "permitted holdings" or, if not allowable, "excess business holdings." However, if effective control of a business rests with unrelated parties, a private foundation and its disqualified persons may hold as much as 35 percent of a business enterprise. For these purposes, the term "business enterprise" does not include a "functionally related business" or a business that derives at least 95 percent of its income from passive sources.

A private foundation may not invest any amount in a manner that will jeopardize the fulfillment of any of its charitable purposes. (The law does not define jeopardizing investments but in context it means highly speculative investments.) The rule does not apply to *program-related investments.*

A private foundation is expected to avoid making "taxable expenditures." Generally, a taxable expenditure is an amount paid or incurred to carry on propaganda, influence legislation, promote a particular outcome of a public election, make a variety of grants to individuals, make a variety of grants to organizations where the foundation has failed to properly exercise "expenditure responsibility," or for any other noncharitable purpose. These rules entail a range of exceptions, involving such matters as voter registration drives, eligible scholarship and fellowship grants, and circulation of the results of nonpartisan analysis, study, or research. (Because of these rules, most private foundations are forced to confine their grant making to public charities, and cannot extend them to other types of organizations or to individuals.)

A private foundation must pay an excise tax equal to 2 percent of its net investment income for each year. "Net investment income" means interest, dividends, rents, royalties, capital gain, and the like, less allowable deductions. As noted earlier, certain operating foundations are excused from the payment of this tax.

THE TAXES

This part of the book summarizes the many instances in which ostensibly tax-exempt organizations are in fact taxable. Tax-exempt organizations that are classified as private foundations, and their managers, are subject to many of these taxes—all considered excise (not income) taxes.

The private foundation rules are underlain with a series of sanctions, imposed in the form of these excise taxes. There are "initial" taxes and "additional" taxes. The additional taxes are payable when an offense has occurred, one or more initial taxes have been imposed, and the offense is not timely corrected.

In a case of self-dealing, the initial tax is 5 percent of the amount involved and is payable by the disqualified person who participated in the wrongful act. If that initial tax is imposed on a self-dealer, the foundation manager who participated in the act is subject to an initial tax (not to exceed $10,000) of $2^1/2$ percent of the amount involved, where he or she knew the act was one of self-dealing and where the participation was willful and not due to reasonable cause. The additional tax on the self-dealer is 200 percent of the amount involved. The additional tax (not to exceed $10,000) on the participating foundation manager, who refused to agree to part or all of the correction, is 50 percent of the amount involved. Two or more individuals may be jointly and severally liable for these taxes.

If a private foundation (that is not an operating foundation) fails to satisfy the payout requirements, it must pay a tax equal to 15 percent of the undistributed income. The additional tax is 100 percent of the undistributed amount.

A private foundation must annually pay a tax equal to 5 percent of its excess business holdings. The additional tax is 200 percent of these holdings.

If a private foundation makes a jeopardizing investment, it must pay a tax equal to 5 percent of the investment. If that initial tax is imposed, a foundation manager who participated in the investment is subject to a tax (not to exceed $5,000) equal to 5 percent of the investment, where he or she knew that the investment was a jeopardizing one and where the participation was willful and not due to reasonable cause. The additional tax on the foundation is 25 percent of the amount of the investment. The additional tax (not to exceed $10,000) on the manager, who refused to agree to part or all of the removal from jeopardy, is 5 percent of the amount of the investment. Two or more individuals may be jointly and severally liable for these taxes.

The initial tax on a private foundation that makes a taxable expenditure is 10 percent of the amount involved. An initial tax (not to exceed $5,000 per taxable expenditure) is also imposed on every foundation manager who agreed to the taxable expenditure, where he or she knew it was a taxable expenditure, where the making of the taxable expenditure was willful, and where it was not due to reasonable cause. The additional tax on the private foundation is 100 percent of the expenditure. The additional tax (not to exceed $10,000 per expenditure) on a manager of a private foundation, where he or she refused to agree to part or all of the correction, is 50 percent of the amount of the taxable expenditure. Again, two or more individuals may be jointly and severally liable for these taxes.

CONCLUSION

There is no advantage to classification as a private foundation. Private foundation status should be avoided whenever possible. This classification brings a battery of stringent rules to restrict the operations of a charitable organization and decrease the tax advantages of charitable gifts to it. A private foundation categorization means that the organization, and in many instances its directors or officers, are subject to very onerous taxes. These tax rules are very technical and it is all too easy for an innocent misstep to lead to heavy taxation. Probably the most useful thing a lawyer or other tax professional can do for a charitable organization is to lead it (if at all possible) to public charity status.

CHECKLIST

☐ Is the (charitable) organization a private
   foundation?   Yes _____ No _____

☐ If yes:

   Is it a private operating foundation?   Yes _____ No _____

   Is it an exempt operating foundation?   Yes _____ No _____

   Has the foundation or its managers been
   subjected to any of the excise taxes?   Yes _____ No _____

☐ If no:

   Is the organization publicly supported?   Yes _____ No _____

   Basis for classification:

   ☐ Donative

   ☐ Service provider

   ☐ Facts and circumstances test

☐ Other

Is the organization an "institution"?	Yes ____	No ____
Is the organization a supporting organization?	Yes ____	No ____
Does the organization have a definitive ruling?	Yes ____	No ____
Does the organization have an advance ruling?	Yes ____	No ____

☐ When does the organization's advance ruling period expire? _____

FOCUS: Campaign to Clean Up America

The Campaign to Clean Up America is organized and will be operated to function as a charitable organization that is not a private foundation. Because of the nature of its programs (see Chapter 6), it does not qualify as one of the institutional charities. Lacking any formal relationship to another nonprofit organization, it does not qualify as a supporting organization.

Because of its funding—principally, grants and contributions—the CCUA is to be qualified as a donative publicly supported charity. This status will be under the general rules; that is, the "facts and circumstances" test will be inapplicable.

Being a new organization, the CCUA is ineligible for a definitive ruling as to its publicly supported organization status. However, it is entitled to an advance ruling on that status.

CHAPTER TWELVE

When Possible, Make It Related

Chapter 11 showed how the tax law applies penalties to the persons involved in violations by private foundations. This chapter deals with the taxation of activities that are unrelated to the tax-exempt functions of nonprofit organizations. The next two chapters cover taxes imposed on lobbying and political campaign activities. In each situation, an organization must tread carefully. The taxes are long-established and they can be heavy.

THE TAXES

Since 1950, the law has divided the activities of tax-exempt organizations into two categories: those that are related to the performance of tax-exempt functions and those that are not. The latter activities, *unrelated activities,* are subject to tax. The gross revenues gained from unrelated activities are taxable, but the IRS will take into account the deductible expenses generated by the activities. No taxes are imposed on the individuals involved.

For organizations that are incorporated, the net revenue from unrelated activities is subject to the regular federal corporate income tax. The federal tax on individuals applies to the unrelated activities of organizations that are not corporations (trusts, for example). Unlike the private foundation rules (see Chapter 11), the current law on related and unrelated activities does not impose any taxes on the directors and officers of nonprofit entities.

To decide whether any of its activities are taxable, an otherwise tax-exempt organization must first ascertain which activities are related to exempt functions and which are not. The judgments that go into assigning activities into these two categories are at the heart of one of the greatest controversies facing nonprofit organizations today. The existing legal structure is simple, intricate, and dynamic. Although the rules were enacted in 1950, it was not until the early 1970s that this body of tax law became of primary importance to nonprofit organizations.

THE UNRELATED INCOME RULES

The unrelated income rules were significantly rewritten by Congress in 1969. The original concept underlying these rules was that of an *outside* business owned and perhaps operated by a tax-exempt organization. However, in 1969, Congress significantly expanded the reach of these rules by authorizing the IRS to evaluate activities conducted by nonprofit organizations internally—*inside* activities.

The objective of the unrelated business income tax is to prevent unfair competition between tax-exempt organizations and for-profit, commercial enterprises. The rules are intended to place the unrelated business activities of an exempt organization on the same tax basis as those of a nonexempt business with which it competes.

To be tax-exempt, a nonprofit organization must be organized and operated primarily for exempt purposes. (See Chapter 4.) The federal tax law allows a tax-exempt organization to engage in a certain amount of income-producing activity that is unrelated to exempt purposes. Where the organization derives net income from one or more unrelated business activities, known formally as *unrelated business taxable income,* it is subject to tax on that income. An organization's tax exemption will be denied or revoked if an inappropriate portion of its activities is not promoting one or more of its exempt purposes.

Business activities may preclude the initial qualification of an otherwise tax-exempt organization. If the organization is not being operated principally for exempt purposes, it will fail the *operational test.* If its articles of organization empower it to carry on substantial activities that are not in furtherance of its exempt purpose, it will not meet the *organizational test.*

A nonprofit organization may still satisfy the operational test, even when it operates a trade or business as a substantial part of its activities, as long as the trade or business promotes the organization's exempt purpose and is not the organization's primary purpose for existing. If the organization's primary purpose is carrying on a trade or business for profit, it is expressly denied exemption on the grounds that it is a *feeder organization,* even if all of its profits are payable to one or more tax-exempt organizations.

The law in this area was, just a few years ago, on the brink of revision. The House Subcommittee on Oversight, a unit of the House Committee on Ways and Means, held five days of hearings on the subject in 1987. Specific alterations were proposed, and they would have been sweeping. Ironically, a large part of the impetus for these hearings was the charge by the business community of unfair competition. The difference between the circumstances in the 1950s and those in the 1980s was that the competing activities of nonprofit organizations in the 1950s were of the unrelated variety; in the 1980s, the competing activities were, under existing law definitions, related to exempt functions. The drive for extensive revision of the unrelated business statutes has stalled; only the IRS and the courts are currently making new law in this area.

Prior to enactment of the unrelated income rules, the law embodied a *destination of income test.* For an organization to be tax-exempt, the net profits of the organization had to be used in furtherance of tax-exempt purposes. Because the test did not consider the source of the profits, it tolerated forms of unfair competition.

In adopting these rules in 1950 and in amplifying them in 1969, Congress has not prohibited commercial ventures by nonprofit organizations nor has it levied taxes only on the receipts of businesses that bear no relation to nonprofit organizations' tax-exempt purposes. Instead, it has struck a balance between, as the Supreme Court phrased it in 1986, "its two objectives of encouraging benevolent enterprise and restraining unfair competition."

Essentially, for an activity of a tax-exempt organization to be taxed, three tests must be satisfied. The activity must constitute a "trade or business," be "regularly carried on," and not be "substantially related" to the tax-exempt purposes of the organization. However, the many exceptions to these rules exempt from taxation certain forms of activity and types of income.

The unrelated income rules are in a peculiar state of affairs these days. The courts are simultaneously developing additional and sometimes different criteria for assessing the presence of unrelated business, and from judicial decisions a doctrine of *commerciality* is emerging. The results: considerable confusion as to what the law in this area is, and extensive judgmental leeway on the part of the courts and the IRS in applying it.

Affected Tax-Exempt Organizations

Nearly all types of tax-exempt organizations are subject to the unrelated income rules. They include religious organizations (including churches), educational organizations (including universities, colleges, and schools), health care organizations (including hospitals), scientific organizations, and other charitable organizations. Beyond the realm of charitable entities, the rules are applicable to social welfare organizations (including advocacy groups), labor organizations (including unions), trade and professional associations, fraternal organizations, employee benefit funds, and veterans' organizations.

Special rules tax all income not related to exempt functions (including investment income) of social clubs, homeowners' associations, and political organizations.

Certain organizations are not generally subject to the unrelated income rules, simply because they are not allowed to engage in any active business endeavors. This is the case, for example, for private foundations and title-holding organizations. The operation of an active business (externally or internally) by a private foundation would likely trigger application of the excess business holdings restrictions. (See Chapter 11.)

Instrumentalities of the United States, like nearly all governmental agencies, are exempt from the unrelated business rules. However, the unrelated income rules are applicable to colleges and universities that are agencies or instrumentalities of a government, as well as to corporations owned by such colleges and universities.

Trade or Business Defined

For the purpose of the federal tax rules, the term *trade or business* includes any activity that is carried on for the production of income from the sale of goods or the performance of services. Most activities that would constitute a trade or business under basic tax law principles are considered a trade or business for purposes of the unrelated income rules.

This definition of the term *trade or business* embraces nearly every activity of a tax-exempt organization; only passive investment activities generally escape this classification. In this sense, every tax-exempt organization should be viewed as a bundle of activities, each of which is a trade or business. (It must be emphasized that this definition has nothing to do with whether a particular activity is related or unrelated; there are related businesses and unrelated businesses.)

The IRS is empowered to examine each of an organization's activities in search of unrelated business. Each activity can be examined as though it existed wholly independently of the others; an unrelated activity cannot, as a matter of law, be hidden from scrutiny by tucking it in among a host of related activities. As Congress chose to state the principle, "an activity does not lose identity as a trade or business merely because it is carried on within a larger aggregate of similar activities or within a larger complex of other endeavors which may, or may not, be related to the exempt purposes of the organization." This is known, in the jargon of tax law professionals, as the *fragmentation rule.* For example, the fragmentation rule allows the IRS to treat the income from the sale of advertising space in an exempt organization's magazine as revenue derived from an unrelated business, even though otherwise the publication of the magazine is a related business.

The federal tax law also states that, "[w]here an activity carried on for profit constitutes an unrelated trade or business, no part of such trade or business shall be excluded from such classification merely because it does not result in profit." In other words, just because an activity results in a loss in a particular year, that is insufficient basis for failing to treat the activity as an unrelated one (including reporting it as such to the IRS). Conversely, simply because an activity generates a profit is not alone supposed to lead to the conclusion that the activity is unrelated (although there are many in the IRS and on court benches who are likely to leap to that conclusion).

Just as *profits* are not built into the formal definition of the term *trade or business,* so too is the element of *unfair competition* missing from that definition. Yet, unfair competition is the driving force behind the unrelated income rules, and the IRS and the courts sometimes use the factor of "competition" in assessing whether an activity is related or unrelated to exempt functions.

Another absent term in the tax law definition of *trade or business* is *commerciality.* Nothing in the statutory law generally authorizes the IRS and judges to conclude that an activity is unrelated solely because it is conducted in a commercial manner, which basically means it is conducted the way a comparable activity is carried on by for-profit businesses. But they do it anyway.

Regularly Carried On

To be considered an unrelated business, an activity must be *regularly carried on* by a tax-exempt organization.

Income from an activity is considered taxable only when (assuming the other criteria are satisfied) the activity is regularly carried on, as distinguished from sporadic or infrequent transactions. The factors that determine whether an activity is regularly carried on are the frequency and continuity of the activities, and the manner in which the activities are pursued. (In this context, the statutory law comes the closest to using a doctrine of *commerciality.*)

These factors must be evaluated in light of the purpose of the unrelated business income tax, which is to place tax-exempt organizations' business activities on the same tax basis as those of their nonexempt business competitors. Specific business activities of a tax-exempt organization will generally be deemed to be regularly carried on if they are frequent and continuous, and are pursued in a manner that is generally similar to comparable commercial activities of nonexempt organizations.

Where an organization duplicates income-producing activities performed by commercial organizations year-round, but performs those activities for a period of only a few weeks, they do not constitute the regular carrying on of a trade or business. Similarly, occasional or annual income-producing activities, such as fund-raising events, do not amount to a business that is regularly carried on. However, the conduct of year-round business activities, such as the operation of a parking lot for one day each week, would constitute the regular carrying on of a business. Where commercial entities normally undertake income-producing activities on a seasonal basis, the conduct of the activities by an exempt organization during a significant portion of the season is deemed the regular conduct of that activity. For this purpose, a "season" may be a portion of the year (such as the summer) or a holiday period.

In summary, a trade or business is regularly carried on by a tax-exempt organization where the attributes of the activity are similar to the commercial activities of nonexempt organizations.

Unrelated Trade or Business

The term *unrelated trade or business* is defined to mean "any trade or business the conduct of which [by a tax-exempt organization] is not substantially related (aside from the need of such organization for income or funds or the use it makes of the profits derived) to the exercise or performance by such organization of its charitable, educational, or other purpose or function constituting the basis for its exemption." The parenthetical clause means that an activity is not related simply because the organization uses the net revenue from the activity for exempt purposes.

The revenue from a regularly conducted trade or business is subject to tax, unless the business activity is substantially related to the accomplishment of the organization's exempt purpose. The key to taxation or nontaxation in this area is the meaning of the words *substantially related*. Yet the law tells us merely that, to be substantially related, the activity must have a *substantial causal relationship* to the accomplishment of an exempt purpose.

The fact that an asset is essential to the conduct of an organization's exempt activities does not shield from taxation the unrelated income produced by that asset. The income-producing activities must still meet the causal relationship test if the income is not to be subject to tax. This issue arises when a tax-exempt organization owns a facility or other assets that are put to a dual use. For example, the operation of an auditorium as a motion picture theater for public entertainment in the evenings is treated as an unrelated activity even though the theater is used exclusively for exempt purposes during the daytime hours. The fragmentation rule allows this type of use of a single asset to be split into two businesses.

Activities should not be conducted on a scale larger than is reasonably necessary for the performance of exempt functions. Activities in excess of the needs of exempt functions constitute unrelated businesses.

There is a host of court cases and IRS rulings providing illustrations of related and unrelated activities. Colleges and universities operate dormitories and bookstores as related activities but can be taxed on travel tours and sports camps. Hospitals may operate gift shops, snack bars, and parking lots as related activities but may be taxable on sales of pharmaceuticals to the general public and on performance of routine tests for physicians. Museums may, without taxation, sell items reflective of their collections but are taxable on the sale of souvenirs and furniture. Trade associations may find themselves taxable on sales of items and particular services to members, while dues and subscription revenue are nontaxable. Fund-raising events may be characterized as unrelated activities, particularly when compensation is paid or when the activity is regularly carried on.

Unrelated Business Taxable Income

As noted earlier, to be subject to the unrelated income rules, an activity must satisfy (or, depending on one's point of view, fail) three tests. These tests are built into the definition of the term *unrelated business taxable income*: "the gross income derived by any [exempt] organization from any unrelated trade or business . . . regularly carried on by it, less the deductions allowed . . . [under federal tax law in general] which are directly connected with the carrying on of such trade or business."

Both this gross income and allowable deductions are computed in conformance with the "modifications" discussed below.

When the organization covered by the unrelated income rules is a foreign organization, its unrelated business taxable income is "its unrelated business taxable income which is derived from sources within the United States and which is not effectively connected with the conduct of a trade or business within the United States" and "its unrelated business taxable income which is effectively connected with the conduct of a trade or business within the United States."

Some tax-exempt organizations are members of partnerships. (See Chapter 16.) If a trade or business regularly carried on by the partnership is an unrelated trade or business, the organization has special reporting requirements. In computing its unrelated business taxable income, it must (subject to the modifications) include its share (whether or not distributed) of the partnership's gross income from the unrelated business and its share of the partnership deductions directly connected with the gross income. (This is an application of what the tax law terms the *look-through rule.*) A tax-exempt organization's share (whether or not distributed) of the gross income of a *publicly traded partnership* must be treated as gross income derived from an unrelated business, and its share of the partnership deductions is allowed in computing unrelated business taxable income.

A tax-exempt organization may own *debt-financed property,* and the use of the property may be unrelated to the organization's exempt function. When the organization computes its unrelated business taxable income, any income from the property has to be included as gross income derived from an unrelated business. The income is subject to tax in the same proportion that the property is financed by debt. The debt involved must be what the tax law terms *acquisition indebtedness.* The most common example is a mortgage.

Exempted Activities

Despite the foregoing general rules, certain businesses conducted by tax-exempt organizations are expressly exempted from taxation. Most frequently exempted from taxation is a trade or business "in which substantially all the work is performed for the organization without compensation." If a tax-exempt organization conducts an unrelated business using services substantially provided by volunteers, the net revenue from that business is not taxable. This exemption protects from taxation many ongoing charitable fund-raising activities.

Also exempted is a trade or business carried on by the organization "primarily for the convenience of its members, students, patients, officers, or employees." However, this exception is only available to organizations that are charitable, educational, and the like, or are governmental colleges and universities.

A further exemption is given to a trade or business "which is the selling of merchandise, substantially all of which has been received by the organization as gifts or contributions." This exemption shelters the work of exempt thrift stores from taxation.

The term *unrelated trade or business* does not include *qualified public entertainment activities.* A public entertainment activity is any entertainment or recreational activity traditionally conducted at fairs or expositions promoting agricultural and educational purposes. Typically, these activities attract the public to fairs or expositions or promote the breeding of animals or the development of products or equipment.

To be *qualified*, a public entertainment activity must be conducted:

- In conjunction with an international, national, state, regional, or local fair or exposition

- In accordance with the provisions of state law which permit the activity to be operated or conducted solely by a qualifying organization or by a governmental agency

- In accordance with the provisions of state law which permit a qualifying organization to be granted a license to conduct no more than 20 days of the activity, on payment to the state of a lower percentage of the revenue from the licensed activity than the state requires from nonqualifying organizations

To earn the public entertainment activities exception, a *qualifying organization* must be a tax-exempt charitable, social welfare, or labor organization that regularly conducts, as one of its substantial exempt purposes, an agricultural and educational fair or exposition.

The term *unrelated trade or business* also does not include qualified convention and trade show activities. These activities, traditionally conducted at conventions, annual meetings, or trade shows, are designed to attract attention from persons in an industry. There is no requirement for those persons to be members of the sponsoring organization. The shows' purposes are to display industry products, to stimulate interest in, and demand for, industry products or services; or to educate persons within the industry in the development of new products and services or new rules and regulations affecting industry practices.

To be *qualified*, a convention and trade show activity must be carried out by a qualifying organization in conjunction with an international, national, state, regional, or local convention, annual meeting, or show that the organization is conducting. One of the purposes of the organization in sponsoring the activity must be: the promotion and stimulation of interest in, and demand for, the products and services of that industry in general, or the education of attendees regarding new developments or products and services related to the exempt activities of the organization. The show must be designed to achieve its purpose through the character of the exhibits and the extent of the industry products displayed.

A *qualifying organization* is a charitable, social welfare, or labor organization, or a trade association, that regularly conducts a show as one of its substantial exempt purposes. The show must be aimed toward stimulating interest in, and demand for, the products of a particular industry, or a segment of an industry, or toward educating attendees on new developments of products and services related to the exempt activities of the organization.

The concept of unrelated trade or business does not include situations where cooperative hospital service organizations furnish services to one or more other tax-exempt hospitals. However, the services: (1) must be furnished solely to hospitals that have facilities for no more than 100 inpatients; (2) if performed on its own behalf by the recipient hospital, must constitute exempt activities of that institution; and (3) must be provided for a fee or cost that does not exceed the actual cost of providing the services. The cost must include straight-line depreciation and a reasonable amount for return on capital goods used to provide the services.

The concept of unrelated trade or business also does not include bingo games. The game must be: (1) of a type in which usually the wagers are placed, the winners are determined, and the prizes or other property are distributed in the presence of all persons placing wagers in the game, (2) not an activity ordinarily carried out on a commercial basis, and (3) not in violation of any state or local law.

For a charitable, veterans', or other organization, to which contributions are deductible, the term *unrelated trade or business* does not include activities relating to a distribution of low-cost articles that is incidental to the solicitation of charitable contributions. A *low-cost article* is one that has a maximum cost of $5.00 (indexed for inflation) to the organization that distributes the item (directly or indirectly). A *distribution* qualifies under this rule if it is not made at the request of the recipients, if it is made without their express consent, and if the articles that are distributed are accompanied by a request for a charitable contribution to the organization and a statement that the recipients may retain the article whether or not a contribution is made.

For a charitable, veterans', or other organization to which contributions are deductible, the term *trade or business* does not include exchanging with another like organization the names and addresses of donors to or members of the organization, or the renting of these lists to another like organization.

Other exemption rules apply to certain local organizations of employees, the conduct of certain games of chance, and the rental of poles by mutual or cooperative telephone or electric companies.

Exempted Income

Certain types of passive income and income derived from research are exempt from the unrelated income tax.

Because the unrelated income tax applies to active businesses conducted by tax-exempt organizations, most types of passive income are exempt from taxation. This exemption generally covers dividends, interest, securities loans payments, annuities, royalties, rents, capital gains, and gains on the lapse or termination of options written by exempt organizations.

However, there are important exceptions to this exemption for passive income:

- Income in the form of rent, royalties, and the like from an active business undertaking is taxable; that is, merely labeling an income flow as rent, royalties, and so forth does not make it tax-free
- The unrelated debt-financed income rules override the general exemption for passive income
- Interest, annuities, royalties, and rents from a controlled corporation may be taxable

The following exemptions pertain to the conduct of research:

- Income derived from research for the United States, or any of its agencies or instrumentalities, or any state or political subdivision of a state
- Income derived from research performed for any person at a college, university, or hospital
- Income derived from research performed for any person at an organization operated primarily for purposes of carrying on fundamental research, the results of which are freely available to the general public

This exemption for research income is under strain. Some organizations do not engage in "research" at all; rather, they are merely testing products for public use just prior to marketing. Other organizations, principally universities and scientific research institutions, are engaging in research, but their discoveries are licensed or otherwise transferred to business organizations for exploitation in the public marketplace. This closeness between businesses and nonprofit organizations—known as "technology transfer"—is raising questions as to how much commercial activity is being sheltered from tax by the research exceptions.

There is a specific deduction of $1,000. This means that the first $1,000 of unrelated income is spared taxation.

Use of Subsidiaries

As discussed more fully in Chapter 15, some tax-exempt organizations elect to spin off their unrelated activities to related taxable subsidiaries. The tax on the net income of the unrelated activity is then not borne directly by the exempt organization. The managers of the tax-exempt organization may be averse to reporting any unrelated income or the unrelated activity may be too large in relation to related activity.

If funds are transferred from a taxable subsidiary to an exempt parent, that income will be taxable as unrelated income to the parent if it is interest, rents, royalties, or capital gains, where the parent has, directly or indirectly, 80 percent or more control of the subsidiary. However, if the subsidiary pays dividends to the tax-exempt parent, the dividends are not taxable to the parent because they are not deductible by the subsidiary.

CONCLUSION

The unrelated income rules represent an attempt by Congress to prevent tax-exempt organizations from unfairly competing with for-profit businesses. These rules generally equalize the tax treatment of unrelated business activities by segregating them, for tax purposes, from the other activities of tax-exempt organizations and taxing them as though they are free-standing business undertakings.

For an activity to be taxable under these rules, it must be a trade or business that is regularly carried on and is not substantially related to the performance of tax-exempt functions. If a tax-exempt organization uses the net revenue from an unrelated business to fund related activities, that use is not enough to convert the unrelated activity into a related one.

The law provides a variety of exemptions that allow certain activities and certain forms of income to be tax-free. The most important of these exemptions is for passive income.

In computing taxable unrelated income, a tax-exempt organization may utilize all business expense deductions, as long as the expenses are directly related to the conduct of the unrelated business.

As tax-exempt organizations struggle to generate additional income in these days of declining governmental support, proposed adverse tax reform, more sophisticated management, and greater pressure for more services, they are increasingly drawn to service-provider activities, some of which may be unrelated to their exempt purposes.

The growth of service-provider activities, the increasing tendencies of the courts to find activities unrelated because they are "commercial," and the unrest over "unfair competition" between tax-exempt organizations and for-profit entities—all of these are clear evidence that this aspect of the law of tax-exempt organizations is constantly evolving and will be reshaped. Indeed, the IRS is currently concentrating its audit force on universities, colleges, and hospitals, hoping to tap unrelated business income as one of the main areas for new revenue.

This subject is among the most fast-paced of any topics covered by federal tax law. All indications are that this trend will continue.

CHECKLIST

☐ Does the organization have one or more
unrelated businesses?   Yes _____ No _____

☐ If yes, identify them:

_____

_____

_____

If yes and if applicable, check one or more of the following:

The organization does not pay any unrelated business income tax because:

☐ The activity is not regularly carried on

☐ The income from the activity is considered passive income

☐ The business is conducted substantially by volunteers

☐ The convenience exception is used

☐ The items sold were donated

☐ The activity is a qualified public entertainment activity

☐ The activity is an exempted game of chance

☐   The standard deduction applies

☐   The expenses are equal to or exceed the unrelated income

☐   One or more other reasons are applicable

Does the organization have any unrelated
debt-financed income?   Yes _____   No _____

FOCUS: Campaign to Clean Up America

The Campaign to Clean Up America does not initially intend to conduct any unrelated business activities. Its service-provider revenue will be insubstantial and is expected to come from related businesses (such as seminars and the sale of publications).

However, as the CCUA grows and becomes known, it may find that it can profitably engage in one or more unrelated businesses. For example, it could sell trash bags and similar supplies and equipment. It could provide property maintenance services for individuals or communities. It could consult with government agencies in the development and maintenance of large-scale beautification programs.

Some of these unrelated activities could be conducted within the organization. Others could be undertaken by means of one or more for-profit subsidiaries.

CHAPTER THIRTEEN

The Lobbying Constraints—and Taxes

Congress has long been concerned with legislative activities—lobbying—by nonprofit organizations. This concern is particularly evident in the federal tax law pertaining to charitable organizations and trade, business, and professional associations. The Treasury Department and the IRS have promulgated extremely stringent regulations and rules in an attempt to restrict lobbying by nonprofit organizations—most notably, charitable groups. The federal courts have upheld the government in its efforts to enforce these constraints.

Regulation in this area is currently very active. Congress, in 1987, introduced new rules in an effort to further limit lobbying by charitable organizations and, to some extent, other nonprofit organizations. The Treasury Department and the IRS have recently issued sweeping regulations in a new effort to curb lobbying by public charities and related organizations. (In 1969, Congress adjusted the tax law by flatly prohibiting lobbying by private foundations.)

In addition to the tax law, other federal law imposes meaningful constraints on lobbying by nonprofit organizations. For example, the U.S. Postal Service will not grant second- or third-class mail privileges to otherwise qualifying nonprofit groups whose primary purpose is lobbying. Under authority of the Federal Regulation of Lobbying Act, lobbying organizations or individual lobbyists are required to register with the clerks of the House of Representatives and the Senate. Still other laws may have an impact in this area; among them are the law requiring registration and reporting by lobbyists for foreign governments, and the laws restricting the use of federal funds for lobbying (such as various rules of the Office of Management and Budget and the "Byrd Amendment").

The principal laws regulating lobbying by nonprofit organizations, however, are the federal tax laws. They are explored in this chapter.

LOBBYING RESTRICTIONS ON CHARITABLE ORGANIZATIONS

Organizations that are tax-exempt because they are "charitable" in nature (this classification includes educational, religious, scientific, and similar entities) must, to preserve the exemption, adhere to a variety of requirements. One of these is that "no substantial part of the activities" of the organization may constitute "carrying on propaganda, or otherwise attempting, to influence legislation." Because of the considerable and continuing uncertainty as to the meaning and scope of this rule, many nonprofit organizations have experienced much anguish in attempting to fathom the "substantial part" test.

The difficulties of compliance with this limitation on legislative activities have been manifold. In reaction to an increasingly intolerable situation, Congress, in 1976, tried to clarify compliance but failed, due in no small part to the insistence of the IRS in proposing broad and onerous rules in interpretation of the statutory law. As is so often the case with "tax reform," the law ends up being much more complicated than it was before.

In its present state, the law in this area has three sets of rules. One set of rules applies to private foundations (no lobbying). The other two sets of rules are available for other types of charitable organizations ("public charities"). (For the distinctions between public and private charities, see Chapter 11.) One of these sets of rules, which is available to most public charities, must be elected by them. This is called the *expenditure test*. The third set of rules, called the *substantial part test*, is applicable to those public charities that have not (or cannot) come within the elective rules.

Why, as a matter of policy, is it inappropriate for a charitable organization to engage in lobbying in pursuit of its exempt purposes? The law on this subject was originally enacted in 1934, without benefit of congressional hearings, in an effort to stop the activities of a particular organization that had antagonized some members of the U.S. Senate. Case law prior to that date suggests that lobbying may be a legitimate way for a charitable organization to pursue its exempt goals; there is nothing in the common law of charitable trusts (on which the tax law of charities is based) that specifies that lobbying by charitable groups is contrary to their status as charities. One clue to the rationale for the prohibition was offered by the U.S. Supreme Court in 1983, when it observed that Congress, in enacting the substantial part test, "was concerned that exempt [charitable] organizations might use tax-deductible contributions to lobby to promote the private interests of their members." Recently, the Treasury Department expressed opposition to any relaxation of the limitation on lobbying by charitable organizations. Liberalization of the rules, said the Treasury, would enable more nonprofit entities to become classified as charitable ones, therefore becoming eligible to attract deductible gifts and in turn helping to aggravate the federal deficit by increasing the use of the charitable contribution deduction!

Philosophical or policy considerations aside, the law is the law. Lobbying by public charities is restricted under either set of rules. If a charitable organization loses its tax exemption because of lobbying activities, it may not convert to a tax-exempt social welfare organization (see below).

General Rules

The general rules pertaining to lobbying by public charities are found in the Treasury Regulations, IRS rulings, and court opinions that comprise the body of law under the substantial part test. These rules label a charitable organization that has lobbying as a substantial activity an "action" organization—and, needless to say, charitable action organizations are not tax-exempt as charities.

Legislative activities can take many forms. Some amount to "direct" lobbying, which occurs when one or more representatives of an organization make contact with a legislator and/or his or her staff, and/or the staff of legislative committees. Direct lobbying includes office visits, presentation of testimony at hearings, correspondence, publication and dissemination of material, and entertainment.

"Grass roots" lobbying is another form. This type of lobbying occurs when the organization urges the public, or a segment of the public, to contact members of a legislative body or their staffs for the purpose of proposing, supporting, or opposing legislation.

The law, under the substantial part test, does not differentiate between lobbying that is related to an organization's exempt purposes and lobbying that is not. The function is still lobbying, and both types are subject to the proscription. However, a charitable organization that does not initiate any action with respect to pending legislation but merely responds to a request from a legislative committee to testify is not, solely because of that activity, considered an action organization. Also, a charitable organization can engage in nonpartisan analysis, study, and research, and publish its results. Even where some of the plans and policies formulated can only be carried out through legislative enactments, as long as the organization does not advocate the adoption of legislation or legislative action to implement its findings, it escapes being an action organization. In both of these instances, the organization is advancing education, not engaging in advocacy activities.

There can be a fine line between nonpartisan analysis, study, or research, and lobbying. An organization may evaluate proposed or pending legislation and present to the public an objective analysis of it, as long as it does not participate in the presentation of suggested bills to a legislature and does not engage in any campaign to secure enactment of the legislation. However, if the organization's primary objective can be attained only by legislative action, it is an action organization. In general, then, promoting activism instead of promoting educational activities can deny an organization classification as a charitable entity.

Because these rules obviously apply to legislative activities—activities undertaken in connection with the championing or opposing of legislation—it is necessary to know what does and does not constitute *legislation*. The term *legislation* refers principally to action by the U.S. Congress, a state legislative body, a local council, or similar governing body, and by the general public in a referendum, initiative, constitutional amendment, or similar procedure. In the view of the IRS, congressional action on cabinet and judicial nominees constitutes *legislating*. Legislation does not generally include action by the executive branch, such as the promulgation of rules and regulations, nor does it include action by the independent regulatory agencies. Charitable organizations can "lobby" executive branch and independent agencies, in support of or opposition to the agencies' rules, and the lobbying will not endanger their tax-exempt status.

The most important concept under the general rules is the meaning of the word *substantial*. As noted earlier, the law offers no formula for computing *substantial* or *insubstantial* legislative undertakings.

There are at least three ways to measure *substantial* in this context:

- Determine what percentage of an organization's annual expenditures are devoted to efforts to influence legislation
- Apply a percentage to the legislative activities themselves, in relation to total activities
- Ascertain (usually with hindsight) whether an organization has had a substantial impact on the legislative process simply by virtue of its prestige and influence

Case law and IRS practice support the use of all three practices.

The IRS being the IRS, substantiality is usually measured in terms of money. Because of the way the term *substantial* is used in other tax contexts, it is likely that a public charity's annual outlays for lobbying can be up to 15 percent of its total expenditures without causing loss of tax-exempt status. (It must be emphasized strongly, however, that this guideline is the author's, based on practical experience, and should not be regarded as a rule of law.)

The true measure of substantiality remains elusive. In reports accompanying tax legislation over the years, the Senate Finance Committee has characterized the state of affairs well. In 1969, the Committee wrote that "the standards as to the permissible level of [legislative] activities under the present law are so vague as to encourage subjective application of the sanction." Later, in 1976, the Finance Committee portrayed the dilemma this way: "Many believe that the standards as to the permissible level of [legislative] activities under present law are too vague and thereby tend to encourage subjective and selective enforcement."

The confusion and frustration with the substantial part test of the general rules led to enactment of the expenditure test, discussed in the next section. The chafing under the restrictions also led to litigation challenging the general rule on constitutional law grounds. Essentially, the courts have upheld the limitation in the face of charges that it violates free speech and equal protection rights. The rationale is that the tax law does not prohibit organizations from engaging in substantial efforts to influence legislation; it merely refrains from allowing the federal treasury to subsidize the lobbying efforts. As the U.S. Supreme Court stated in 1983, the constraints pass constitutional muster and "Congress has merely refused to pay for the lobbying out of public moneys."

Lobbying by charitable organizations, or on their behalf by related nonprofit organizations, was the subject of congressional hearings in 1987. The result was enactment of even more legislation, designed to give the general rules more strength, as part of the Revenue Act of 1987.

The 1987 legislation, which is applicable to most public charities, introduced a system of excise taxes on excess lobbying outlays. Under these rules, if a charitable organization loses its tax exemption because of attempts to influence legislation, a tax of 5 percent of the *lobbying expenditures* is imposed on the organization. (This tax *does not apply* to any organization that is under the expenditure test described below or that is ineligible to make that election.) A lobbying expenditure is any amount paid or incurred by a charitable organization in carrying on propaganda or otherwise attempting to influence legislation.

A separate 5 percent tax is applicable to each of the organization's managers (its officers, directors, and key employees) who agreed to the lobbying expenditures (knowing they were likely to result in revocation of its exemption), unless the agreement was not willful and was due to reasonable cause. The burden of proof for whether a manager knowingly participated in the lobbying expenditure is on the IRS. The imposition of an excise tax on an organization does not itself establish that any manager of the organization is subject to the excise tax.

Expenditure Test

The expenditure test regarding permissible lobbying by charitable organizations arose from a desire to clarify the law that had been made unclear by the substantial part test. In other words, the purpose of this test is to offer charitable groups some certainty on how much lobbying they can undertake without endangering their tax-exempt status. This purpose has not been fulfilled: the IRS has made the rules sweeping and onerous, and few organizations have elected to use the rules. (One day, Congress may make the expenditure test rules mandatory, as a definition of the substantial part standard.)

The expenditure test utilizes a tax system as well, although none of the taxes falls on individuals involved. These rules are not a substitute for the general rules (embodied in the substantial part test) but act as a "safe harbor" guideline, so that a charitable organization that is in compliance with the expenditure test is deemed to be in conformance with the general rules.

These rules are termed *elective* because charitable organizations must elect to come under these standards. Organizations that choose not to make the election are governed by the substantial part test, with all of its uncertainties. Churches, conventions or associations of churches, integrated auxiliaries of churches, certain supporting organizations, and (of course) private foundations may not elect to come under the expenditure test.

The expenditure test rules provide a definition of terms such as *legislation, influencing legislation, direct lobbying,* and *grass roots lobbying.* These terms are essentially the same as those used in connection with the substantial part test. However, in an attempt to define when the legislative process begins (and, therefore, when a lobbying process begins), the expenditure test offers a definition of legislative *action:* the "introduction, amendment, enactment, defeat, or repeal of Acts, bills, resolutions, or similar items."

The expenditure test measures permissible and impermissible legislative activities of charitable organizations in terms of sets of declining percentages of total exempt purpose expenditures. (These do not include fund-raising expenses.) The basic permitted annual level of expenditures for legislative efforts (termed the "lobbying nontaxable amount") is 20 percent of the first $500,000 of an organization's expenditures for an exempt purpose (including legislative activities), plus 15 percent of the next $500,000, 10 percent of the next $500,000, and 5 percent of any remaining expenditures. The total amount spent for legislative activities in any one year by an electing charitable organization may not exceed $1 million. A separate limitation—amounting to one-fourth of the foregoing amounts—is imposed on grass roots lobbying expenditures.

Here is where the taxes come in. A charitable organization that has elected these limitations and exceeds either the general lobbying ceiling amount or the grass roots lobbying ceiling amount becomes subject to an excise tax of 25 percent of the excess lobbying expenditures. The tax falls on the greater of the two excesses. If an electing organization's lobbying expenditures normally (an average over a four-year period) exceed 150 percent of either limitation, it will lose its tax-exempt status as a charitable organization.

The expenditure test rules contain exemptions for five categories of activities. The term *influencing legislation* does not include:

- Making available the results of nonpartisan analysis, study, or research
- Providing technical advice or assistance in response to a written request by a governmental body
- Appearances before, or communications to, any legislative body in connection with a possible decision of that body that might affect the existence of the organization, its powers and duties, its tax-exempt status, or the deductibility of contributions to it
- Communications between the organization and its bona fide members regarding legislation or proposed legislation that is of direct interest to them, unless the communications directly encourage the members to influence legislation or to urge nonmembers to influence legislation
- Routine communications with government officials or employees

The expenditure test contains a method of aggregating the expenditures of related organizations. The intent is to forestall the creation of numerous organizations for the purpose of avoiding the expenditure test.

Where two or more charitable organizations are members of an "affiliated group" and at least one of the members has elected coverage under these provisions, the calculations of lobbying and exempt purpose expenditures must take into account the expenditures of the group. If these expenditures exceed the permitted limits, each of the electing member organizations must pay a proportionate share of the penalty excise tax. The nonelecting members are treated under the substantial part test.

Generally, two organizations are "affiliated" where (1) one organization is bound by decisions of the other on legislative issues as stated in its governing instrument or (2) the governing board of one organization includes enough representatives of the other (that is, there is an interlocking directorate) to cause or prevent action on legislative issues by the first organization. Where a number of organizations are affiliated, even in chain fashion, all of them are treated as one group of affiliated organizations. However, if a group of autonomous organizations controls an organization but no one member of the group has exclusive control of the organization, the group is not considered an affiliated group by reason of the interlocking directorates rule.

Special reporting requirements are imposed on charitable organizations that engage in lobbying. One set of obligations is for those under the substantial part test; the other set is for organizations that have elected the expenditure test. The record-keeping and reporting requirements are more onerous for charitable organizations that are under the expenditure test, although the IRS is working to bring approximately equal reporting burdens to groups under the substantial part test.

Should the Election Be Made?

There is some controversy as to whether, or when, a charitable organization should elect to come under the expenditure test. The IRS strenuously advocates the election (so it can obtain the additional information on lobbying that must be reported). The biggest advantages to the election are:

- The test can offer greater certainty on the amount of permissible lobbying
- The tax rules enacted in 1987 are not applicable
- Various statutory exceptions apply
- The time of volunteers is excluded from the computation of lobbying time

The biggest disadvantages are:

- Record-keeping and reporting requirements are more extensive
- Assessment of permissible lobbying is still sometimes uncertain
- The election can be particularly onerous for grass-roots lobbying organizations
- The 1987 tax rules potentially apply
- The rules concerning affiliated organizations apply

LOBBYING RESTRICTIONS ON OTHER NONPROFIT ORGANIZATIONS

The federal law pertaining to tax-exempt status imposes lobbying restrictions only on charitable organizations, not on other nonprofit organizations. The only constraint (if it can even be called that) is that the
organization must pursue its exempt functions (whatever they may be)
as its primary purpose and that any lobbying it may do must not inter-
fere with that principal requirement. Basically, entities such as social
welfare organizations, labor organizations, business and professional
associations (business leagues), and veterans' organizations may lobby
without restriction.

Indeed, this stark contrast in the law between charitable organizations and other types of tax-exempt organizations (even those to which
deductible gifts can be made) gave rise to challenges to the general
rules on equal protection grounds. But the U.S. Supreme Court ruled
that "[l]egislatures have especially broad latitude in creating classifications and distinctions in tax statutes."

Because of these distinctions, charitable organizations are afforded a
major opportunity to sidestep the rigorous rules regulating lobbying by
them: A charitable organization can create a related social welfare organization and use it as a lobbying arm. Some Justices of the U.S. Supreme
Court believe that the easy availability of tax-exempt lobbying arms of
charitable organizations is the feature of the tax law that prevents the
lobbying restrictions on charities from being unconstitutional.

A few other aspects of the federal tax laws bear on this matter. These
are described next.

Associations

Nonprofit membership associations are generally tax-exempt. Most of
these are trade, business, or professional associations (business leagues)
or charitable organizations. Others are labor organizations or social welfare organizations. The pertinent common element is that all of these
associations receive dues revenue and, in many cases, the dues are deductible as business expenses.

The rules concerning the deductibility of business expenses limit
the amount that may be expended for lobbying. In short, these rules
have an impact on the way the recipient associations can use the dues
revenue.

A deduction is permitted for two categories of ordinary and necessary
business expenses paid or incurred for legislative efforts: expenses in
direct connection with appearances before, submission of statements to,

or communications sent to members or committees of legislative bodies regarding legislation or proposed legislation that is of direct interest to the taxpayer; or expenses directly connected with communication of information between the taxpayer and an organization of which the taxpayer is a member, regarding legislation or proposed legislation that is of direct interest to the taxpayer and the organization.

If the taxpayer is a dues-paying member of an organization, these rules apply to the portion of dues paid or incurred by the taxpayer that is attributable to the expenses of legislative activities.

There is no business deduction for amounts paid or incurred in connection with any attempt to influence the general public, or segments of the public, with respect to legislative matters (or elections or referenda). No deduction is allowed for any expenses incurred in grass roots campaigns or any other attempt to urge or encourage the public to contact members of a legislative body for the purpose of proposing, supporting, or opposing legislation. Communications between an association and its members generally do not constitute influencing the general public. However, the employees and customers of members of the association are a segment of the general public. Consequently, a communication from a business league that is intended to go beyond its members and, directly or through its membership, targets a segment of the public will constitute grass roots lobbying. The expenses attributable to that type of lobbying (including the allocable portion of members' dues) are not deductible as business expenses.

An association, as a practical matter, normally avoids grass roots lobbying, so as not to risk a possible audit of its membership, particularly where the members are business corporations and the dues are substantial.

Political Organizations

One type of tax-exempt organization is the "political organization." A political organization, such as a political action committee (PAC), is unlikely to engage in lobbying. Legislative activities are not "exempt functions" for a political organization and may cause taxation if they are undertaken.

To qualify for exemption, a political organization must be organized and operated primarily for the purpose of directly or indirectly accepting contributions and making expenditures for an "exempt function." In this context, an exempt function is influencing or attempting to influence the selection, nomination, election, or appointment of any individual to any federal, state, or local public office. Lobbying, then, is not an exempt function for a political committee. If lobbying is done in an insubstantial amount by a political committee, the outcome from a tax law viewpoint would be the payment of some tax; if done in violation of the primary purpose standard, the outcome would be loss of tax-exempt status.

Other Organizations

As observed earlier, nearly all forms of tax-exempt organizations may engage in lobbying without endangering their tax exemption under federal law. The exceptions, in varying degrees, are charitable organizations, membership associations, and political organizations.

There are a few instances where lobbying activities are inconsistent with tax-exempt status. One example is the title-holding corporation—either single-parent or multi-parent (see Chapter 4)—which must be operated for the exclusive purpose of holding title to property and paying over the income from the property to its parent. Lobbying by this type of entity would be contrary to the "exclusivity" requirement and inconsistent with the passive nature of the organization. Some governmental units may operate under restrictions that preclude lobbying. However, no type of tax-exempt organization, other than the charitable one, is expressly prohibited from engaging in activities to influence legislation.

Other federal, state, or local law may operate to prevent or restrict a nonprofit organization from engaging in activities to influence the legislative process.

CHECKLIST

☐ Does the organization engage in legislative activities?   Yes_____ No_____

☐ If yes, how much money was expended for legislative activities over the past year? $_____

☐ What percentage of total annual expenditures is this amount?   _____%

☐ If yes:

How much was spent for direct lobbying? $_____

How much was spent for grass roots lobbying? $_____

What was the total value of volunteer time? $_____

☐ If a charitable organization, has it elected
the expenditure test?   Yes＿＿ No＿＿

☐ Does the organization keep its board of
directors informed as to its legislative
activities?   Yes＿＿ No＿＿

☐ Does the organization have a related and/or
affiliated organization that engages in
lobbying?   Yes＿＿ No＿＿

FOCUS: Campaign to Clean Up America

The Campaign to Clean Up America has exempt purposes that clearly can be furthered by lobbying. However, its primary purposes—volunteer clean-up programs and public education—enable it to qualify as a charitable organization. Still, the CCUA would like to press for federal, state, and local law changes, such as tougher penalties for those who litter and incentive programs for those who collect and dispose of trash found in public places.

You, as president, and your CCUA managers have a decision to make: Should you elect to bring the CCUA under the expenditure test for public charities? After consulting with legal counsel, you and your managers choose not to make the election at this time, because the amount of lobbying that is contemplated is less than 10 percent of total activities. Also, a substantial portion of the lobbying that is to be done may be grass roots lobbying and the CCUA would like to avoid the narrower range of percentages that the elective rules impose on that type of lobbying. Besides, because of this decision, the CCUA is not subject to the detailed IRS regulations that accompany the expenditure test and it need not annually report its legislative activities to the IRS in the detailed form required of electing organizations.

Indeed, you and the management of the CCUA have decided to seriously consider organizing and operating a related social welfare organization for the purpose of conducting lobbying activities, should the level of lobbying increase beyond the 10 to 15 percent range.

CHAPTER FOURTEEN

Political Activities— and More Taxes

Congress and the IRS, as troubled as they are about nonprofit entities' lobbying activities, are even more concerned about political campaign activities by nonprofit organizations, particularly charitable ones. There are vagaries and uncertainties associated with its constraints on lobbying activities, but the federal tax law regulating political campaign activities is relatively clear.

An extensive federal statute—the Federal Election Campaign Act—regulates political campaign activity, and a federal agency—the Federal Election Commission—enforces the law in this area. The election laws and the tax laws are clearly separate sets of requirements, yet there is interplay between them. Nonprofit organizations are very much subject to the federal election laws and must arrange their activities to conform with those laws as well as the tax laws. State laws operate to regulate intrastate political campaign activity.

POLITICAL ACTIVITIES BY CHARITABLE ORGANIZATIONS

Congress has flatly decreed that charitable organizations may not engage in political campaign activity.

The General Rules

The congressional prohibition states that charitable organizations must "not participate in, or intervene in (including the publishing or distributing of statements), any political campaign on behalf of or in opposition to any candidate for public office." Coincidentally, this restriction originated in the U.S. Senate, as did the lobbying limitations on charitable organizations. There were no hearings on the restriction, and its enactment can be traced to one senator's interest in preventing campaign activity (against him) by a particular organization. (As described in Chapter 11, there are separate and more stringent rules against electioneering that are applicable only to private foundations.)

The prohibition on charitable organizations' involvement in political campaigns is said by the IRS to be absolute; the rules do not use a substantiality test. As a practical matter, a minor involvement in a political campaign may not trigger loss of exemption because, as one court put it, "a slight and comparatively unimportant deviation from the narrow furrow of tax approved activity is not fatal."

The concept of an *action organization* (see Chapter 13) is used in the political campaign context. An action organization is one that participates or intervenes, directly or indirectly, in any political campaign on behalf of or in opposition to any candidate for public office. An action organization cannot qualify as a charitable organization. No charitable organization may make a contribution to a political candidate's campaign, endorse or oppose a candidate, or otherwise support a political candidacy.

Most of the law amplifying the political campaign proscription for charitable groups is in IRS rulings. These rulings, over the years, have been uniformly rigid in their finding that nearly any activity relating to the political process will prevent charitable organizations from being tax-exempt. For example, the evaluation of candidates, the administration of a fair campaign practices code, and assistance to individuals after they have been elected have been found to be prohibited activities.

In recent years, the IRS has relented somewhat, conceding that voter education activities are permissible for charitable organizations. As an illustration, a charitable organization can prepare and disseminate a compilation of the voting records of legislators on a variety of subjects, as long as there is no editorial comment and no approval or disapproval of the voting records is implied. A charitable organization may also conduct public forums where there is a fair and impartial treatment of political candidates. In practice, some charitable organizations have disseminated information about candidates' voting records and positions on issues in formats that clearly reflect approval and disapproval, but the IRS has not acted to stop them. While this practice remains risky, it is less so where the opinionated material is not widely distributed to the general public or not timed to be disseminated on the eve of an election.

Despite the stringent prohibition on their political campaign activities, the law permits charitable organizations to engage in educational undertakings, such as instruction of the public on matters useful to individuals and beneficial to communities. There is an inherent tension between political campaign activities and educational activities—just as there is within the constraints on legislative activities.

Some charitable organizations have cautiously entered the political milieu, as part of the process of advancing education. For example, charitable organizations have been permitted to assemble and donate to libraries the campaign speeches, interviews, and other materials of a candidate for a historically important elective office, and to conduct public forums at which debates and lectures on social, political, and international questions are considered.

However, in performing this type of educational activity, charitable organizations are expected to present a balanced view of the pertinent facts. Members of the public must be permitted to form their own opinion or conclusion independent of any presented by the organization. The organization may advocate a particular position or viewpoint, but not a particular candidate. A charitable organization may seek to educate the public on patriotic, political, and civic matters, but it may not do so by using disparaging terms, insinuations, innuendos, or suggested implications drawn from incomplete facts. In a sense, this aspect of the prohibition on political activity is not unlike the prohibition on propagandizing that is part of the constraints on lobbying by charitable groups.

Taxation of Political Expenditures

Until recently, the only legal sanction for charitable organizations' violation of the political campaign activities proscription was revocation of their tax-exempt status. Congress came to see that sanction as somewhat ineffective. The IRS had little revenue incentive to take such drastic action. The organizations involved, and those who managed them, had little incentive to strictly adhere to the rules: they could simply start anew with a successor organization. The enactment of a new law in 1987 dramatically changed the rules of this game.

The federal tax law now levies taxes in situations where a charitable organization makes a "political expenditure." Generally, a political expenditure is any amount paid or incurred by a charitable organization in any participation or intervention (including the publication or distribution of statements) in any political campaign, on behalf of or in opposition to any candidate for public office.

In an effort to discourage ostensibly "educational" organizations from operating in tandem with political campaigns, the term "political expenditure" also applies with respect to "an organization which is formed primarily for purposes of promoting the candidacy (or prospective candidacy) of an individual for public office (or which is effectively controlled by a candidate or prospective candidate and which is availed of primarily for such purposes)." In these circumstances, a political expenditure includes any of the following:

- Amounts paid to or incurred by the individual for speeches or other services
- The travel expenses of the individual
- The expenses of conducting polls, surveys, or other studies, or the preparation of papers or other materials, for use by the individual
- The expenses of advertising, publicity, and fund-raising for the individual
- Any other expense "which has the primary effect of promoting public recognition, or otherwise primarily accruing to the benefit of" the individual

"Initial" taxes and "additional" taxes similar to the private foundation taxes are applicable in the political activities context. A political expenditure triggers an initial tax, payable by the organization, of 10 percent of the amount of the expenditure. An initial tax of $2^1/_2$ percent of the expenditure is also imposed on each of the organization's managers (such as directors and officers), where these individuals knew it was a political expenditure, unless the agreement to make the expenditure was not willful or was due to reasonable cause. The IRS has the discretionary authority to abate these initial taxes where the organization is able to establish that the violation was due to reasonable cause and not to willful neglect, and timely corrects the violation.

An additional tax is levied on a charitable organization, at a rate of 100 percent of the political expenditure, where the initial tax was imposed and the expenditure was not timely corrected. An additional tax is levied on the organization's manager, at a rate of 50 percent of the expenditure, where the additional tax was imposed on the organization and the manager refused to agree to part or all of the correction.

An organization that loses its status as a charitable organization because of political campaign activities is precluded from becoming tax-exempt as a social welfare organization. (This rule is identical to the rule concerning a charity's inability to convert to social welfare status after engaging in substantial lobbying.)

Under certain circumstances, the IRS is empowered to commence an action in federal district court to enjoin a charitable organization from making further political expenditures and for other relief to ensure that the assets of the organization are preserved for charitable purposes.

If the IRS finds that a charitable organization has "flagrantly" violated the prohibition against political expenditures, the IRS is required to immediately determine and assess any income and/or excise tax(es) due, by terminating the organization's taxable year.

The discussion to this point has been deliberately written to refer only to "political campaign activity." Let's turn now to "political activity." Essentially, there are two types.

The first type is "activism." This term embraces a wide range of "political" undertakings constitutionally protected as free speech. These activities have a variety of forms—writings, demonstrations, boycotts, strikes, picketing, and litigation. These activities frequently give the IRS pause, but, unless the activities can be fairly characterized as being lobbying or electioneering, the IRS has no basis in the tax law for denying tax-exempt status to organizations that engage in them or for revoking the organizations' tax-exempt status.

Activist activities are usually a permissible method for furthering a charitable organization's tax-exempt purposes. These activities often are not inherently exempt functions but are viewed by the law as being means to further the end result of achieving exempt purposes. As the U.S. Tax Court once wrote, "the purpose towards which an organization's activities are directed, and not the activities themselves, is ultimately dispositive of the organization's right to be classified as a . . . [charitable] organization." However, such activities will jeopardize tax exemption where they are illegal or are otherwise contrary to public policy.

The second type of political activity is "tax-triggering" activity. The taxes involved are by-products of the rules defining the tax-exempt "political organization."

Political Organization Taxes

The law defines political organizations' "exempt function" as, essentially, to engage in political activity. This exempt function involves actions of influencing or attempting to influence the selection, nomination, election, or appointment of any individual to any federal, state, or local public office. The wording of this definition makes the term "political activity" broader than "political campaign activity." "Political activity" includes words such as "selection" and "appointment," which can mean processes other than electioneering. For example, if a representative of a charitable organization testifies for or against a presidential appointment to a cabinet position or a judgeship, the organization is not engaging in political campaign activity (because there is no "campaign" and no "election") but it is engaging in political activity.

When a charitable organization engages in a political activity that is not a political campaign activity, it will presumably not forfeit its tax-exempt status but will have to pay a tax. The tax is determined by computing an amount equal to the lesser of the organization's net investment income for the year involved or the amount expended for the political activity. This amount, characterized as "political organization taxable income," is taxed at the highest corporate rates.

Unlike the restrictions on lobbying by charitable organizations, which allow a charitable entity to operate a related lobbying organization, a charitable organization is not permitted to operate a related political campaign organization—namely, a political action committee (PAC). Under present law, the activity of the PAC is attributable to the parent charity and it will lose its tax exemption. However, individuals who are involved with a charitable organization may be able to establish and utilize an "independent" PAC. The IRS has not addressed the matter, but the Federal Election Commission has issued guidelines by which such a committee—technically termed a "nonconnected political committee"—may be created and used. A charitable or other tax-exempt organization may operate a PAC for the purpose of conducting political activities that are not political campaign activities.

POLITICAL ACTIVITIES BY OTHER EXEMPT ORGANIZATIONS

Federal tax law does not completely impede political campaign activities by tax-exempt organizations other than charitable ones. However, federal and state election laws limit the extent to which nonprofit organizations can directly participate in the political campaign process. For example, the Federal Election Campaign Act makes it unlawful for a corporation—including a nonprofit corporation—to make a contribution or expenditure for a political candidate in a federal election.

Because of the campaign law restrictions, most nonprofit organizations do not directly engage in political campaign activities; instead, they use PACs. The nonprofit organizations that most commonly use PACs are trade, business, and professional associations, and labor organizations; a few social welfare organizations maintain PACs as well.

The federal election laws term these adjunct political committees "separate segregated funds" and permit the "establishment, administration, and solicitation of contributions to a separate segregated fund to be utilized for political purposes by a . . . membership organization." However, the costs of establishing and administering a separate segregated fund (political action committee) are not contributions or expenditures that are prohibited under the federal election laws. These costs, termed "soft-dollar expenditures," are contrasted with "hard-dollar expenditures," which are direct outlays for political purposes (monies given by the membership and expended for the benefit of candidates).

The tax laws get confused with the federal election laws on these points, because of the double meaning given the term "exempt function." As described in the tax laws, the exempt function of a political organization basically is the funding of campaigns (put another way, the making of hard-dollar expenditures). (See Chapter 4.) That exempt function is also recognized by the federal election laws. A nonprofit organization that has (without endangering its exemption) a PAC may make soft-dollar political expenditures but may not, because of the federal election laws, make hard-dollar political expenditures. Yet, under the tax laws, if a nonprofit organization (other than a political organization) engages in an "exempt function" (as that term is defined in the federal laws context), it is subject to tax, even though it may be engaging in an "exempt function" (as that term is defined in the law pertaining to its tax-exempt status).

The dichotomy between political campaign activities and political activities carries over to nonprofit organizations other than charitable ones. Even though the federal campaign laws prohibit a social welfare, labor, trade, business, or professional organization from making a political campaign contribution (hard-dollar expenditure), that type of organization may make a "political" expenditure under the tax laws. In this setting, a political activity includes the function of influencing or attempting to influence the selection, nomination, election, or appointment of an individual to any federal, state, or local public office (an "exempt function"). These types of membership organizations may, for example, support or oppose a presidential nominee for a cabinet position or judgeship—a political activity and not a political campaign activity. Therefore, the federal election laws are not a factor but the tax laws may force the payment of a tax (but not loss of tax exemption) as the result of participation in that type of activity. For example, if an organization that is primarily engaged in social welfare functions also carries on activities involving participation and intervention in political campaigns on behalf of or in opposition to candidates for public office, it will not lose its tax-exempt status, but it may have to pay a political activities tax.

CHECKLIST

☐ Does your organization engage in political
   campaign activities?   Yes____ No____

☐ If yes:

   How much money was expended for political
   campaign activities over the past year? $_____

   Is the organization certain that the Federal
   Election Campaign Act was not violated?   Yes____ No____

☐ If the organization has engaged in political
   activities that are not political campaign
   activities, describe them: _____

☐ Does the organization have a political
   action committee (PAC)?   Yes____ No____

☐ Does the organization have any other
   related or affiliated organization that
   engages in political activities?   Yes____ No____

☐ Does the organization keep its board of
   directors informed as to its political
   activities?   Yes____ No____

FOCUS: Campaign to Clean Up America

The Campaign to Clean Up America has no plans to engage in political campaign activities. As with lobbying activities, the exempt purposes of the CCUA can clearly be furthered by involvement in political campaigns. Its purposes can be advanced by those in government who agree with its principles and programs, so the CCUA is rightfully concerned about those who are elected and appointed to public office.

Yet, at this stage in its formation, the CCUA cannot afford to jeopardize its eligibility for deductible charitable gifts. It will not participate in any campaigns for candidates for public office.

The management of the CCUA remains well aware of the relationship between the success of its programs and those who hold public office. It is seriously considering undertaking political activities that are not political campaign activities and are in advancement of its program objectives. At some point, it may prove feasible to establish a political action committee (PAC) for this purpose.

The management of the CCUA is considering the establishment of an independent PAC, for the purpose of electing those whose vision of the future includes a litter-free America.

PART FOUR

Helpful Hints and Successful Techniques

CHAPTER FIFTEEN

For-Profit Subsidiaries

I t is becoming commonplace, and is frequently essential, for a tax-exempt organization to utilize a for-profit, taxable subsidiary. The reasons include situations where:

- The activity to be housed in the subsidiary is an unrelated one (see Chapter 12) and is too extensive to be conducted within the tax-exempt organization
- The management of an exempt organization does not want to report the receipt of any unrelated income and so shifts it to a separate subsidiary
- The management of an exempt organization is enamored with the idea of using a for-profit subsidiary

In most instances, the first reason is the true reason, if not the only one. An unrelated business may be operated as an activity within an exempt organization, as long as the primary purpose of the organization is to carry out one or more exempt functions. (See Chapter 4.) There is no fixed percentage of unrelated activity that may be engaged in by a tax-exempt organization, but it is clear that at least 51 percent of its activities must be in furtherance of exempt purposes.

Therefore, if a tax-exempt organization engages in one or more unrelated activities and the activities are *substantial* in relation to its exempt activities (for example, constituting more than half of its total activities), the use of a for-profit subsidiary is unavoidable.

ESTABLISHING A FOR-PROFIT SUBSIDIARY

When should a particular activity be housed in a tax-exempt organization or a for-profit organization? The factors to be considered are the
same as those weighed at the startup of a business, when deciding
whether it will be conducted in a tax-exempt or a for-profit form:

- The value of or need for tax exemption
- The true motives of those involved in the enterprise (for example,
  profit)
- The desirability of creating an asset (such as stock that is appreci-
  ating in value) for equity owners (shareholders) of the enterprise
- The compensatory arrangements contemplated for the employees

The law is clear: a tax-exempt organization can have one or more tax-
exempt (or at least nonprofit) subsidiaries and/or one or more for-profit
subsidiaries. In the latter situation, the tax-exempt parent organization
can own some or all of the equity (usually, stock) of the for-profit subsidiary (unless the parent is a private foundation, in which case special
rules apply).

If an activity of a tax-exempt organization is unrelated to its exempt
purpose or functions but is not a principal activity, it may be conducted
within the exempt organization without impairment of its tax-exempt
status (although taxes would have to be paid on the net income generated by the activity).

STRUCTURAL CONSIDERATIONS

Several matters of structure must be taken into account when contemplating the use of a for-profit subsidiary by a tax-exempt organization.
These include choice of form and the control mechanism.

Choice of Form

Just as in forming nonprofit organizations, the choice of organizational
form is important when establishing for-profit subsidiaries. Most will
be corporations—the most common business form and one that enables
the exempt parent to own the subsidiary by holding all or at least a majority of its stock.

A few taxable businesses are sole proprietorships; however, this form
is of no avail in the exempt organization context. A business activity

operating as a sole proprietorship is an undertaking conducted directly by the exempt organization and does not lead to the desired goal of having an unrelated activity in a separate entity.

Some taxable businesses are partnerships, but an exempt organization's participation in a partnership may involve additional legal difficulties. (See Chapter 16.)

Because several states allow businesses to be conducted by means of business trusts, this approach may be available to a nonprofit organization. However, before this approach (or any other approach other than forming a corporation) is used, those involved must be absolutely certain that the corporate form is not the most beneficial. One important consideration must be stock ownership: a share of stock in and of itself is an asset that can appreciate in value and can be sold in whole or in part.

A potential compromise is to house the business activity within a taxable nonprofit organization. This approach is a product of the distinction between a nonprofit organization (a state law concept) and a tax-exempt organization (a federal tax law concept). Assuming state law permits (an activity may be "nonprofit" yet still be "unrelated" to the parent's exempt functions), a business activity may be placed in a nonprofit, yet taxable, organization.

In the general business context, those forming a corporation must make an additional decision on whether to qualify the entity as an S corporation—a corporation that is treated for federal tax purposes the same as a partnership. The S corporation decision need not detain the managers of a tax-exempt organization, because tax-exempt organizations are not permitted to hold stock in an S corporation.

Control

Presumably, a tax-exempt organization will, when forming a taxable subsidiary, intend to maintain control over the subsidiary. After capitalizing the enterprise, nurturing its growth and success, and desiring to enjoy some profits from the business, the exempt organization parent would not want to give up its control.

Where the taxable subsidiary is structured as a business corporation, the tax-exempt organization parent can own the entity and ultimately control it simply by owning the stock (received in exchange for the capital contributed). The exempt organization parent, as the stockholder, can thereafter select the board of directors of the corporation and, if desired, its officers.

If the taxable subsidiary is structured as a nonprofit corporation, two choices are available. The entity can be structured as a conventional nonprofit organization; the exempt organization parent would then control the subsidiary by means of interlocking directorates. Alternatively, the entity can be structured as a nonprofit organization that can issue stock; the exempt organization parent would then control the subsidiary by holding its stock. If the latter structure is chosen and if the nonprofit subsidiary is to be headquartered in a state where stock-based nonprofits are not authorized, the subsidiary can be incorporated in a state that allows nonprofits to issue stock and thereafter be qualified to do business in the home state.

Attribution Considerations

For federal income tax purposes, a parent corporation and its subsidiary are treated as separate entities as long as the purpose for which the subsidiary is formed is reflected in true business activities. Where an organization is established with the bona fide intention that it will have some real and substantial business function, its existence will generally not be disregarded for tax purposes. By contrast, where the parent organization so controls the affairs of the subsidiary that it is merely an extension of the parent, the subsidiary may not be regarded as a separate entity. In an extreme situation, the establishment of an ostensibly separate subsidiary may be regarded as a sham.

The IRS generally will respect the separateness of closely related entities, even in situations where the tax-exempt parent wholly owns the for-profit subsidiary.

FINANCIAL CONSIDERATIONS

The principal financial considerations that a nonprofit organization should keep in mind when contemplating the establishment of a for-profit subsidiary are capitalization, compensation, and liquidation.

Capitalization

Assets that are currently being used in an unrelated activity (if any) may be spun off into a related, for-profit organization. However, the extent to which a for-profit corporation can be capitalized using exempt assets involves far more strenuous limitations.

A tax-exempt organization can invest a portion of its assets and engage in a certain amount of unrelated activities. At the same time, the governing board of a tax-exempt organization must act in conformance with basic fiduciary responsibilities and the organization cannot operate for the benefit of private interests.

Recent IRS private letter rulings suggest that perhaps only a very small percentage of an organization's resources ought to be transferred to controlled subsidiaries. The percentages approved by the IRS are usually unduly low and probably pertain only to cash. A specific asset may be best utilized—in some cases, it must be utilized—in an unrelated activity, even though its value represents a meaningful portion of the organization's total resources.

The best guiding standard in capitalizing a subsidiary is that of the prudent investor (once known as "the prudent man rule"). A tax-exempt organization should only part with an amount of resources that is reasonable under the circumstances and can be rationalized in relation to amounts devoted to programs and invested in other ways. Relevant to this decision is the projected return on the investment, in terms of both income and capital appreciation. If a contribution to a subsidiary's capital seems unwise, the parent-to-be should consider a loan bearing a fair rate of interest and accompanied by adequate security.

Compensation

The structure of a tax-exempt parent and a taxable subsidiary may generate questions and issues regarding compensation of employees.

The compensation of employees of a taxable subsidiary is subject to an overall requirement that the amounts paid may not exceed a reasonable salary or wage. To be deductible, all business expenses must be "ordinary and necessary." The compensation of the employees of the parent exempt organization is subject to a similar limitation, under the private inurement doctrine. (See Chapter 5.)

The employees of the tax-exempt parent could participate in deferred compensation plans or tax-sheltered annuity programs. The subsidiary may also use deferred salary plans or qualified pension plans, including "401(k) plans." (See Chapter 10.)

Use of a taxable subsidiary may facilitate an offering of stock options to employees, to enable them to share in the growth of the corporation. Another possibility may be an employee stock ownership plan—a plan that invests in the stock of the sponsoring company. The subsidiary may issue unqualified options to buy stock or qualified incentive stock options.

Tax-exempt organizations must annually report to the IRS the amount of compensation received by an individual from both the exempt organization and a related organization where the total amount of compensation is at least $100,000 and the amount of compensation from the related organization is at least $10,000.

Liquidation

Under the federal tax law, a corporation must recognize its gain or loss on a liquidating distribution of its assets (as if the corporation had sold the assets to the distributee at fair market value) and on liquidating sales. There is a nonrecognition exception for liquidating transfers within an affiliated group (which is regarded as a single economic unit), so that the distributee's basis in the property is carried over.

This nonrecognition exception is modified for eligible liquidations in which an 80 percent corporate shareholder receives property with a carryover basis. Nonrecognition of gain or loss is allowed on any property actually distributed to that shareholder. This exception for 80 percent corporate shareholders is generally not available where the shareholder is a tax-exempt organization. However, nonrecognition treatment is available to tax-exempt organizations where the property distributed is used by the tax-exempt organization in an unrelated business immediately after the distribution. If the property later ceases to be used in an unrelated business, the tax-exempt organization will be taxed on the gain at that time.

TREATMENT OF REVENUE FROM SUBSIDIARY

Most tax-exempt organizations develop an unrelated activity in anticipation of its serving as a source of revenue. When the unrelated business is developed into or shifted to a taxable subsidiary, it should be done in such a way that the flow of income from the subsidiary to the parent is not slowed down or stopped.

The staff and other resources of an affiliated business are usually those of the exempt organization parent; the headquarters used are likely to be the parent's. This means that the taxable subsidiary will have to reimburse the parent for the subsidiary's occupancy costs, share of employees' time, and use of the parent's equipment and supplies. Dollars can flow from the subsidiary to the parent in the form of reimbursement, which would include rent.

A lender–borrower relationship may exist between an exempt organization parent and its taxable subsidiary; that is, in addition to funding its subsidiary by means of a capital contribution (with the parent holding the equity), the parent may lend money to its subsidiary. Because a no-interest loan to a for-profit subsidiary by an exempt organization parent may endanger the parent's tax-exempt status and trigger problems under the imputed interest rules, the loan should bear a fair market rate of interest. Interest is another way for dollars to flow from the subsidiary to the parent.

The business activities of a for-profit subsidiary may be marketing and selling a product or service. When done in conformance with its tax-exempt status, the parent can license the use of its name, logo, acronym, or some other feature that would enhance the sale of the product or service provided by the subsidiary. For this license, the subsidiary would pay the parent a royalty—another way of transferring dollars from subsidiary to parent.

A conventional way of transferring money from a corporation to its stockholders is for the corporation to distribute its earnings and profits to them. These distributions, or dividends, represent still another way in which a taxable subsidiary can transfer dollars to its tax-exempt parent.

As mentioned earlier, certain types of income are exempted from taxation as unrelated income—principally, the various forms of passive income. Were it not for a special rule of federal tax law, a tax-exempt organization could have it both ways: avoid taxation on unrelated income by housing the activity in a subsidiary, and receive passive, nontaxable income thereafter from the subsidiary.

Congress was mindful of this potential double benefit and legislated an exception to the general rule that exempts passive income from taxation: Otherwise passive nontaxable income that is derived from a controlled taxable subsidiary is taxed as unrelated income. When an exempt organization parent receives rents, interest, or most other forms of passive income from a controlled taxable subsidiary, those revenues will generally be taxable. In this instance, *controlled* means a direct or indirect 80 percent ownership.

As is typical of the tax laws, there is an exception to the exception—a rule predicated on the fact that the payment of rents, interest, or royalties creates a tax deduction for the payor corporation. So, for example, when a for-profit subsidiary pays interest to its exempt organization parent in connection with a loan, the interest payments are deductible by the subsidiary.

However, there is no tax deduction for the payment of dividends. When a for-profit subsidiary pays dividends to its exempt organization parent, the dividend payments are not deductible by the subsidiary. Congress determined that it would not be appropriate to tax revenue to an exempt organization parent where it is not deductible by the taxable subsidiary.

The following principle has developed and it has eased tax planning regarding which entity, if any, is to be taxed: If the income paid to an exempt organization parent is deductible by the subsidiary, it is unrelated income to the parent. If the income paid is not deductible by the subsidiary, it is not taxable to the parent. The exception to the exception is for dividend income: it is not taxable to an exempt organization parent even when derived from a controlled taxable subsidiary.

SUBSIDIARIES IN PARTNERSHIPS

In the discussion of exempt organizations in partnerships in Chapter 16, we alluded to another use of a taxable subsidiary by a tax-exempt organization parent. A charitable organization, which would endanger its tax-exempt status if it were a general partner in a partnership, can cause its taxable subsidiary to be the general partner instead.

This can be an effective strategy as long as all the laws are satisfied, including the requirement that the subsidiary must be an authentic business entity. However, if the exempt organization parent is too intimately involved in the day-to-day management of the subsidiary, the IRS may impute the activities of the subsidiary to the parent and treat it as if it were directly involved as the general partner of the partnership. Its tax-exempt status would be at high risk.

In the federal tax law concerning the depreciation deduction, there are rules that reduce the deduction in situations where otherwise depreciable property is being used for the benefit of tax-exempt organizations. These rules are the *tax-exempt entity leasing rules.* They force investors to compute their depreciation deduction over a longer recovery period where the property is *tax-exempt use property.* The tax-exempt entity leasing rules can cause property to be tax-exempt use property where the property is owned by a partnership in which a tax-exempt organization is a partner or where the property is owned by a partnership in which a for-profit subsidiary owned by a tax-exempt organization is a partner.

Suppose a property that would not otherwise be tax-exempt use property is owned by a partnership that has both a tax-exempt organization and a nonexempt entity as partners. An amount equal to the tax-exempt organization's proportionate share of the property is treated as tax-exempt use property, unless there is a *qualified allocation* of the partnership items (such as gains and losses). In an attempt to prevent property from becoming tax-exempt use property, some exempt organizations did not enter into partnership arrangements directly but used for-profit subsidiaries as the partners instead. Congress reacted to thwart this technique by causing taxable subsidiaries to be considered tax-exempt organizations for purposes of the tax-exempt entity leasing rules. Such subsidiaries are termed "tax-exempt controlled entities."

TITLE-HOLDING CORPORATIONS

This discussion of the use of subsidiaries by tax-exempt organizations has been confined to the use of for-profit subsidiaries. We have not directly focused on situations where a subsidiary also is a tax-exempt organization, such as a membership organization utilizing a related foundation, or a charitable organization utilizing a related advocacy organization.

One type of subsidiary related to an exempt organization parent warrants mention—the *title-holding corporation*, which is somewhat of a hybrid. This entity's activities are generally in the business context, yet it is tax-exempt by reason of a relationship with a tax-exempt parent.

Essentially, the function of a title-holding corporation is a passive one: to hold title to property, to pay expenses associated with maintenance of the property, and, at least annually, to remit any net revenue to the parent organization. A title-holding corporation cannot be engaged in an active business undertaking, although, under certain circumstances, it can serve two or more tax-exempt parent organizations. This type of subsidiary can be useful in the administration of property and as a device for limiting liability.

CHECKLIST

☐ If the organization has any of the following, identify each entity:

For-profit subsidiary _____

For-profit subsidiary in a partnership _____

For-profit subsidiary in a joint venture _____

Title-holding corporation _____

☐ Describe any existing compensation arrangements where an individual is being paid by both a tax-exempt organization and a for-profit subsidiary. _____

_____

FOCUS: Campaign to Clean Up America

At present, the Campaign to Clean Up America does not have any plans to utilize a for-profit subsidiary. As discussed in the unrelated income context (see Chapter 12), there are potential unrelated businesses for the CCUA. Some of these may ultimately be housed in a subsidiary.

As the CCUA grows, and if federal tax laws allow, the organization may find it productive to utilize one or more for-profit subsidiaries in advancement of businesses selling supplies, equipment, and/or consulting services.

CHAPTER SIXTEEN

Tax-Exempt Organizations and Partnerships

One of the most important current phenomena involving tax-exempt organizations is their use of related organizations. There is nothing particularly revolutionary about this technique; we have just seen in Chapter 15 how tax-exempt organizations use subsidiaries. What is fairly new and different is the willingness of tax-exempt organizations to simultaneously use so many different forms of related entities—for-profit or nonprofit, trust or corporation, taxable or nontaxable.

Some observers ascribe this development to the economic pressures on tax-exempt organizations that have resulted from the decline in government funding. Others trace it to tax reform. There is ample cause in both of these sources, but they do not explain, for example, the trade association surrounded by a charitable foundation, a political action committee, and two for-profit business subsidiaries, one of which is a general partner in a real estate limited partnership. This typical cast of characters was not born of the mother-of-invention theory. It is attributable to another factor: sophistication. Tax-exempt organizations are better managed and better advised than ever before.

Exempt organizations have discovered that partnerships are available to facilitate almost anything they would like to do. That is, a partnership is essentially a financing technique.

REAL ESTATE ACQUISITIONS

Managers of tax-exempt organizations are more frequently concluding that their organizations should own real estate, usually for purposes of housing their offices. These are the financial advantages:

- A preferable position, economically, if occupancy costs are fixed rather than subject to the vagaries of the rental market
- A stronger portfolio if real property is among the assets of an organization
- An opportunity to conduct program activities at an organization's own location and/or utilize the property to generate additional revenue
- An improved image to the membership, contributors, or perhaps the general public, because of the prestige associated with owning the organization's headquarters

For some nonprofit organizations, ownership of real property has a long history. Many churches, universities, colleges, schools, hospitals, country clubs, and some major charities and associations were founded on the land where they are still operating. However, real estate ownership—particularly for office headquarters purposes—is becoming more commonplace for a wide variety of newer charitable, educational, religious, scientific, trade, business, professional, veterans', and other categories of nonprofit organizations.

There are several aspects of real estate ownership by nonprofit organizations. As a general proposition, it is clear that a nonprofit organization will not jeopardize its tax exemption because of acquisition, ownership, and maintenance of real property. In some states, real property owned by a nonprofit organization will be exempt from property tax. As a general rule, there is no likelihood that tax exemption will be impaired where a nonprofit organization leases space in property it owns, whether to other nonprofit entities or to the general public.

Still, a variety of potential unrelated income tax considerations are associated with the acquisition, ownership, and maintenance of real property by nonprofit organizations.

In the simplest of circumstances, where a nonprofit organization acquires real property with no financing and uses the property wholly for its tax-exempt purposes, there would be no adverse consequences to its tax-exempt status and no unrelated income taxation. Federal tax considerations come into play where the property is acquired with the assistance of others (such as by means of a partnership or other joint venture), rental or other income is involved, financing is utilized, and/or the property is put to an unrelated use.

In the property acquisition phase, tax considerations can be prominent, and the issue is likely to be whether tax-exempt status would be jeopardized. Unrelated income taxation is a much smaller threat.

A common way for an organization (nonprofit or not) to acquire real property, where the organization is unable or unwilling to do so using only its own resources, is to utilize a partnership. The partnership may well be comprised of the organization, the person(s) providing the financing, and the construction company. In many instances, there will be a limited partnership, with the tax-exempt organization being the general partner or one of the general partners. The partnership is the entity that acquires the property, develops it (if necessary), and sometimes continues to operate and maintain it. Subsequently, the nonprofit organization involved may acquire the property from the partnership, by purchase or (if the organization is a charitable one) by being the recipient of gifts of the partnership interests.

Not all partnerships utilized by tax-exempt organizations involve the acquisition and maintenance of real estate. (Others are used to acquire and operate capital equipment.) However, because most of these partnerships are employed in the real estate context, this use is appropriate for examining the underlying rationale for this technique.

Assume that a charitable organization has decided that it no longer wishes to pay rent for its office space. Instead, it wants to own a building for its own use. These are its options for deriving the necessary funds:

- Use money it has saved and held for investment
- Embark on a capital campaign and raise the money from gifts and grants
- Utilize tax-exempt bonds
- Acquire the property by means of a real estate partnership
- Combine two or more of the foregoing approaches

The drawbacks for most of these options are that the tax-exempt organization usually does not have or cannot get the money, and/or lacks the time or other resources to attract the funding. The pluses of the partnership approach include the ability of the organization to acquire the building using the funds of others. As observed earlier, a partnership is a financing mechanism—a means to an end.

SOME BASICS ABOUT PARTNERSHIPS

A partnership is a business form that is recognized as an entity under the law just as is a corporation or trust. Its formal document is a partnership agreement. The agreement is between "persons" who are the partners; the persons may be individuals, corporations, and/or other partnerships. Each partner owns one or more interests, called units, in the partnership.

Partners are of two types: general and limited. Every partnership must have at least one general partner. Where there is more than one general partner, one of them is designated the managing general partner.

Many partnerships have only general partners, and they contribute cash, property, and/or services. The interests of the general partners may or may not be equal. This type of partnership is essentially a joint venture: generally, all of the partners are equally liable for satisfaction of the obligations of the partnership and can be called on to make additional capital contributions to the partnership.

Some partnerships need or want to attract capital from sources other than the general partners. This capital can come from investors, called *limited partners*. Their interest in the partnership is limited in the sense that their liability is limited. The liability of a limited partner is confined to the amount of the capital contributed—the investment. General liability for the acts of the partnership rests with the general partner or partners. A partnership with both general and limited partners is a *limited partnership.*

When the partners decide to buy real estate, the partnership acquires the property, develops it (if necessary), and sometimes continues to operate and maintain it. Where a tax-exempt organization is a general partner, it is not the owner of the property (the partnership is) but it can enjoy many of the perks of ownership, such as participation in the cash flow generated by the property, a preferential leasing arrangement, and/or the general perception by the outside world that the property is owned by the tax-exempt organization (often furthered by giving the building the organization's name). The tax-exempt organization leases space in the property owned by the partnership; often, the organization will have an option to purchase the property from the partnership after the passage of a few years.

Partnerships do not pay taxes. They are merely conduits of net revenue to the partners, who bear the responsibility for paying tax on their share of the net income. Partnerships are also conduits of the tax advantages of the ownership of property; they pass through preference items such as depreciation and interest deductions.

If an entity fails to qualify under the federal tax laws as a partnership, it will be treated as an *association*, which means it will be taxed as a corporation. When that happens, the entity usually has to pay taxes and the ability to pass through tax advantages to the equity owners is lost.

As a general rule, a partnership is a very useful and beneficial way for one or more individuals or organizations to acquire, own, and operate a property. However, tax-exempt organizations can face problems with this approach.

THE TAX EXEMPTION ISSUE

The IRS is not thrilled with the presence of nonprofit organizations in partnerships, unless they are limited partners in a prudent investment vehicle. To date, all of the controversy on partnerships has focused on charitable organizations, although some or all of the principles of law being developed may become applicable to other types of tax-exempt organizations, such as social welfare organizations and membership associations.

In the view of the IRS, substantial benefits can be provided to the for-profit participants in a partnership (usually the limited partners) where a tax-exempt organization is a general partner. This concern has its origins in arrangements involving hospitals and physicians. An example would be a partnership formed to build and manage a medical office building, with a hospital as the general partner and investing physicians as limited partners. Where these substantial benefits are present, the IRS—upon discovering them—will not be hesitant to assert private inurement and private benefit.

The IRS's current position is that a charitable organization will lose its federal income tax exemption if it is a general partner in a partnership, unless the principal purpose of the partnership itself is to further charitable purposes. Even where the partnership can so qualify, the exemption is revoked if the charitable organization/general partner is not adequately insulated from the day-to-day management responsibilities of the partnership and/or if the limited partners are receiving an unwarranted return.

The IRS's position on tax-exempt organizations in partnerships is questionable, somewhat unfair, and in conflict with basic legal principles. Still, its present position is far more enlightened than its original position. Indeed, it is apparent that the views of the IRS on this subject are changing. The IRS now concedes that a charitable organization can (as required) be operated exclusively for exempt purposes and simultaneously be a general partner and satisfy its fiduciary responsibilities to the other partners. (The IRS's original view was predicated on the private inurement doctrine.)

The courts have forced the IRS to relax its stance on participation of tax-exempt organizations in partnerships. The IRS's lawyers have opined that it is possible for a charitable organization to participate as a general partner in a limited partnership without jeopardizing its tax exemption. The lawyers have advised that two aspects of the arrangement should be particularly reviewed:

- Was the participation in conflict with the goals and purposes of the charitable organization?
- Did the terms of the partnership agreement contain provisions that "insulated" the charitable organization from certain obligations imposed on a general partner?

This position of the IRS's legal counsel opened the way for many favorable private letter rulings concerning charitable organizations in partnerships. Each of these partnerships, however, has been held to be in furtherance of charitable objectives: the construction and operation of a medical office building on the grounds of a hospital, the purchase and operation of medical equipment at a hospital, and the initiation of low-income housing projects. To date, the IRS has yet to issue a private letter ruling denying a charitable organization tax-exempt status because of its involvement as a general partner in a limited partnership.

In summary, the current position of the IRS on whether a charitable organization will have its tax-exempt status revoked (or recognition denied) if it functions as a general partner in a limited partnership is the subject of a *two-part test* (really a three-part test). The IRS first looks to determine whether the charitable organization/general partner is serving a charitable purpose by means of the partnership. If the partnership is serving a charitable purpose, the IRS applies the second portion of the test. If the partnership fails to adhere to the charitability standard, however, the charitable organization/general partner will be deprived of its tax-exempt status.

The second part of the two-part test is designed to ascertain whether the charity's role as general partner inhibits its charitable purposes. Here, the IRS looks to means by which the organization may, under particular facts and circumstances, be insulated from the day-to-day responsibilities as general partner and (the true third part of the test) whether limited partners are receiving an "undue" economic benefit from the partnership. In the view of the IRS, there is an inherent tension between the ability of a charitable organization to function exclusively in furtherance of its exempt functions and the obligation of a general partner to operate the partnership for the benefit of the limited partners. This tension is the same perceived phenomenon that the IRS, at the outset, chose to characterize as a conflict of interest.

SOME ALTERNATIVES TO PARTNERSHIPS

Until or unless the IRS revises its rules in this area, charitable organizations must avoid participation in partnerships where the purpose of the partnership is not itself charitable (or else be prepared to test the government's position in court).

One way for a charitable organization to avoid the dilemma is to establish a wholly owned organization, usually a for-profit corporation, that would serve as the general partner in the partnership. This approach has been upheld by the IRS in private letter rulings. However, as mentioned earlier, the tax-exempt entity leasing rules have been revised to make this approach somewhat less attractive.

Some charitable organizations are using a pooled income fund (discussed in the next chapter). Donors transfer cash and/or property to a pooled income fund and receive a charitable contribution deduction. The assets of the fund are used to purchase and maintain real property; the depreciation deduction flows through the fund and to the income beneficiaries for their use in computing income tax liability. Under some circumstances, the tax-exempt entity leasing rules will be applicable in determining the depreciation deduction. Sometimes, these benefits will be reduced because of the recent insistence by the IRS that pooled income funds holding depreciable property must establish depreciation reserve funds.

Another approach is to avoid partnerships or other "pass-through" entities altogether and set up a leasing arrangement. This works best where a tax-exempt organization acquires unimproved land and subsequently desires to have it improved (often, for its offices). The organization can acquire land and enter into a long-term ground lease with a developer or development group. The developer would construct the building, perhaps giving it the organization's name and otherwise providing all external appearances that the structure is the organization's own building. The developer or development group is in the position of fully utilizing all of the tax benefits. The nonprofit organization leases space in the building, perhaps pursuant to a "sweetheart" lease, and may be accorded an option to purchase the building after the passage of a few years.

CHECKLIST

☐ If the organization has any of the following, identify those in each category:

Participation in partnership as general partner _____

_____

Participation in partnership as limited partner _____

_____

Participation in joint venture _____

_____

Use of pooled income fund _____

_____

Other leasing arrangements _____

_____

FOCUS: Campaign to Clean Up America

The Campaign to Clean Up America is not ready, at this stage in its development, for participation in a joint venture or other type of partnership.

There will be opportunities in the future for advancement of the programs of the CCUA by means of one or more joint ventures with other nonprofit organizations. Perhaps a general partnership with a for-profit entity will prove advantageous or a limited partnership may become available as a financing vehicle. Part of this depends on the success of the CCUA itself and part depends on forthcoming developments in the law of tax-exempt organizations.

CHAPTER SEVENTEEN

The World of Planned Giving

One of the great mysteries in the world of charity is why so few nonprofit organizations take advantage of the most remunerative fund-raising technique there is—planned giving. Those that do venture into the realm of planned giving are inevitably successful if they have given the attempt even half a chance. We know that the managers of nonprofit organizations do talk to one another. Why is planned giving not commonplace throughout the charitable community?

One reason is that planned giving has, over the years, been seen as mysterious and very complicated. Management, at many organizations, has grown fearful of it. The other reason is a consequence of the "nonprofit mentality"—the frequent tendency of the management of nonprofit organizations to think small and to see short-sightedly. These two reasons are actually tightly interwoven. Most organizations think about planned giving from time to time but put off implementing a planned giving program to another day—a tomorrow that never comes. Perhaps this is why the old term—deferred giving—is more accurate!

APPRECIATED PROPERTY GIFTS—A REPRISE

One of the chief principles undergirding the advantages of charitable gifts of securities, real estate, and other property is that the deductible amount is generally equal to the full fair market value of the property at the time of the gift. The amount of appreciation in the property (the amount exceeding the donor's basis), which would be taxed if sold, escapes income taxation. (As noted in Chapter 8, there may be some alternative minimum tax complications.) For this favorable result to occur, the property must constitute long-term capital gain property.

Consequently, the key to wise charitable giving is to give property that is long-term capital gain property and has substantially appreciated in value. The greater the appreciation, the greater the charitable deduction and other income tax savings. The appreciated property gift is, therefore, a core concept of planned giving.

PLANNED GIFTS—AN INTRODUCTION

There are two basic types of planned gifts. One type is a legacy: under a will, a gift comes out of a decedent's estate (as a bequest or devise). The other type is a gift made during the donor's lifetime, using a trust or other agreement.

These gifts are often called *deferred gifts* because the actual receipt of the contribution by the charity is deferred until the happening of some event (usually the donor's death). But the term *deferred giving* has fallen out of favor. Some donors (to the chagrin of the gift-seeking charities) have gained the impression that it is their tax benefits that are being deferred.

A planned gift usually is a contribution of a donor's interest in money or an item of property, rather than an outright gift of the money or property in its entirety. (The word *usually* is used because gifts using insurance do not neatly fit this definition and because an outright gift of property, in some circumstances, is treated as a planned gift.) Technically, this type of gift conveys a partial interest in property; planned giving is (usually) partial interest giving.

An item of property has within it two interests: an *income interest* and a *remainder interest.*

The income interest within an item of property is a function of the income generated by the property. A person may be entitled to all of the income from a property or to some portion of the income—for example, income equal to 6 percent of the fair market value of the property, even though the property is producing income at the rate of 9 percent. This person is said to have the (or an) income interest in the property. Two or more persons (such as husband and wife) may have income interests in the same property and these interests may be held concurrently or consecutively.

The remainder interest within an item of property is the projected value of the property, or the property produced by reinvestments, at some future date. Put another way, the remainder interest in property is an amount equal to the present value of the property (or its off-spring) when it is to be received at a subsequent point in time.

These interests are measured by the value of the property, the age of the donor(s), and the period of time that the income interests will exist. The actual computation is made by means of actuarial tables, usually those promulgated by the Department of the Treasury.

An income interest or a remainder interest in property may be contributed to charity, but a deduction is almost never available for a charitable gift of an income interest in property. By contrast, the charitable contribution of a remainder interest in an item of property will—assuming all of the technical requirements are met—give rise to a (frequently sizable) charitable deduction.

When a gift of a remainder interest in property is made to a charity, the charity will not acquire that interest until the income interests have expired. The donor receives the charitable deduction for the tax year in which the recipient charity's remainder interest in the property is established. When a gift of an income interest in property is made to a charity, the charity acquires that interest immediately and retains it until such time (sometimes measured by a term of years) as the remainder interest commences. Again, any resulting charitable deduction is available for the tax year in which the charity's income interest in the property is established.

Basically, under the federal tax law, a planned gift must be made by means of a trust if a charitable deduction is to be available. The trust used to facilitate a planned gift is known as a *split-interest trust* because it is the mechanism for satisfying the requirements involving the income and remainder interests. In other words, the trust is the medium for splitting the property into its two component interests. Split-interest trusts are charitable remainder trusts, pooled income funds, and charitable lead trusts (explained in a separate section below).

There are some exceptions to the general requirements on using a split-interest trust in planned giving. The principal exception is the charitable gift annuity, which uses a contract rather than a trust. Individuals may give a remainder interest in their personal residence or farm to charity and receive a charitable deduction without utilizing a trust. A trust is also not required for a deductible gift of a remainder interest in real property when the gift is granted to a public charity or certain operating foundations exclusively for conservation purposes. Similarly, a donor may contribute a lease on, an option to purchase, or an easement with respect to real property, granted in perpetuity to a public charity or certain foundations exclusively for conservation purposes, and receive a charitable contribution deduction without a trust. A contribution of an undivided portion of one's entire interest in property is not regarded as a contribution of a partial interest in property.

A donor, although wishing to support a particular charity, may be unwilling or unable to fully part with property, either because of a present or perceived need for the income that the property provides and/or because of the capital gains taxes that would be experienced if the property were sold. The planned gift is likely to be the answer in this situation: the donor may satisfy his or her charitable desires and yet continue to receive income from the property. The donor also receives a charitable deduction for the gift of the remainder interest, which will reduce or eliminate the tax on the income from the gift property. No regular income tax on the capital gain is inherent in the property (although there may be some alternative minimum tax consequences). If the gift property is not throwing off sufficient income, the trustee of the split-interest trust may dispose of the property and reinvest the proceeds in more productive property. The donor will then receive more income from the property than was received prior to the making of the gift.

The various planned giving vehicles are explored next.

CHARITABLE REMAINDER TRUSTS

The most widespread form of planned giving involves a split-interest trust known as the *charitable remainder trust*. The term is nearly self-explanatory: the entity is a trust that has created a remainder interest destined for charity. Each charitable remainder trust is arranged specifically for the particular circumstances of the donor(s), with the remainder interest in the gift property designated for one or more charities.

A qualified charitable remainder trust must provide for a specified distribution of income, at least annually, to or for the use of one or more beneficiaries (at least one of which is not a charity). The flow of income must be for life or for a term of no more than 20 years, with an irrevocable remainder interest to be held for the benefit of the charity or paid over to it. The beneficiaries are the holders of the income interests and the charity has the remainder interest.

How the income interests in a charitable remainder trust are ascertained depends on whether the trust is a *charitable remainder annuity trust* (income payments are in the form of a fixed amount, an *annuity*), or a *charitable remainder unitrust* (income payments are in the form of an amount equal to a percentage of the fair market value of the assets in the trust).

All categories of charitable organizations—both public charities and private foundations—are eligible to be remainder beneficiaries of as many charitable remainder trusts as they can muster. However, the allowability of the charitable deduction will vary for different types of charitable organizations, because of the percentage limitations. (See Chapter 8.)

Usually, a bank or similar financial institution serves as the trustee of a charitable remainder trust. The financial institution should have the capacity to administer the trust, make appropriate investments, and timely adhere to all income distribution and reporting requirements. It is not unusual, however, for the charitable organization that is the remainder beneficiary to act as trustee. If the donor or a related person is named the trustee, the *grantor trust* rules may apply: the gain from the trust's sale of appreciated property is taxed to the donor.

Conventionally, once the income interest expires, the assets in a charitable remainder trust are distributed to the charitable organization that is the remainder beneficiary. If the assets (or a portion of them) are retained in the trust, the trust will be classified as a private foundation, unless it can sidestep the retention rules.

POOLED INCOME FUNDS

A popular planned giving technique involves gifts to a *pooled income fund*. Like a charitable remainder trust, a pooled income fund is a form of split-interest trust.

A donor to a qualified pooled income fund receives a charitable deduction for giving the remainder interest in the donated property to charity. The gift creates income interests in one or more noncharitable beneficiaries, and the remainder interest in the gift property is designated for the charity that maintains the fund.

The pooled income fund's basic instrument (a trust agreement or a declaration of trust) is written to facilitate gifts from an unlimited number of donors, so the essential terms of the transaction must be established in advance for all participants. The terms of the transfer cannot be tailored to fit any one donor's particular circumstances (as they can with the charitable remainder trust). The pooled income fund is, literally, a pooling of gifts.

Contributions to a pooled income fund may be considerably smaller amounts than those to a charitable remainder trust. Gifts to pooled income funds are generally confined to cash and readily marketable securities (other than tax-exempt bonds).

Each donor to a pooled income fund contributes an irrevocable remainder interest in the gift property to (or for the use of) an eligible charity. Each donor creates an income interest for the life of one or more beneficiaries, who must be living at the time of the transfer. The properties transferred by the donors must be commingled in the fund (to create the necessary pool).

Each income interest beneficiary must receive income at least once each year. The pool amount is determined by the rate of return earned by the fund for the year. Beneficiaries receive their proportionate share of the fund's income. The dollar amount of the income share is based on the number of units owned by the beneficiary, and each unit must be based on the fair market value of the assets when transferred.

A pooled income fund is essentially an investment vehicle whose funding is motivated by charitable intents.

A pooled income fund must be maintained by one or more charitable organizations. The charity must exercise control over the fund; it does not have to be the trustee of the fund (although it can be), but it must have the power to remove and replace the trustee. A donor or an income beneficiary of the fund may not be a trustee. However, a donor may be a trustee or officer of the charitable organization that maintains the fund, as long as he or she does not have the general responsibilities toward the fund that are ordinarily exercised by a trustee.

Unlike other forms of planned giving, a pooled income fund is restricted to only certain categories of charitable organizations. Most types of public charities can maintain a pooled income fund; private foundations and some nonprivate foundations cannot. (The distinctions between public and private charities are summarized in Chapter 11.)

The same general tax advantages that are available as the result of gifts to charitable remainder trusts are available for gifts to pooled income funds. The advantages are particularly solid when the gift consists of fully marketable and appreciated securities. A pooled income fund transfer may accommodate a smaller amount (value) of securities than a transfer to a remainder trust. However, if fixed income is an important consideration, a charitable remainder annuity trust (see above) or a charitable gift annuity (see below) will be preferable to a gift to a charitable remainder unitrust or pooled income fund.

A qualified charitable organization can have as many pooled income funds as it wishes. One or more funds may be for general fundraising purposes, and one or more for use in lieu of a partnership (see Chapter 16).

CHARITABLE LEAD TRUSTS

Most forms of planned giving have a common element: The donor transfers to a charitable organization the remainder interest in a property, and one or more noncharitable beneficiaries retain the income interest. However, a reverse sequence may occur—and that is the essence of the *charitable lead trust*.

The property transferred to a charitable lead trust is apportioned into an income interest and a remainder interest. Like the charitable remainder trust and the pooled income fund, this is a split-interest trust. An income interest in property is contributed to a charitable organization, either for a term of years or for the life of one individual (or the lives of more than one individual). The remainder interest in the property is reserved to return, at the expiration of the income interest (the "lead period"), to the donor or some other noncharitable beneficiary or beneficiaries; often, the property passes from one generation (the donor's) to another.

The charitable lead trust can be used to accelerate into one year a series of charitable contributions that would otherwise be made annually. There is a corresponding single-year deduction for the "bunched" amount of charitable gifts.

In some circumstances, a charitable deduction is available for the transfer of an income interest in property to a charitable organization. There are stringent limitations, however, on the deductible amount of charitable contributions of these income interests.

CHARITABLE GIFT ANNUITIES

Another form of planned giving is the *charitable gift annuity*. It is not based on use of a split-interest trust. Instead, the annuity is arranged in an agreement between the donor and donee. The donor agrees to make a gift and the donee agrees, in return, to provide the donor (and/or someone else) with an annuity.

With one payment, the donor is engaging in two transactions: the purchase of an annuity and the making of a charitable gift. The gift gives rise to the charitable deduction. One sum is transferred; the money in excess of the amount necessary to purchase the annuity is the charitable gift portion. Because of the dual nature of the transaction, the charitable gift annuity transfer constitutes a *bargain sale*.

The annuity resulting from the creation of a charitable gift annuity arrangement is a fixed amount paid at regular intervals. The exact amount paid depends on the age of the beneficiary, which is determined at the time the contribution is made.

A portion of the annuity paid is tax-free because it is a return of capital. Where appreciated securities are given, there will be capital gain on the appreciation that is attributable to the value of the annuity.

If the donor is the annuitant, the capital gain can be reported ratably over the individual's life expectancy. However, the tax savings occasioned by the charitable contribution deduction may shelter the capital gain (resulting from the creation of a charitable gift annuity) from taxation.

Because the arrangement is by contract between the donor and donee, all of the assets of the charitable organization are on the line for ongoing payment of the annuities. (With most planned giving techniques, the resources for payment of income are confined to those in a split-interest trust.) That is why a few states impose a requirement that charities must establish a reserve for the payment of gift annuities—and why many charitable organizations are reluctant to embark on a gift annuity program. This outcome is unfortunate; millions of dollars are lost annually by charitable organizations that fail to use charitable gift annuities. Even those that are reluctant to commit to the ongoing payment of annuities can eliminate the risk by reinsuring them.

LIFE INSURANCE

An underutilized form of planned giving is the donation of individual (not group) life insurance. A gift of life insurance is an excellent way for a person who has a relatively small amount of present resources to make a major contribution to a charitable organization. Gifts of life insurance are particularly attractive for younger donors.

If the life insurance policy is fully paid up, the donor will receive a charitable deduction for the cash surrender value or the replacement value of the policy. If the premiums are still being paid, the donor receives a deduction on his or her annual tax return for the premium payments made during the taxable year. For the deduction to be available, however, the donee charity must be both the beneficiary and the owner of the insurance policy.

There is some uncertainty in legal circles as to whether a gift of life insurance is valid (and thus deductible), because of the necessity of *insurable interest*—the owner and beneficiary of the policy must be more economically advantaged with the insured alive rather than dead. (Examples of relationships where insurable interests exist are healthy marriages and employment of key individuals.) In many instances, a charitable organization is advantaged by having a donor of a life insurance policy alive: he or she may be a key volunteer (such as a trustee or officer) or a potential donor of other, larger gifts.

STARTING A PROGRAM

Knowing something about the various planned giving techniques is only a start. A planned giving program must be implemented, and that takes more than knowing about income and remainder interests.

Some tips on how to launch a planned giving program are found in the next chapter.

CHECKLIST

☐ If the organization has any of the following, identify those in each category:

One or more charitable remainder annuity trusts _____

One or more charitable remainder unitrusts _____

One or more pooled income funds _____

One or more charitable gift annuity contracts _____

One or more charitable lead trusts _____

One or more donated life insurance contracts _____

Other forms of a "planned gift" _____

FOCUS: Campaign to Clean Up America

The Campaign to Clean Up America is implementing a planned giving program at the very outset of its operations. The CCUA does not have a defined constituency (like a church's parish or a university's graduates), but it will be able, over time, to identify sources of planned gifts from its developing donor base.

The CCUA is presently prepared to accept gifts by means of charitable remainder trusts, charitable lead trusts, and life insurance. It is in the process of establishing a pooled income fund. The CCUA is holding off on implementing a full-scale effort to secure charitable gift annuities until it can satisfy the various state laws on this form of giving.

CHAPTER EIGHTEEN

Putting Ideas into Action

I t is one thing to have an idea; putting the idea into actual practice is something else. The chapters in this part of the book are offered to stimulate ideas rather than to prescribe firm solutions for particular problems. Starting and operating a nonprofit organization is a relatively common undertaking. However, planned giving, subsidiaries, joint ventures, and partnerships are not so common, and not all of these possibilities are suitable for all nonprofit organizations at all times. The intent is not to overlook a possibility that can prove useful for a particular organization.

When approaching key decisions of this sort, professional guidance is a must. Fees for lawyers, accountants, and/or management or fundraising consultants may seem unaffordable at first, but the money is usually well-spent.

JOINT VENTURES

A *joint venture* is any undertaking involving two (or more) organizations. In the context of nonprofit organizations, the venturers can both be nonprofits, or one can be a nonprofit and one a for-profit organization.

Most joint ventures are the products of decisions that two heads are better than one. A pooling of resources occurs. Partnerships, more so than other forms of joint ventures, pool financial resources. Most often, a joint venture is an aggregation of programs: one organization has a program resource and the other organization has another program resource, and the purpose of the joint venture can only be accomplished (or can be better accomplished) through a blending of the two.

From the standpoint of a nonprofit organization, two general outcomes are possible:

- It will be approached by another organization that is seeking access to one of its resources
- It will seek out a resource of another organization, to carry out one of its own desired programs

The management of a nonprofit organization should always have an ongoing business plan that includes an inventory of what the organization is doing or wishes to do. From the inventory, management may discover that the organization lacks the resources to undertake a particular project. Some nonprofit managers might give up at this point. Others may expend the effort needed to purchase the personnel, equipment, or other resources necessary to tackle the project.

A third option is possible: use of the existing resources of another organization. Despite the effort and ingenuity required, this alternative can be preferable to the others. When one nonprofit organization joins with another organization to advance a particular undertaking, a joint venture results.

Besides being a medium for furthering program objectives, a joint venture can be a way to further management objectives. However, if one nonprofit organization is merely providing management services to another; the provision of services may be an unrelated business of the provider. (See Chapter 12.)

A joint venture can be used to advance fund-raising objectives. This is often done with another nonprofit organization, but can also be done with a for-profit organization—for example, in a *commercial co-venture*. This is an unfortunate term, because of the connotation (usually inaccurate) that the nonprofit organization involved is engaged in some activity that is commercial. Often, a commercial co-venture is not really a venture—although it can be (and increasingly is).

A commercial co-venture is an arrangement between a business and a charitable organization whereby the business agrees to make a contribution to the charity. The gift's amount is related to the volume of sales of the company's service or product during a particular period of time. That is, the company agrees to donate to the charity an amount equal to a percentage of sales during the time of the promotion, and the fact of the prospective gift is advertised to the consuming public. The charity benefits because of the gift, and the business benefits because of the positive marketing and (it hopes) an increase in the sales volume. The relationship can turn into a true joint venture if the charity itself becomes involved in the promotional aspects of the sales campaign. A word of caution: As the charity becomes more involved in this type of joint venture, the likelihood increases that the business's payments to the charity will be treated as a taxable payment for services rendered rather than a charitable contribution.

PARTNERSHIPS

The concept of a partnership is described in Chapter 16. A partnership can be general or limited.

As a practical matter, there is little difference between a general partnership and a joint venture. Both involve a pooling of resources, often programmatic ones. Astute managers of nonprofit organizations will always be alert to opportunities to achieve something by using the resources of others. This is not a selfish or unilateral approach; the other party to the venture, by definition, also will be entering into the arrangement for the purpose of achieving some desired end.

Whenever programs and objectives are reviewed, nonprofit management should determine whether something can be better accomplished (or just plain accomplished) working in tandem with one or more other organizations.

Sometimes, because of the nature of the relationship, one or more of the partners is bringing to the arrangement something other than programmatic resources. The resource brought may be money, and in this context a partnership is used as a financing device. As noted in Chapter 16, when a limited partnership is utilized, the limited partners are investors and the resource they bring to the arrangement is money. When a nonprofit organization is involved, the limited partners will most likely be strong supporters of the organization—people who are particularly interested in its programs and objectives and who are then acting in a dual capacity. They desire to make an investment and receive an economic return, and they wish to assist the organization. These limited partners tend to be directors, trustees, and/or officers of the organization, and/or its substantial contributors. Nonprofit organizations have unique opportunities in limited partnerships.

The management of a nonprofit organization should approach the possibility of a partnership, particularly a limited partnership, as a search for funding, perhaps blended with a fund-raising program. Limited partners and donors can be drawn from the same constituency. For example, an individual can become a limited partner in a partnership where a charitable organization is a general partner, and then subsequently donate his or her limited partnership interest to the organization.

When considering the possibilities of a limited partnership, the management of a nonprofit organization should do the following:

- Review all program, administrative, and fund-raising objectives, with a view to the best way of funding them
- Develop a schedule of priority for financing each of the objectives
- Identify those that may be clearly fundable with contributions (in the case of charitable organizations), those that may be funded with service-provider revenue, those that may be funded with membership fees (assuming a membership), and those that may be funded with investment income (funded out of an endowment)
- Earmark any programs or functions that cannot be fully funded using one or more of these approaches (or cannot be funded at all) as possibilities for a limited partnership

Does the organization need or want its own building? A new computer system? Other major equipment or capital assets? What about a facility to further its programs, such as a research center or conference facility? A limited partnership can be used as a financing mechanism to accomplish these ends.

The process of deciding whether to utilize a partnership or joint venture is really one of matching means to ends. It requires the management of a nonprofit organization to take an expansive view of its objectives and opportunities and to seek the fullest available exploitation of the organization's potential.

As an illustration, some nonprofit organizations' management only dream of having their own building for their offices. They fear a conventional fund-raising program to that end, believing (in some instances, correctly) that they lack the donor base to accumulate the necessary funds through gifts and grants. Others take a broader view. They assemble board members and other supporters and persuade them to become limited partners in a partnership. Using the capital thus acquired and/or borrowed by the partnership, the partnership acquires the property, creates the offices, leases them (presumably on some favorable basis) to the organization, and passes along to the limited partners all or some of the cash flow of the property and the tax advantages of owning property. In the meantime, the organization can (particularly if a charitable one) raise funds to ultimately purchase the property from the partnership. When the process is completed, the organization has done a remarkable thing: It has acquired its own headquarters, which it can now occupy rent-free, solely using the funds of others.

Some programs of nonprofit organizations can be enhanced by administering them by means of a general partnership. Some functions of nonprofit organizations can be best financed using a limited partnership, but that choice must be weighed against and integrated with other financing techniques. Without intending to be too opportunistic, a limited partnership is a legitimate way of utilizing the money of others to achieve one's own ends. That ability can be doubly enhanced when coupled with the charitable deduction.

PLANNED GIVING

In Chapter 17, we observed that charitable organizations are underutilizing planned giving, often because of an aura of mystery that surrounds it. Many managers perceive planned giving as far too complex for their organizations, or as not dynamic enough to generate badly needed current dollars. The implementation of a planned giving program usually gets deferred to another day—one that never seems to come.

There is also an erroneous belief that planned giving is only for the larger charities, those that have been in existence for some time and have an existing constituency. Finally, the initial process of establishing a planned giving program is thought to be too expensive.

None of these reasons for delaying a planned gift is truly valid. Nearly every charitable organization, no matter how small or how new, should have a planned giving program.

The very term *planned giving* usually causes some uncertainty. The pairing of these two words does not mean that all other gifts are unplanned. As noted in Chapter 8, a far better term would be *integrated giving*. The concept of planned giving means that a gift is of sufficient magnitude that the transfer of it is integrated with the donor's personal financial plan or estate plan. A planned gift is not an impulse gift; its consequences (other than to the charity) relate, for example, to the donor's family or business and are taken into account before the gift is made, when determining the type of gift that it will be.

Probably the simplest of planned gifts is a bequest in a will. The larger the gift or the more complicated the terms (one or more trusts may be included), the greater the extent of the planning. Writing a will or setting up a trust means formulating a plan.

Usually, an outright gift of cash or property is not regarded as a planned gift, although sometimes an outright contribution of property can be, if it is a gift of a business or a partnership interest. A mere gift of an insurance policy may not be regarded by some as a planned gift, but the process of deliberately selecting a particular policy for donation to charity and the circumstances of giving it can easily entail some serious planning.

Most planned gifts are based on the fundamental principle that property consists of two interests: an income interest and a remainder interest. Planned gifts usually involve the donation to charity of either an income interest or a remainder interest.

A gift of an income interest is made by means of a charitable lead trust. Most remainder interest gifts are made using a charitable remainder trust, a pooled income fund, or a charitable gift annuity.

A knowledgeable fund-raiser can do more in the planned giving field than ask for gifts and collect them. He or she can simultaneously render to the donor valuable services that can have these beneficial effects:

- The donor may end up with more income as the result of the gift
- The donor's earnings may be shifted from taxable income to non-taxable income
- The donor becomes enabled to dispose of property without paying taxes—in many cases, property that he or she did not really need
- The donor may be able to pass property to other family members without incurring estate taxes

Planned giving can yield professional money and property management without cost to the income beneficiaries. It can be the foundation for retirement plans, tuition payments, and memorial gifts. The list goes on and on.

How to Start a Planned Giving Program

If planned giving is so great, why is every charity not using it? The principal reasons have already been stated. However, another reason may be that the organization simply does not quite know how to begin. Here are the ten easy steps to implementation of a successful planned giving program.

Step 1. The members of the organization's board of directors *must* be involved. At this point, *being involved* does not mean as donors—that comes later. It means involved in the launching of the program.

The best way to start this process is to have the board pass a planned giving launch resolution. This resolution should state that there is to be such a program, who on the staff and among the officers is principally responsible for it, and, most importantly, what planned giving methods are going to be used. The resolution should expressly identify the vehicles: wills, charitable remainder trusts, insurance, pooled income fund, or whatever.

Step 2. Most of the board members will not have heard of these vehicles. At a board meeting, set some time aside for a brief presentation on the basics of planned giving. The presentation should be made by an outsider—a lawyer, professional development counselor, or bank trust officer, for example. The board members should be given some written material to peruse at their leisure.

Step 3. Once the board has received its initial training and has adopted the launch resolution, develop some prototype instruments—documents, with the organization's name in the appropriate places, that can be shown to interested parties. These documents may be will clauses, charitable remainder trust models (both annuity trust and unitrust, and one-life and two-lives versions), stock powers, pooled income fund transfer agreements, and/or charitable gift annuity contracts.

Donors will rarely be interested in these prototype documents; some of the board members may be. However, those who are going to be asking for planned gifts should have some basic familiarity with them. The greatest use of these instruments will be to provide them to a potential donor's professional counselor, whether a lawyer, accountant, financial planner, insurance agent, or securities broker. These persons may be unfamiliar with planned giving and will find actual documents very helpful.

Step 4. Government regulation of planned giving programs is unavoidable, so this step is to adhere to the requirements of the law. Asking for a planned gift is still asking for a gift, and it is important to register in each of the states that have charitable solicitation acts, if the charity has not already done so. (See Chapter 9.) If a pooled income fund is to be in the arsenal of planned giving methods, management should be certain to secure a favorable ruling from the IRS as to qualification of the fund *before* gifts are made. If charitable gift annuities are to be used, state insurance law requirements must be complied with. Where gifts of insurance policies are involved, it is necessary to be able to establish that the charity has an insurable interest in the lives of the donors.

Step 5. The marketing phase begins here. This step may involve a myriad of alternatives, but the first concern must be acquisition of some easy-to-understand brochures on the concept and methods of planned giving, to be distributed to prospective donors. Separate brochures on each of the techniques are far preferable to having one large booklet.

The organization can either write and print its own brochures or have brochures prepared commercially.

Back to the board of directors, who have now been provided copies of the literature. The process of getting some (preferably all) of the directors to commit to some form of planned gift begins here and should be concluded without hedging or postponements. How can others be expected to give when the organization's own leadership has not (or worse, will not)?

Step 6. Start the process of building a network or cadre of volunteers who will be planned giving advocates to the outside world. This group should be comprised in part of members of the organization's board of directors; other possibilities include individuals from the organization's prior leadership, active members, community leaders, and volunteer professionals (such as lawyers and accountants). These individuals will assist in procuring planned gifts by making them themselves, by asking others, and/or by influencing others who will do the asking.

The volunteers will need some training before they are sent out looking for planned gifts. Special sessions with someone knowledgeable about planned giving are essential, as are comprehensible printed materials. The intent is not to make these persons instant planned giving experts or even expect them to procure the gift. Their job is to become sufficiently familiar with the concept and techniques of planned giving that they know the basics about each method and something about how to correlate these basics with the facts and circumstances of each prospect's situation. The actual "ask" will probably be done by a staff person or a professional planned giving consultant.

Step 7. Identify prospective planned gift donors. This step is actually an ongoing process. If the organization has a membership, those individuals form the base with which to begin. The giving history of donors (frequency and amount of gifts) should be reviewed to identify planned giving prospects. Others who are interested in the organization's programs are prospects as well. Even new organizations have dedicated supporters who are thus potential planned givers.

Step 8. Once the prospective donors are identified, they must be contacted. This is the essence of the marketing phase, and how it is done will vary from group to group. One tried-and-true approach is to send letters to the prospects explaining the planned giving program and inviting them to request additional information; those who respond are sent the appropriate brochures. Another approach is to concentrate on one vehicle, such as the pooled income fund, or insurance, and market just that method by sending a brochure with the introductory letter. Some organizations like to lead with a wills program; others have had success opening with a pooled income fund program.

There are many marketing techniques. Some organizations have had success with financial planning seminars, where planned giving is stressed. Others hold seminars for those in the community who advise donors—lawyers, financial planners, accountants, and so on. If the organization has a magazine or newsletter, it should regularly publish items on planned giving. If the organization has an annual meeting or convention, a presentation on planned giving should be on the agenda. One favorite technique at the annual membership meeting is to have a planned giving booth among the other displays in the exhibit hall, as part of the "trade show."

The marketing aspects of planned giving must be ongoing practices. Some organizations can use all of the techniques described above. For launching a planned giving program, a combination of a special mailing, a seminar, and coverage in the organization's regular publications can be powerful.

Step 9.   The next process is to obtain the gift once a bona fide prospect has signaled some interest. Advice here is hard to generalize. For organizations with an emerging planned giving program, the best way to proceed is to have a staff person or a volunteer meet with the prospective donor and work out a general plan, then have a subsequent session with a planned giving professional who can advise the parties as to the specific method that is best for all concerned. A lawyer can prepare the specific instrument. As the organization matures, it can build planned giving expertise into its in-house operations.

Here is an example of a typical planned gift. An individual has been contacted about a charitable organization's planned giving program. Having coincidentally received a large amount of money as the result of a sale of property, he or she is looking for some tax relief. The prospective donor has an interest in the programs of the organization, so he or she and a staff person meet and work out these general guidelines: the donor needs a charitable deduction of X amount and annual income of Y amount. The parties subsequently meet with a lawyer, the numbers are run on a computer, the deduction and income amounts for each planned giving method are reviewed, and a specific arrangement (in this case, perhaps a charitable remainder annuity trust) is developed.

One thing is clear: The organization's staff and volunteers will only learn by doing. As the gifts come in and the various processes that lead to the gifts are experienced, the parties involved will gain greater confidence and will need to rely less on the outside professional. It is advisable to have a planned giving professional on call at the outset and available thereafter as circumstances warrant.

Step 10. This step may have occurred much earlier in the process: the selection of legal counsel or another professional who can work with the organization in the launching and ongoing administration of the program.

Excuses and Misunderstandings

One of the excuses frequently given for postponing the inauguration of a planned giving program (or altogether ignoring the idea of such a program) is that it is not suitable for a new organization. There is no question that a university with decades of graduations has a larger and more solid donor base than a community service group incorporated last week. But the service group's relative disadvantage is not an arguable reason for doing nothing. Every organization has a support base or it would not exist. It may be that, on day 1, there is only one planned gift prospect, yet that is no reason not to approach that one prospect. The largest planned giving program started with one gift.

Another excuse for not implementing a planned giving program is that the organization must channel all of its fund-raising energies into the generation of current dollars. Of all the excuses for not beginning, this is the most plausible. Still, it's an excuse, not a reason.

Two aspects of planned giving are misunderstood when it comes to the need for current support. There *are* some forms of planned giving that produce current dollars; planned giving is not simply waiting 30 years for someone to die. The planned giving methods that yield current dollars are:

- The charitable lead trust, where the charity is provided immediate income out of the trust, rather than a deferred remainder interest
- The charitable remainder trust, where the donor (in addition to giving the remainder interest) gives the portion that is income interest to charity
- Gifts of life insurance (or gifts based on life insurance), where the policy can be surrendered if necessary for its cash value, or the charity can borrow money using the policy's cash value as collateral

The other fact that is often misunderstood is that planned gifts generate usable support much more quickly than is usually realized. Without becoming too morbid or grasping about it, individuals can die sooner than expected. Or, to state the matter more charitably, not everyone reaches his or her life expectancy. The odds being what they are, the larger the portfolio of planned gifts, the greater the likelihood of a speedy return.

The planned gift is ideal for an organization that is amassing a general endowment, scholarship, memorial, research, building, or similar fund. Everyone likes current gift dollars, but once a base of investment assets (principal) is established, the investment income can nicely complement the gift support, and the organization has the security of knowing that the assets remain in place.

The more it is understood that planned giving means service to the donors and receipt of large gifts, the more appreciated it will be. Some money will have to be expended at the outset, but it will be minimal in relation to the gifts received. The hurdle is simply getting started—taking the "deferral" out of this form of giving. Once the program is launched, the mystery will fall away and planned giving will become the most enjoyable and remunerative component of the fund-raising and development program.

FINDING THE BEST BLEND

Innovative and energetic management of nonprofit organizations may well utilize all of these ideas—and more. A contemporary nonprofit organization may have subsidiaries, be involved in a partnership, and have a successful planned giving program.

Once again, it cannot be stressed enough that all of these techniques are means to ends. They are ways for an organization to acquire what it wants and needs. Usually, the need is for money, and all of these suggestions are fund-raising techniques.

The place to begin is the organization's wish list. What does it want? A building? A computer? An endowment? Thereafter, the technique is matched with the wish, and the sky is the limit.

These techniques can be blended. A partnership may be the best way to acquire the organization's offices; an ongoing fund-raising program (including planned giving) can be used to buy out partnership interests, so as to own the property directly someday. A conventional fund-raising program may be used to acquire a computer system, but an endowment fund (fueled in part by planned giving) may secure future upgrades and replacements of equipment. A subsidiary or other separate organization may be appropriate to house a particular activity, but, as the organization grows, it may be able to absorb the activity within its basic operations, and an ongoing fund-raising program can provide the wherewithal to buy out shareholders or otherwise acquire the assets supporting the activity.

Fund-raising programs are not the only option. A joint venture or subsidiary may be preferable to any fund-raising.

Generalizations are difficult here. There are many opportunities and many techniques. All an organization has to do is match its wants and needs to these techniques, and the rest is relatively simple.

CHAPTER NINETEEN

Avoiding Personal Liability

O f all the labels that might be applied to U.S. society in the closing decades of the twentieth century, the Age of Litigation often seems the most appropriate. These days, it seems, anyone can sue someone else for just about any reason and for enormous amounts of money. The only restraint (which is rarely applied) is a judge's rejection of a frivolous lawsuit or a state's principles of legal ethics limiting a lawyer's ability to bring unwarranted litigation.

LAWSUITS AGAINST NONPROFIT ORGANIZATIONS

Nonprofit organizations can be sued—under federal, state, and local law—and they often are. Criminal prosecutions are rare, but the civil laws contain many crevices that cause missteps leading to lawsuits. For the most part, nonprofit organizations can be sued for the same reasons as for-profit organizations.

Here are the usual bases on which a nonprofit organization can be sued:

- Nonpayment of income or property taxes. These suits are brought by governments seeking unpaid tax revenues. The nonprofit organization may be generally tax-exempt, but the IRS may be after some unrelated business income tax; or a state may be looking for real estate tax on a parcel of real property that allegedly is not being used for exempt (usually charitable) purposes.

- Violation of a state's charitable solicitation act. A charitable (or similar) organization may be raising funds in a state without complying with the registration, reporting, or other requirements. A state will not proceed directly to litigation for a violation of this nature. However, if, after a few requests, the organization refuses to obey this law, an injunction or some other form of civil litigation may be initiated.

- Defamation. If an organization produces a libelous publication or one of its spokespersons uses terms or makes statements that another person or organization finds offensive, it is not uncommon for a defamation or bias suit to erupt in retaliation.

- Antitrust law violations. Membership organizations are particularly susceptible to this charge. For example, an association may wrongfully exclude or expel a person from its membership. (This can be a form of restraint of trade.) Or, the association may enforce a code of ethics and conclude that a member acted unethically. This finding could lead to a defamation charge and, if the person is expelled from the membership, to an antitrust law violation complaint.

- Employment discrimination, wrongful termination, personal injury, and breach of a lease or other contract. These are increasingly common bases for lawsuits, and the damages sought can run into the millions.

In most lawsuits, the only party sued is the organization itself; however, there are exceptions, such as the liability incurred by an organization as the result of something done (commission) or not done (omission) by another organization. For example, two (or more) nonprofit organizations may be involved in a *partnership* or a *joint venture*. As a result of this arrangement, the conduct of one organization may bring liability to it and/or to another organization. Technically, the liability may be the partnership's or joint venture's, but the liability can quickly attach to the underlying parties.

Another example concerns national organizations and their chapters. It is possible for a chapter to incur liability and cause the national organization to be sued as well. (This is termed *ascending liability*.) The national organization may have actually done something or failed to do something in conjunction with the chapter. More commonly, however, the national organization is sued simply because it has more resources than any of its chapters (lawyers would say it has "deeper pockets"). The outcome of this type of litigation often depends on whether the chapters are considered separate legal entities or whether they are integral parts of the national organization. (The same analysis can be applied to statewide associations that have local units throughout the state.)

DEFENDING AGAINST LAWSUITS

It probably goes without saying that a lawsuit brought is not necessarily a lawsuit won. It is one thing to be sued; it is another to have a lawsuit ripen into a court-imposed judgment. However, the nonprofit organization will still have to defend against the suit (usually by filing a motion to dismiss, an answer to the complaint, and/or a countercomplaint). The services of a lawyer are commonly required, and the organization can face some high legal fees and costs without having committed any wrong.

As a case in point, a nonprofit, charitable organization annually gives an award honoring an individual in a particular field of business. One year, the organization narrowed the candidates to three and, after much deliberation, decided on a finalist. One of the other two semifinalists became so angry at the organization for not awarding the honor to him that he filed a lawsuit, claiming abuse by the organization of its own procedural rules. The organization was shocked to find itself a target of a lawsuit as the result of its making an award (essentially, a gift). The matter was resolved before the case got to court, but the organization had to pay several thousands of dollars in legal fees to end the suit. It was not clear why the plaintiff wanted the award so much that he sued to try to obtain it, but his action underlined the fact that it does not take much these days to create a defendant, even a charitable one.

INDIVIDUALS AS DEFENDANTS

For the most part, the defendants in lawsuits involving nonprofit organizations are the organizations themselves; seldom will the charges include other parties, such as individuals. It can happen, though, and when it does, the following categories of individuals (including those acting as volunteers) can be dragged into the fray:

- Trustees
- Directors
- Officers
- Key employees

Conduct by most employees in their role as employees is considered conduct by the organization itself. If the employees' actions are outside the scope of their employment, however, they can be held entirely responsible as individuals.

When an individual is personally sued because of something done or not done in the name of a nonprofit organization, the potential liability is termed *personal liability*. Its occurrence is rare, but when it happens, it is usually for one or more of the following reasons:

- An individual had a responsibility to do something in connection with the operation of a nonprofit organization and failed to meet that responsibility
- An individual had a responsibility to refrain from doing something in connection with a nonprofit organization and did it anyway
- An individual failed to dissociate himself or herself from the wrongful conduct of others
- An individual actively participated in a wrongful conduct

For example, a nonprofit organization may have wrongfully terminated the employment of an individual on a discriminatory basis. If the termination was the result of discrimination by a manager who is also an employee of the organization, the organization may be found to be the only wrongdoer. However, if a member of the organization's board of directors actively conspired with the manager to cause the firing on a discriminatory basis, the director may be found personally liable. If another member of the board knew of the discriminatory action (and the conspiracy underlying it) and did nothing to thwart it, that board member may be found personally liable as well.

This example involves *commission:* One or more individuals committed a wrongful act and were found liable along with the organization. But liability can also result from a failure to act. The members of the finance committee of a nonprofit organization may fail in their obligation to oversee adequately the investment practices of the organization. Money may be lost or valuable resources may be squandered as a result. These individuals could be found personally liable for their *omission*.

This concept of personal liability flows out of a principle that has been in the law for centuries: Trustees of charitable trusts are deemed to have the same obligation toward the assets of the trusts as they do toward their personal assets. Their obligation is to *act prudently* in their handling of the nonprofit organization's resources. The trustees are *fiduciaries,* and the law imposes on them standards of conduct and management that, together, comprise *fiduciary responsibility.* Most state laws, by statute or court opinion, now impose the standards of fiduciary responsibility on directors of nonprofit organizations, whether or not the organizations are trusts and whether or not they are charitable.

Some forms of personal liability are imposed by statute. For example, if a nonprofit organization fails to deposit withheld income taxes or social security taxes as required by law, the IRS has the authority to extract the taxes from the organization's directors or trustees personally. When this happens, it is because of a conclusion that the individuals are *responsible parties*.

In a nutshell, personal liability can result when a director, trustee, officer, and/or key employee of a nonprofit organization breaches the standards of fiduciary responsibility.

How can an individual who is serving a nonprofit organization (or wants to serve one) avoid the ravages of personal liability? Cynics would say that the safest way is not to participate in the good works of a nonprofit organization in the first place. Happily, as explained in the first chapter, that is contrary to the American way.

AVOIDING PERSONAL LIABILITY

There are six ways in which an individual who is a director (or trustee) and/or officer of a nonprofit organization can avoid personal liability. Five of these ways are listed below and amplified with checklists and chapter references. The sixth way is this: The individual should, at all times, engage in behavior that prevents (or at least significantly minimizes) the possibility of personal liability even if the organization itself is found liable. The individual is a fiduciary and has a duty to act in a prudent manner. Constant awareness of that duty offers a measure of self-protection.

Here are the ways to avoid personal liability while fulfilling the spirit and the rules of fiduciary responsibility.

Understand the Organization

Learn about the legal form of the organization and its structure. For example, if the organization is a corporation, obtain copies of its articles of incorporation and bylaws, and *read them*. Compare the organization's operating methods with the structure and procedures that are reflected in these documents. (One common problem is that an organization is operating as a membership organization even though its articles of incorporation state that it shall not have members. In an extreme example, a venerable organization was happily operating for decades, until one of its new directors happened to read the articles of incorporation. The document stated that the organization "shall cease to exist" as of 1946!)

CHECKLIST

- ☐ Articles of incorporation and bylaws
- ☐ Application filed with the IRS to secure recognition of tax-exempt status (Chapter 6)
- ☐ Similar applications filed with state authorities, principally for income tax or real property tax exemptions
- ☐ Annual financial statements prepared by accountants, accompanying auditors' letters, and notes to the financial statements
- ☐ Annual information returns filed with the IRS (Chapter 7)
- ☐ Annual reports filed as required in some states
- ☐ Minutes of directors' meetings, particularly those held since beginning of personal service or election to office
- ☐ Any other documents, correspondence, or memos preserved and made available by the organization's secretary or librarian

Understand the Organization's Activities

Learn how the organization operates—the purposes of its programs, their rank order of priority (as shown by budgeted allowances), their number, possible overlap, and membership support.

CHECKLIST

- ☐ Review the documents that state the organization's purpose. Is each of its programs being operated in furtherance of that purpose? Yes_____ No_____
- ☐ If no:

  Should one or more of the organization's programs be discontinued? Yes_____ No_____

  Alternatively, should the organization's statement of purpose be expanded to accommodate the current scope of activities? Yes_____ No_____
- ☐ Review the annual information returns the organization has filed with the IRS. Are the programs being accurately and adequately described? Yes_____ No_____

☐   Is the organization making an accurate distinction between its lobbying efforts (if any) and its other programs? (Chapter 13)   Yes_____ No_____

Understand the Organization's Other Operations

Committees, subsidiaries, directors' "pet projects," members' personal interests or contacts, or community needs may have introduced activities (and budget expenditures) that were not authorized in the normal way. Some may deserve more recognition and support, others may be innocently jeopardizing the tax-exempt status. Find out exactly what the organization is *doing*.

CHECKLIST

☐   Are all necessary returns and reports being filed on time?   Yes_____ No_____

☐   If the organization is involved in fund-raising, are all of the state laws being followed? (Chapter 9)   Yes_____ No_____

☐   If you are a director, are you comfortable with all of the compensation arrangements? (Chapters 4 and 10)   Yes_____ No_____

☐   Does the organization have one or more for-profit subsidiaries? (Chapter 15)   Yes_____ No_____

☐   Does it participate in:

Any partnerships? (Chapter 16)   Yes_____ No_____

Any joint ventures?   Yes_____ No_____

☐   Does it have:

A related lobbying organization?   Yes_____ No_____

A related political action committee?   Yes_____ No_____

A related fund-raising foundation?   Yes_____ No_____

☐   Are you comfortable with each and every one of these arrangements?   Yes_____ No_____

Ask Questions

Directors should never be afraid to ask about any arrangement or information that is unclear to them. An individual with fiduciary responsibility should not fret about asking "dumb questions" in front of the other directors; many of them probably have the same question on their minds. Review the structural arrangements. Study the organization's finances. It's part of your duties.

CHECKLIST

☐ Do you understand the committee structure? Yes_____ No_____

☐ Do you fully understand the work of the committee (or committees) that you serve on? Yes_____ No_____

☐ Who is available at board meetings to answer questions?

   The organization's lawyer? Yes_____ No_____

   The accountant? Yes_____ No_____

   The investment adviser? Yes_____ No_____

   The fund-raising consultant? Yes_____ No_____

   (Beware of too many No answers.)

☐ In your opinion, does the organization have too many directors? Yes_____ No_____

☐ Is there a conflict-of-interest policy for directors? Yes_____ No_____

☐ Does the organization have a planned giving program? (Chapter 17) Yes_____ No_____

☐ Does the board have a "retreat" once in a while to reflect on what the organization is doing and why? Yes_____ No_____

☐ If you are a director or officer, do you contribute money or property to the organization? Yes_____ No_____

   If no, why not?

☐ Are you opposed to any policy of the organization? Yes_____ No_____

(If you were on the board when the policy was adopted, is your opposition recorded in the minutes?)

☐ If you are a director, do you miss meetings of the board?   Yes_____ No_____

(If yes, be sure that the reason for your missing a meeting is stated in the minutes.)

Read Current Relevant Materials

Magazine articles and books describing the proper role for directors and officers of nonprofit organizations will help to update your knowledge of permissible and innovative practices and applicable legal opinions. Periodically, attend a seminar or conference for directors of nonprofit organizations. At almost any time, if someone were to ask you, you should be prepared to answer the questions listed here.

CHECKLIST

☐ What is the tax-exempt status of the organization?
(IRC § _____; usually § 501(c)(____))

☐ If the organization is a charitable one, is it "public" _____ or "private" _____? (Chapter 11)

☐ If it is a public charity, which type is it?
   ☐ Donative public charity
   ☐ Service-provider public charity
   ☐ Supporting organization
   ☐ Other

☐ When was the last time you read the fundraising literature of the organization? Are you aware of what is currently being circulated?   Yes_____ No_____

☐ Has the organization been audited by state authorities in the past five years?   Yes_____ No_____

☐ Has the organization been audited by the IRS in the past five years?   Yes_____ No_____

☐ Has the organization recently had a *legal audit*—a thorough analysis, by a lawyer, of the organization's structure, operations, and law compliance?   Yes___ No___

☐ Are you aware of any activity (or lack of activity) within the organization that you suspect may bring liability to the organization and/or any of its directors or officers?   Yes___ No___

☐ Can you honestly say that you are treating the assets and other resources of the organization as you are treating your own?   Yes___ No___
(This answer has positive meaning only if you are treating your own resources in a prudent manner.)

No one can guarantee that a nonprofit organization will not be sued, or that its directors and officers will not be sued. But if these techniques for achieving and maintaining fiduciary responsibility are followed, there is little possibility that personal liability will be found.

PROTECTIONS AGAINST PERSONAL LIABILITY

As mentioned earlier, self-protection, stemming from prudent behavior and fulfillment of fiduciary responsibility, can ensure that personal liability is avoided. A key source of protection is overlooked too often: Be certain that the organization is incorporated. This is critical. Remember that the incorporated organization is clearly a separate legal entity, and the corporate form usually serves as a shield against personal liability. Most lawyers advise their individual clients not to sit on the board of directors of a nonprofit organization that is not incorporated. If you are an officer and/or director of a nonprofit organization and it is not incorporated, find out why not. Do not accept reasons for unincorporation lightly. In the case of the organization that was sued because an individual did not receive an award (discussed above), the organization was not incorporated and its volunteer president was personally sued. (Soon afterward, the organization became incorporated.)

CHECKLIST

☐ Is the organization incorporated?   Yes_____ No_____

☐ If it is not incorporated, are you comfortable
with that?   Yes_____ No_____

☐ Does the organization have an indemnifica-
tion clause in its articles of organization?   Yes_____ No_____

If not, why not?

☐ Are you satisfied with the scope of the indemnification?   Yes_____ No_____

☐ Does the organization have adequate assets
to back up this indemnification?   Yes_____ No_____

☐ Does the organization have an officers' and
directors' liability insurance policy?   Yes_____ No_____

If not, why not?

☐ Have you read the policy?   Yes_____ No_____

☐ Are you aware that the largest single section
of the policy is likely to be the portion that
details *exclusions*—what the policy does *not*
cover?   Yes_____ No_____

☐ Do you know and understand the exclusions
in your policy?   Yes_____ No_____

☐ Are you comfortable with these exclusions?   Yes_____ No_____

☐ Is the indemnification broader than the in-
surance coverage?   Yes_____ No_____

☐ Is the insurance coverage broader?   Yes_____ No_____

☐ Does the law in your state provide some form
of statutory immunity by which personal liability arising out of service for a nonprofit organization is avoided as a matter of law?   Yes_____ No_____

☐ If conditions are attached to the immunity,
do you (and/or the organization) satisfy
these conditions?   Yes_____ No_____

☐ In some states, the language that triggers the
immunity must be in the organization's articles of incorporation/organization or bylaws.

If this is required, does your organization's
organizational documents contain this lan-
guage?   Yes_____   No_____
(If the organization operates in more than
one state, be certain to check on the immunity laws in each of those states.)

If a director or officer follows these guidelines and maximizes use of
the "four I"s—indemnification, insurance, immunity, and incorporation—he or she can almost be guaranteed that personal liability for service for a nonprofit organization will be avoided. In any event, the
individual will know that he or she did everything possible to avoid liability.

Nonprofit organizations need and deserve the best leadership they
can find. It is important to serve. It is also important to serve prudently.

PART FIVE

The Future of Nonprofits

CHAPTER TWENTY

Nonprofits: A Short-Range Look

Nonprofit organizations are an expanding component of today's American society. They affect the lives of people nationwide. They are, as stressed in Chapter 1, a most distinguishing characteristic that differentiates the United States from all other countries. When grappling with problems, our nation is willing to rely on institutions other than governmental ones. They are a treasured national resource . . . or are they?

Many individuals truly treasure nonprofit organizations—and demonstrate this feeling by giving of their money, expertise, and time—for they comprehend the value of pluralism and voluntarism. Most Americans generally have a positive attitude toward nonprofit entities—their church, synagogue, hospital, or old alma mater. Yet, a growing minority is not particularly sympathetic toward nonprofits, and is, in some instances, hostile toward them. Persons in this latter category serve in legislatures, are employees of legislators, preside in courtrooms, or are federal, state, or local regulators. There are some in the U.S. Congress, for example, who see nonprofit organizations as the most unregulated of sectors in our society—and they are working to remedy that perceived "deficiency."

Nonprofit organizations are not on the brink of extinction; they undoubtedly have decades of service yet to come. However, some troubling signs suggest that the climate for nonprofit organizations may soon be dramatically different. The philosophy underlying the law that regulates them is shifting—as is the substance of that law. This chapter explores three of these signs: competition with for-profit organizations (and resulting tax policy), fund-raising regulation, and self-regulation. These developments are leading to a fundamental problem: the non-profits' identity crisis, which is explored in Chapter 21.

THE COMPETITION ISSUE

Without doubt, the greatest single issue facing nonprofit organizations today is the charge that they are unfairly competing with for-profit businesses (frequently portrayed as "small business"). The legal issues associated with this allegation range across federal, state, and local law topics and involve constitutional, statutory, and administrative law considerations. Here is just a sampling:

- The reach of the IRS for revenue by classifying activities as unrelated to tax-exempt purposes
- The right of charitable organizations to engage in fund-raising as an act of free speech
- The determination by governments as to what entities are to be entitled to be recipients of grants and contracts
- The permission to pay preferential postal rates
- The question as to what, if any, changes in the federal tax law are warranted in light of the current service-provider activities of nonprofit organizations

Yet, despite this range of topics, the matter is essentially one of federal tax policy: Will nonprofit organizations be able to remain exempt from federal, state, and local income, sales, use, and property taxes?

This subject has attracted little research. Despite many months of allegations and comprehensive congressional hearings in 1987, a substantive inquiry into the matter of competition by nonprofit organizations has yet to be done. There have been some studies and general articles but there has been little true research. Instead, the subject is flavored with misconceptions, predispositions, a great amount of emotion, and—the element that will determine much of the nature of the evolving law on the subject—politics.

Recently, there has been great pressure from the small business community for review of this issue at both the federal and state levels. The federal government itself is participating in the review effort through the U.S. Small Business Administration (SBA). In November 1983, the SBA's Office of Advocacy issued a report (subsequently updated) concluding that many types of tax-exempt organizations are engaging in commercial activities in competition with the nation's small businesses and that this competition is increasing. Institutions cited in the report for engaging in unfair competition included educational institutions, healthcare providers, and nursing homes. Competitive activities were found to include audiovisual services, analytical testing, research, computer services, and the sale of hearing aids. The report singled out technological services provided by colleges and universities in the name of research, sales of health products by clinics, sales of excess computer capacity, operation of tours, and a variety of studies and services generally denominated consulting.

Following the release of this report, the small business community began organizing its campaign. A Business Coalition for Fair Competition was formed and is now spearheading efforts to revise the relevant federal and state laws. This issue was a prominent topic at the 1986 White House Conference on Small Business. The subject is of growing interest in both the popular media and specialized publications.

All too many people believe that this entire set of issues boils down to the federal tax treatment of unrelated business income. This is understandable: The unrelated trade or business rules presently in the law were written as the result of charges of unfair competition. (See Chapter 12.) However, today's allegations of unfair competition are complaints about activities that, under existing law, are related to the tax-exempt organizations' functions. As a consequence, much of the debate is shifting the discussion to whether overall qualification for tax-exempt status should be allowed to continue. Congress seems ready to revise the law if necessary, to accommodate these concerns.

The core of the legal issues involving competition between nonprofit and for-profit organizations is found here. Will emerging law provide more specific definitions of the term *unrelated business?* Will there be overarching rules, such as an equation of competitive activities with unrelated ones, or will new rules focus on particular activities, such as publishing, consulting, research, and/or product sales? Will activities now denominated fund-raising, cause-related marketing, or commercial co-venturing be considered taxable or disqualifying activities? Will specific limitations be placed on the ability of tax-exempt organizations to incur unrelated income? To what extent will the law prohibit or require the use of for-profit subsidiaries or joint ventures? The immediate future probably holds the answers to these questions.

Concurrently, the courts have been more disposed to finding activities nonexempt or unrelated functions of tax-exempt organizations—not through the application of the conventional unrelated income rules but rather because of the conclusion that the activities are commercial or competitive with tax-paying organizations. Recent developments reflect this trend, whether it involves the marketing of insurance programs to members of associations, the selling of advertising, or the publishing

activities of allegedly educational or religious organizations. At about
the same time that the doctrines of commerciality and competitiveness
in the tax-exempt organizations law context are taking hold in the court
opinions, Congress may be embarking on a process of grafting these concepts onto the statutory law.

Only educated guesswork is available at this point to predict what
all of this activity will yield in the way of new law. A vast amount and
variety of proposals are under examination. The SBA analysis, for example, urged these possibilities (some inconsistent with others): an
outright prohibition, in the federal tax laws, on unrelated business activities; a higher income tax on unrelated business activities; a more
specific federal tax law definition of the term "unrelated trade or business"; a percentage limitation on allowable unrelated business activities; repeal of some of the statutory exceptions to the unrelated income
rules; and use of tax differentiation factors, between nonprofit and for-
profit organizations, in the cost comparison process followed under the
federal procurement law. The SBA concluded that federal policymakers
"must undertake a thorough evaluation of the changing role of the nonprofit [organization] in our society and economy." The report found
that "[a]ppropriate revisions in federal statutes and regulations governing nonprofits are necessary to reflect the existence of the commercial nonprofit sector, and to remedy the unfair competition now
imposed on for-profit small business."

No matter how the nonprofit community reacts to those propositions,
that is the way the issue is being framed for debate. There is a potential
that all of this will lead to nothing—or it could bring an in-depth inquiry
into the federal and state law distinctions between for-profit and nonprofit organizations, the rationale for the tax exemption of certain types
of nonprofit organizations, and whether some existing tax exemptions
are outmoded and some new forms of tax exemption are required. It is
probable that this legislative process will introduce many new aspects of
the law of tax-exempt organizations, including perhaps some rewriting
of the criteria for achieving and maintaining tax-exempt status.

A major battle is shaping up; on the line is the future of the terms in
law of nonprofit and tax-exempt organizations. Along with these impending law changes is the potential for a substantial alteration in the
entire economic and regulatory climate for nonprofit organizations.

FUND-RAISING REGULATION

Fund-raising regulation, at the federal and state levels, is experiencing
another great surge. (See Chapter 9.) More and more states are getting

into charitable solicitation regulation, imposing registration, reporting, and a myriad of other requirements on charities and those who assist them in the fund-raising process. (Today, only five states do not regulate in this area.) States that have formerly forgone the desire for a fund-raising law have suddenly decided that their citizens now need one. States with fund-raising regulation laws are making them tougher. Those who administer these laws—the state regulators—are applying them with new vigor.

These state laws require a charitable organization that engages in fund-raising to comply with the law of the state in which the organization is located and the law of each of the other states in which the organization solicits contributions. Further, these laws directly impact charities by regulating those who help them raise funds—professional fund-raisers, paid solicitors, and commercial co-venturers.

Without doubt, these charitable solicitation acts are generally well-intentioned. Most state legislators vote for them, thinking they are performing a public service. There *are* fund-raising abuses taking place, and the public needs and deserves a place to lodge complaints and be assured that the frauds are prosecuted and punished. The law is clear that each state, in the exercise of its police power, has the authority to enact and enforce this type of law. Indeed, the states' attorneys general have considerable inherent authority to regulate in this field, even without statutory backup.

Sometimes, however, the cure is worse than the disease. Fund-raising regulation, under today's version, is one of those instances. The typical contemporary state charitable solicitation act is a monster: unnecessarily complex, onerous, stringent, burdensome, written by a legislator or regulator with a motive to "get" someone, or otherwise ill-conceived. These laws are frequently authored by individuals who have a dim idea of what they are doing and administered by bureaucrats who have a negative view toward philanthropy. In too many cases, the zeal to control fund-raising is leading to the creation of little regulatory empires staffed (at taxpayers' expense) by lawyers and investigators whose skills are sorely needed in far more important government service. The paperwork and the costs imposed on charities and their professional consultants exceed any value these overreaching laws may provide.

The ridiculousness of the situation can be readily seen when one stops to think about what is being regulated. We are not talking about public health and safety here. This is not drug trafficking or nuclear waste disposal. This is charitable giving! Some public education and disclosure by soliciting charities are all that is needed. If an individual is uncertain about a particular charity and cannot obtain some wanted information, there is a very simple solution: Don't give.

The shame of it all is that the legislators and regulators have lost perspective on what it is they are regulating. Philanthropy is the lifeblood of the American pluralistic system. Billions of dollars are annually provided for services and other benefits that government cannot and will not supply. Giving to charity is, obviously, what fuels this machine. But fund-raising regulation is damaging the legitimate gift solicitation process. (Do not forget that charitable fund-raising is a constitutionally protected act of free speech.) In short, charitable fund-raising is over-regulated—unnecessarily, harmfully, and counterproductively.

Return for a moment to two examples referenced in Chapter 9: the improper use of percentages as a means of regulating limitations on fund-raising costs, and the nonsensical definitions of the terms professional fund-raiser and professional solicitor.

The use of percentages in this setting has been repeatedly criticized and found unconstitutional by federal and state courts all the way up to the U.S. Supreme Court. Yet the legislators and regulators persist in using these restrictions anyway. The regulators are absolutely rabid about fund-raising expenses, even though it has been repeatedly shown (and common sense dictates) that the relative size of an organization's fund-raising costs bears no correlation to the quality of its program.

The foolishness in the applicability of the definitions can be seen, for example, in the impact of the state charitable solicitation acts on telemarketers who assist charitable organizations in fund-raising. Most of the fund-raising regulation zealotry is being directed at quickie promoters—those who roll into town for a weekend with a circus, or some similar attraction, and roll out of town on Monday with most of the money. The statute-writers cannot seem to find the ability to develop law regulating these types. It is a virtual scandal that all of fund-raising—whether capital, annual giving, direct mail, or planned giving programs—is heavily regulated so that purveyors of tickets to vaudeville acts can be monitored.

Chapter 9 refers to the meaning of the terms *professional fund-raiser* and *solicitor*. When it is remembered that the term *solicit* includes the seeking of gifts over the telephone, a telemarketer becomes a solicitor in the eyes of most of the regulators. (To their credit, a few regulators refuse to apply their laws in this extreme fashion.) Generically, a telemarketer is not a solicitor. In saying that, the assumption is that the telemarketer does not receive the funds from the solicitation. That is an important distinguishing characteristic. A true *professional solicitor* is one who requests a contribution on behalf of a charity, receives all of the gift proceeds, retains a fee and the amount needed to cover expenses, and remits the balance to the charity. Frequently, another characteristic of a solicitor is that compensation is determined on the basis of a percentage of funds received. Further, because of the way the transactions usually are conducted, the donor realizes that the solicitor is not an employee or volunteer of the donee charity but is functioning in an independent capacity.

Under normal circumstances, when a gift is made to a charity as the result of a telemarketing effort, the gift is—literally—made to the charity. Compensation is on a set fee basis, rather than on the contributions received. And those called believe (harmlessly) that the caller is a direct representative of the charity, not some independent taker of most of the gift amounts. In fact, the usual telemarketer is such a representative, functioning as an agent of the soliciting charity.

Except for the disparaging connotation usually associated in the fund-raising context with the term *solicitor*, there would be no harm in classifying telemarketers as solicitors if it were merely a matter of definitions. However, the matter is far more than that, simply because, in their craze to drive out the circus promoters, the statute writers have made life miserable for anyone categorized as a solicitor, by imposing a battery of tough requirements that are not imposed on others.

What is to be done? First, charities and those who support them must come to more fully appreciate this dilemma, just as there needs to be greater recognition of the law warp the telemarketers are in. The states are overreacting and overregulating—and the public (and federal legislators) are concluding with greater frequency that increasing regulation reflects a *need* for increasing regulation, not realizing that the regulation is feeding on itself. In other words, there is no problem of great magnitude here, but the expanding scope of regulation is conveying the impression that there is—an instance of the law developing backward.

Second, there must be some organized effort to change these laws. One charity or telemarketing firm cannot do it alone.

Third, any remedial efforts must not make the same mistake that many legislatures are currently making; that is, sweeping definitions will not do. The corrective legislation must be narrow and precise, to rectify the particular problems without ignoring the abuse situations. It can be done but it will take much work.

Couple all of this with the emerging reach of federal regulation of fund-raising (see Chapter 9), and it is clear that whether or not the fund-raising regulation system is altered will have a great bearing on the process of raising funds for charitable purposes and on the success of nonprofit organizations in general. No one—not donors, donees, consultants to charities, regulators, or the public—is served by this present state of affairs. It cries out for correction and the status of nonprofit entities in the future will be shaped by the outcome.

SELF-REGULATION

Some people believe that the nonprofit community escaped some forms of regulation by government because of the extent to which it regulated itself. They now tend to admit that self-regulation of the nonprofit sector is no longer adequate to do the job—that government must regulate the sector even more than it presently does.

Apart from whether this view is valid, the fact is that self-regulation in the nonprofit sector is on the rise—dramatically so. But because the word on this does not seem to be getting out, the sector will, ironically, likely be facing the prospect of more governmental regulation at a time when nongovernmental regulation is increasing.

Nongovernmental regulation of nonprofit entities comes in three basic forms: *watchdog groups, codes of ethics,* and *certification.* Watchdog groups are self-appointed bodies that call themselves voluntary agencies and serve as a source of information about nonprofit organizations for the media, researchers, and the general public. They promulgate standards, prepare and disseminate reports on nonprofit organizations, and distribute lists identifying the entities that do and do not meet the standards. The public, including donors and grantors, tend to give these ratings and reports considerable credibility and act (give or do not give) accordingly, thereby giving the voluntary agencies a degree of real-life clout and leverage that they would not otherwise have.

The two best-known watchdog groups are the Philanthropic Advisory Service of the Council of Better Business Bureaus, and the National Charities Information Bureau. These agencies endeavor to monitor most of the charities that solicit contributions from the general public. Other agencies established to provide standards for smaller groupings of nonprofit organizations include the Evangelical Council on Financial Accountability.

The problem has been that sometimes these watchdog groups have been unfair in their practices. They have set standards that lack common sense or are inconsistent with points of law. Organizations that operate in a perfectly lawful manner and have meaningful programs find themselves on a widely distributed list of organizations that "fail to meet standards"—and the general public believes the organizations are poorly run and directs its support elsewhere. The reports are sometimes inadequately researched and unfairly written, with heavy emphasis on negative points, some of which are immaterial. On occasion, the agencies are poorly staffed, using the services of individuals who lack adequate training on the subject and/or who have an antiphilanthropic mind-set.

For better or worse, the reach and the numbers of these watchdog groups are increasing. So too is this form of self-regulation.

The second form of self-regulation is through codes of ethics. These statements of principles established by membership organizations (associations) apply only to those individuals who are members. The point of these codes is to hold the members to at least minimal standards of ethical conduct, all for the ultimate protection of the public. One problem, quite obviously, is the determination of what is ethical behavior for a particular group of individuals representing one profession, business, trade, discipline, field of interest, or whatever. Because so many considerations must be accommodated, the typical code of ethics tends to be a very general and vague statement of broad principles. It becomes very difficult to interpret and apply in relation to a particular set of facts.

Even where a nonprofit organization devises a detailed code of ethics, another problem arises: What to do with it. There are two basic choices: Ignore it (rendering the process of writing it rather pointless) or enforce it. If a code of ethics is properly enforced, the organization must have an ethics committee that reviews cases (sometimes by holding hearings), a detailed statement of the procedures for processing a case, an appeals procedure, and a series of meaningful sanctions (reprimand, censure, suspension, expulsion). Here, a phenomenon sets in: If an ethics enforcement mechanism is in place, people will use it, and that will lead to more people using it, which will lead to the nonprofit organization's having to expend a meaningful portion of its time acting as a court system. Proper enforcement is a substantial commitment.

Enforcement of a code of ethics does not occur in a legal vacuum. There are serious antitrust and defamation considerations. An individual who has been found "guilty" of violating a code of ethics is likely to be unhappy about being embarrassed in front of his or her peers, losing a job, failing to be promoted, or whatever, because of (or allegedly because of) the ethics violation. This individual is a potential plaintiff, with all of the implications for organizational and personal liability.

Despite the legal considerations, the development and enforcement of codes of ethics are on the rise, as organizations strive to make their constituency more professional. The nonprofit sector is actively engaged in self-regulation and self-improvement.

The third form of self-regulation in the nonprofit world is certification. This form, also known as credentialing and accreditation, essentially means the conferring of a designation on an individual who has met particular criteria. The certification process is akin to licensure and, again, evidences a desire to enhance the professionalism of a particular group. The designation is intended to benefit the public by identifying those in a particular field who are accomplished and suitable for selection when their services are needed. For example, there are certified financial planners, certified association executives, and certified fund-raising executives.

Unlike codes of ethics, to which all members of an association are expected to adhere, a certification program is voluntary: a member of a group can (but need not) pursue certification. Still, when a certification program is in place, there is a natural pressure to become certified or else risk the perception of "second class" status. Here again, a form of self-regulation is operating in the nonprofit sector.

The ramifications in the administration of a certification program are not unlike those in the administration of a code of ethics. There is always the prospect of lawsuits by unhappy individuals who fail to achieve accreditation or who lose it. Charges of defamation, antitrust violations, and due process transgressions are all possible. Some organizations compound this risk by making compliance with a code of ethics a requirement for ongoing certification.

One thing is clear: In the years to come, nonprofit organizations will be laboring under the burden of more regulation. Much of it will come from government, but a lot of it will flow from the nonprofit community itself, with nonprofits being the regulators and their constituencies the regulated.

WHERE ARE NONPROFITS HEADED?

From a lawyer's vantage point, this question is easy to answer: They are headed for more regulation. More regulation does not (necessarily) mean extinction, but additional regulation is a threat. It raises suspicions in the minds of some public donors, tempts more than a few legislators into seeking even more regulatory control, and generally is a drag on the system (most notably, when it comes to charitable giving).

There are two things the members of the nonprofit community can do to improve their prospects for keeping some autonomy. Probably neither will be done, in part because the recommendations are somewhat inconsistent but largely because of human nature's adherence to the status quo, inertia, and fear of the unknown. One entails self-restraint; the other, more involvement in the political process.

Addressing the second point first, the nonprofit community has come a long way in recent years in participation in the legislative process at the federal level. It is more adept than ever in influencing the legislative process as practiced by the U.S. Congress. And this is not easy. If approaches are not handled with some sensitivity and skill, the nonprofit world's emissaries to the legislatures become perceived as merely another pack of lobbyists—often a counterproductive development—instead of a well-intentioned group pursuing the public weal. Also, as Chapters 13 and 14 point out, when nonprofit organizations venture into the realm of legislative and political campaign activities, they face considerable sanctions.

Still, much more action can be taken. Here are some suggestions.

- More interaction with grass roots resources. Federal legislators (particularly those in the House of Representatives) pay attention to their constituency. Representatives of nonprofit organizations must befriend their members of Congress and visit them often, in Washington and in the local districts. These legislators can become informed as to the organizations' programs and other activities, including fund-raising plans and problems. (Legislators can identify with this: They are fund-raisers too.) Nonprofits must learn to lobby when adverse legislation is not imminent; keeping up the relationships month to month, year in and year out, makes the real lobbying easier and more effective—and, in the long run, less necessary. Not all of this type of activity is involvement in the legislative process, so the sanctions are not always a problem. Besides, nonprofit organizations, including charitable ones, can usually lobby much more than they believe they can.

- More activities that affect public opinion. Ideally, there would be ongoing media coverage of nonprofit organizations' good works. Articles, press releases, studies, op-ed columns, and the like should routinely flow. Nonprofit organizations can engage in research activities and other projects that yield substantive results to community and business leaders, and legislators and their staffs. Expanded public relations would enhance the image of nonprofits, educate and remind the public of their heritage and role in contemporary society, and—in the process—probably pave the way for more successful fund-raising. When the public is favorable toward a particular subject, the politicians tend to be as well, and the opponents find the opposing harder going.

- More self-education. Those who manage and advise nonprofit organizations must learn more about the basics of the law affecting them. (This book is written in that spirit.) Much difficulty could be avoided—whether from an IRS audit or a suit of personal liability against a director—if just the fundamentals were mastered. Conferences and seminars abound but, for some reason, those who need the word are not getting it. There are massive gaps in understanding of, for example, fund-raising regulation (and techniques), the requirements for keeping tax-exempt status, the unrelated income rules, and the annual reporting obligations. A very current illustration of this is the growing tendency of charitable organizations to regard every payment to them as a deductible charitable gift, when that is clearly not the case. Some members of Congress have challenged the nonprofit sector to rid itself of this problem, through dissemination of corrective information—before Congress takes on the cause through more stringent legislation. This and comparable efforts must be launched, and soon.

- Make better use of political action committees (PACs). Like nonprofit organizations, members of Congress and other legislators need financial support—and they tend to be responsive to those who provide it to them. The world needs some PACs for the nonprofits' causes. Even those in the charitable community could experiment with the use of independent PACs.

Regarding self-restraint, one aspect has already been discussed: the hope for a cooling of the regulatory zeal associated with self-regulation. Another dimension is directly associated with the *pig theory*. This theory has it that a good idea can evolve into a massive mistake that adversely affects everyone, when the idea is pushed to its outer limits. The idea as implemented in the early stages is a good one; but, as others begin to use it, the idea becomes transformed into something different and certainly something more extensive. The practice expands until it attracts the attention of a legislature, which either taxes the income involved or outlaws the practice altogether. The lawmakers may pass very restrictive legislation that not only wipes out the entire undertaking (including the original good idea) but leaves the community more restricted and regulated than it was before the good idea was initially implemented. An example of the pig theory can be seen in the evolving doctrine of commerciality. This doctrine cuts across tax exemption and unrelated income issues, and applies to nearly all forms of nonprofit organizations.

Many nonprofit organizations have become obligated to sustain themselves and their beneficiaries by pursuing funding from new sources, now that some of the conventional ones are proving insufficient. (This is, by the way, no secret in Washington, DC; the General Accounting Office recently observed that "[a]s a result of growing federal deficits and reduced government spending for social services, tax-exempt organizations are being asked to assume a greater share in the funding of these services" and "[t]herefore, it is likely that in seeking sources of funds, tax-exempt organizations will continue to increase their UBI [unrelated business income] activity.") As they turn to the service-provider approach, they embark on fund-raising ventures that, while innocent enough at the outset, expand economically and in visibility until the business community is antagonized and until some legislative body is activated.

Two cases in point are the enactment by Congress, in 1984, of the tax-exempt entity leasing rules and, in 1986, of the tax rule causing the offering of "commercial-type insurance" to be either a basis for loss of tax exemption or an unrelated business. Other cases in point that are shaping up are income-producing affinity card programs and multi-charity commercial co-venturing. Before the doctrine of commerciality matures, it is likely to challenge many existing notions of what is required to qualify as a tax-exempt organization, rewrite portions of the law of unrelated income taxation, and pit some nonprofit organizations against others.

The overall future for nonprofit organizations is bright, although along the way they are going to have to achieve a better public understanding of their role in society and, to some extent, learn to live with a redefinition of that role. There is much that nonprofit organizations can do to affect these developments. The proactive techniques suggested above can be blended with self-restraint. It is, admittedly, a tall order.

CHAPTER TWENTY-ONE

Nonprofits: A Long-Range Look

Despite the problems and challenges for non-profit organizations chronicled in Chapter 20, it is expected that most nonprofit entities will, overall, fare quite well over the coming decades. What separates the nonprofit organization of today from the successful nonprofit organization of tomorrow is resolution of the nonprofits' identity crisis. The seeds of that process were sown in 1987—an extraordinary year in the development of the law of tax-exempt organizations. Unfortunately, from the standpoint of nonprofit organizations, much of the development was in negative contexts. Indeed, 1987 may be characterized as the year of charity bashing.

1987: AN IDENTITY CRISIS SURFACES

Not since 1969 had there been such a spate of general antipathy toward tax-exempt organizations. However, the 1969 bashing was focused especially on private foundations. (See Chapter 11.) In 1987, the hostility against charitable organizations was widespread and generally indiscriminate.

Why this negativism? The answer is far from clear, although several theories are plausible. Probably all of them involve legitimate factors and some others that are questionable. The relative importance to be assigned to the elements that can be identified is difficult.

No special events in 1987 caused the negativism, and it is curious that so much happened within that year.

The official displays of an intense review of the law of tax-exempt organizations came in three sets of hearings held before the House Subcommittee on Oversight of the House Ways and Means Committee. These hearings examined these practices by charities: legislative activities, political campaign involvements, fund-raising, private inurement, and commercial and competitive activities. The first set of hearings resulted in the adoption of tax legislation concerning lobbying and political activities. (See Chapters 13 and 14.) The hearings on television evangelism did not lead to any legislative recommendations, nor did the hearings on the unrelated activities rules.

Other manifestations included proposals contained in the many revenue-raising options being developed by congressional committee staffs and the continuing flow of developments in the regulation of fund-raising for charity at the state level. (See Chapter 9.)

A great amount of the activity in 1987 had its origins in developments that had commenced months and even years beforehand. What happened legislatively in 1987 in this area spilled over into 1988 and is continuing.

Still, an unusual amount of anti-nonprofit organization activity unfolded in 1987, and it is interesting to speculate on the reasons.

One factor that may seem superficially to be perhaps the most important is *coincidence.* How else to explain, within the same year, the guilty pleas of those who (allegedly) misused the National Endowment for the Preservation of Liberty, and the collapse of Jim and Tammie Bakker's Praise The Lord (PTL) empire? Complaints about lobbying and political campaign activities by charitable organizations and about commercial and competitive practices by charities and other nonprofit organizations had been rumbling for some time. But why congressional hearings on both subjects (plus the hearings on television evangelism) in the same year?

Another factor was the simultaneous convergence, for purposes of policy resolution, of (seemingly) unrelated tax-exempt organization *policy issues.* These included the need to confront the proper tax treatment of nonprofit hospitals, the distinctions between commercial testing and exempt function research, the sales of certain items in university bookstores and museum gift shops, and the pressures building between commercial fitness centers and traditional charitable institutions such as the YM/WCAs.

The *media coverage* accorded charitable organizations had widespread, mostly negative effect. The coverage of tax-exempt (particularly charitable) organizations by the print and broadcast media rarely focuses on the good works of these organizations. Instead, all too often they are portrayed as commercial entities (usually because of their investment practices), or borderline fraudulent entities (the conclusion put forward in stories about alleged inappropriate fund-raising practices), or objects of scorn and ridicule (such as the television evangelists).

The factor of media coverage in 1987 was of great import because of its influence on other developments.

Still another factor is the (ostensible) need of the federal government for *more revenue*. The issue of the need to reduce the federal deficit is growing, and tax-exempt organizations are increasingly being looked to as sources of revenue. The proposed law changes emanating from this development are not being advocated out of substantive policy deliberations; rather, they are being propelled by the sheer need for the revenue that would be derived. A recurring proposal that surfaces all too regularly is a tax on the net investment income of nearly all tax-exempt organizations.

The foregoing factors are all, to some degree, superficial and do not seem to get to the heart of the matter. But they are real and important, and they tended to reflect and, in some instances, facilitated more deep-seated reasons for the focus on tax-exempt organizations in 1987.

There seems to be an ongoing alteration in the thinking of the political leadership in this country on the subject of nonprofit organizations. Nonprofits do not appear to be as sacrosanct in their eyes as these organizations once were. The universities, the hospitals, even the churches, seem more vulnerable to their challenge; thus the attacks on the YM/WCAs and the hospitals.

Why did the political leaders become so emboldened? When the late Representative Wright Patman took on private foundations 20 years before, that undertaking was frequently characterized as a populist's battle against entrenched and unproductive wealth. That stance was popular (and politically easy to assume) throughout most of America. But taking on charities and other tax-exempt organizations across the board was another matter.

Several reasons underlie politicians' bold attacks on charities and other tax-exempt organizations. Some are necessarily superficial. One is desperation—the (alleged) need for additional federal revenue. Another is grandstanding—many nonprofit organizations are not part of a voting constituency. Another is frustration—some members of Congress really do not like the idea of charities engaging in lobbying. Another is successful government relations by others—the small business community is well-represented in Congress. Another is resentment—anger with one nonprofit organization (for example, the PTL) spills over onto other nonprofit organizations.

But these are relatively superficial considerations. Probably something more profound is taking place and accounts for this current boldness in our politicians. A possibility is a decline in the respect previously accorded nonprofit organizations by the general public. Most members of Congress take stances on political issues only to the extent those stances are encouraged, or at least tolerated, by the voters.

Why would the general public lose some degree of respect for nonprofit organizations? Again, the superficial reasons are the easiest to identify. One possibility is that the general public is beginning to take nonprofit organizations for granted, forgetting what a unique American institution they are and how crucial they are to the preservation and enhancement of American societal values. Another possibility is tax reform's increased pressure for more revenue, which has triggered greater resentment in those who must pay taxes. They, in turn, focus more attention on those who do not pay taxes (including tax-exempt organizations). Another possibility is the negative media coverage that has been directed toward all nonprofit organizations in recent years.

Still, these reasons do not explain it all. At a deeper level, the general public may be confused. The precise identity once ascribed to nonprofit organizations is, in many instances, gone. Today, many nonprofit organizations and small or large businesses look the same. Hospitals may be the most stark example, but other illustrations abound. Research, fitness, publishing, conferencing, touring, product sales, counseling—all these and much more are done by nonprofit organizations and for-profit organizations. An identity loss at the organizational level is producing an identity crisis at the individual level of perception.

The analysis cannot stop at this point. What started the public confusion? Partly, apparently, it just happened, as nonprofit organizations evolved in an increasingly complex and competitive society. As America moved from an industrial (manufacturing) economy to a services (information) economy, nonprofits became involved in industries that were once solely the province of for-profits. More sophisticated management has changed the character of many nonprofit organizations. Tax reform, government funding cutbacks, and demands for more services have played a role.

However, some of this confusion is a product of actions by the nonprofit community. Tax-exempt organizations are not necessarily a band of innocents. Some, with huge endowments, physical plants, massive staffs, government relations programs, high-profile fund-raising and development programs, and aggressive investment activities (including involvements in joint ventures and creative uses of for-profit subsidiaries) have shaken the general public's traditional view of what a nonprofit organization is.

This is not to imply that charitable (and other nonprofit) organizations have done anything wrong or otherwise illegal by engaging in these confusion-producing activities. However, nonprofit organizations are changing in character and activities (but not purposes) faster than much of the general public is able to favorably perceive them. Some may even be thinking that nonprofit organizations are anachronisms.

Some confusion is also being caused by the inability of the statutory law to keep pace with the contemporary and evolving practices of nonprofit organizations. Oddly, the courts are developing different principles and are having little difficulty in keeping up with the innovative activities of nonprofit organizations.

The heart of the matter may be a loss of identity for nonprofit organizations. Developments in the federal tax law in the coming years may redefine the role of nonprofit organizations in general, or at least some of them. But how different will the new definition be? Will the criteria for tax exemption remain the same? How about the criteria for charitable giving? Will there be an expansion of reporting and other disclosure requirements and of penalties? What about a rewriting of the definition of related and unrelated activities? What will be the use of criteria such as commerciality and competition with business?

The nonprofit community is being forced to explain what it means to be *nonprofit* and *tax-exempt*, and why it differs from being *for-profit*, and why the present law of tax exemptions, tax deductions, and the like should remain. If abuses of tax-exempt status are occurring—particularly any that cannot be corrected under existing law—the nonprofit community should be forthright about it. A battle is shaping up, and on the line is the future of the legal terms *nonprofit* organizations and *tax-exempt* organizations.

The emerging doctrine of *commerciality* seems to presume that, because for-profit organizations obviously engage in commercial activities, if an activity is duplicated in the for-profit sector, it is an impermissible (taxable) activity when and if conducted in the nonprofit sector.

Should this presumption be the rule? If so, wouldn't some exceptions have to be made for traditional activities conducted in the nonprofit sector? Two clear instances of historical conduct are nonprofit schools and hospitals, even though there are proprietary counterparts. The existence of one proprietary school or hospital would not preempt the field for nonprofits, so that there could no longer be nonprofit (nontaxable) schools or hospitals. Presumably, the same would be true for other institutions, such as museums and libraries.

But what about program activities such as conferences, publications, and consulting, which have counterparts in the for-profit sector? Are they inherently commercial activities and thus automatically unrelated ones? If so, the commerciality concept bears directly on eligibility for tax-exempt status as well as on unrelated income taxation because, in many instances, these activities are the primary (if not the only) ones.

What about the new entry of one or more for-profit organizations into a field previously occupied solely by nonprofit organizations? Does that introduce commerciality into the field, making the activity taxable when conducted by nonprofit organizations? And does the field become nontaxable for nonprofits only when and if the for-profit organizations abandon that field?

Congress has been leery about writing the commerciality test into the tax law. To date, it has done it only once, legislating on situations where charitable or social welfare organizations issue *commercial-type insurance*. But the courts and other policy makers have not been so reticent. Here are the top areas today where the commerciality doctrine could well reshape the tax law as it applies to nonprofit organizations:

- The tax status of nonprofit hospitals. There are tax-exempt hospitals and for-profit hospitals. What is the difference between them? Some government officials are struggling with that one. The present controversy is whether to keep the existing criterion for tax exemption (the *community benefit standard*) in place or to insist that tax-exempt hospitals provide more services to the poor (the *charity care standard*).

- The tax status of nonprofit credit unions. These institutions have been tax-exempt for years. Today, however, other financial institutions are complaining about this tax privilege. What sets nonprofit credit unions apart? The administrations of Jimmy Carter and George Bush advocated repeal of their tax exemption.

- The tax status of insurance activities of fraternal beneficiary societies. Here again, the issue is the distinction between these insurance activities and those of taxable commercial insurers. A 1993 report from the Department of the Treasury found the activities to be similar and serving the same markets (although the report stopped short of recommending taxation of the societies' insurance activities).

One of the challenges for the nonprofit sector over the coming years will be whether it can succeed in satisfactorily defining its role in American society to the general public, and thus to legislators and regulators.

This is a capitalist society, and perhaps nonprofit organizations are to be secondary to for-profit ones when it comes to similar activities. However, the concern is that, in our zeal to protect small business or otherwise address particular legislators' pet peeves, the nation's nonprofit organizations will be significantly harmed and society will suffer from loss of their services. Any corresponding benefit would require augmentation of the role of government in providing social and other services. Others may champion that outcome (and that philosophy may underlie some of the recent proposals to revamp the law of unrelated income taxation), but it would be shortsighted and would dramatically alter for the worse the manner in which our society is organized and operated and the already heavy demands on the federal budget.

EXAMPLE: TAX PENALTIES

Sometimes the best defense is a good offense. In recent years, the nonprofit sector has been on the defense, time and time again, in relation to the development of federal tax law, particularly by Congress. Others have proposed new rules to meet new problems and, for the most part, the nonprofit community has opposed them. This has led to a view among legislators that the independent sector is interested only in protectionism, rather than problem solving, which in turn lowers the sector's credibility and its effectiveness with the legislatures. Reduced effectiveness frequently stimulates more adverse legislation, and the cycle continues—or worsens.

What can nonprofit organizations do to seize the moment and stop this slide in credibility and effectiveness? One idea lies in the nature of the sanctions used to enforce the law of tax-exempt organizations. Traditionally, the sanction used to enforce the federal tax law in this area has been revocation of tax exemption. Over the years, less draconian (usually) sanctions have crept into the law, in the form of taxes (principally excise taxes) and civil penalties.

This process began in 1950, when Congress enacted the income tax on unrelated business activities. (See Chapter 12.) In 1969, Congress enacted a battery of penalties in the form of excise taxes applicable to private foundations. (See Chapter 11.) Legislation in 1987 brought a panoply of taxes and penalties for exempt organizations, for transgressions ranging from lobbying and political campaign activities to fundraising disclosure. (See Chapters 13 and 14.) With these and other penalties—such as those for failure to timely file complete annual information returns or for failure to make those returns or the application for recognition of exemption available for public inspection (see Chapters 6 and 7)—the regulatory emphasis has shifted away from the all-or-nothing sanction of loss of exemption to the use of penalties.

Perhaps the nonprofit sector should build on this trend, to show a willingness to cope with real problems and, not incidentally, to curb some abuses before they grow into major issues and massive legislation. Here are some ideas.

The IRS is rightfully concerned about the manner in which annual information returns are being prepared these days. All too often, the returns are late, incomplete, sloppily prepared, and unresponsive to the questions. Part of the fault for this lies with the IRS, because the return is often vague or confusing. The IRS is constantly revising the return, with or without more legislation, and Congress will be legislating expansions of the return. In conjunction with this revamping of the return, consideration should be given to a strengthening of the penalties, to induce compliance. The penalty of $10 per day (maximum of the lesser of $5,000 or 5 percent of the gross receipts of the organization for the year) may have to be increased. The per-day penalty may go to $100 and/or the maximum penalty to be paid with respect to any one return may be increased. Under certain circumstances, perhaps the individuals responsible for nonfilings or incomplete filings should be personally penalized. Hardly anyone outside of government likes to advocate greater penalties on tax-exempt organizations, but the noncompliance problem is a serious and worsening one, and a higher penalty is likely to be one of the solutions.

Another penalty structure that warrants revisiting is the one levied for failure to comply with the fund-raising disclosure rules. (See Chapter 9.) Here, the penalty ($1,000 per day, up to $10,000 annually) is too stringent, particularly now that the IRS is interpreting the rule to apply to solicitations of membership dues and assessments. Nonprofit organizations should advocate a reduction of that penalty, such as to $100 per day. Why should the penalty be higher for failure to make the fund-raising disclosure than for failure to timely file a complete annual return? At the same time, the nonprofit sector should advocate extension of the disclosure rule and the accompanying penalty to charitable organizations, where they solicit payments that are not deductible as charitable gifts. (See Chapter 8.) This, too, is a growing problem and needs to be nipped now, rather than waiting for more restrictive legislation later.

Many of the well-publicized and embarrassing episodes adversely affecting the nonprofit sector involve violations of the private inurement doctrine. (See Chapter 5.) Perhaps the time has come to develop penalties for public charities along the lines of what Congress did in 1987 with respect to impermissible lobbying and political campaign activities: enact taxes that are potentially imposable on the individuals who willfully cause the exempt organization to engage in the forbidden act(s). The independent sector could advocate sanctions imposed on the individuals who engage in acts of private inurement, instead of more rules on the organizations being manipulated by these individuals. One way to do this would be to underlie the private inurement rules with a series of penalty taxes somewhat akin to those imposed in connection with the self-dealing rules applicable to private foundations. (See Chapter 11.) This would not be a popular stance within the nonprofit community, but it would show leadership in addressing a pressing problem and again ward off the very real possibility of more repressive legislation later. This same approach could be engrafted on the revisions of the unrelated income rules, which are being written.

Probably there is little enthusiasm within the top levels of the independent sector for advocating—of all things—more penalties on their memberships. Yet something must be done, and the sector must do more itself toward contributing to solutions.

THE LONGER VIEW

Too many people regard tax-exempt organizations as quaint anachronisms of another era—forms of institutional life no longer suited for the organizations of today and the future. The thought that exempt organizations, or most of them, are destined for extinction may be tested against the thinking of futurists.

For example, Alvin Toffler, writing in *The Third Wave*, envisioned great change in the nature of "increased diversity" in "ideas, political convictions, sexual proclivities, educational methods, eating habits, religious views, ethnic attitudes, musical tastes, fashions, and family forms." This development (stimulated by what he termed the "de-massification" of society), he believed, will lead to a splintering and/or reshaping of many of society's institutions—both a decentralizing and a fragmenting process. If nothing else, this result would mean more tax-exempt (or at least, nonprofit) organizations. As an illustration, Toffler saw this de-massification occurring in U.S. political life, when he described the "sudden, bewildering proliferation of high-powered splinter groups." Concerning the future of nonprofit organizations, Toffler clearly expected not only more of them but an expanded role for them.

Toffler predicted a greater diversity in organized religion and the emergence of new religions. He expected that a "host of new religions, new conceptions of science, new images of human nature, new forms of art will arise—in far richer diversity than was possible or necessary during the industrial age." He foresaw new educational organizations and new educational methods. Toffler predicted restructuring of curricula, revisions in the concept of grading, increased parental influence on the schools, and a lessening in the number of years of compulsory schooling; in general, he expected new forms of consultancies, massive changes in the modes of educational instruction (because of the advent of word processors, home computers, and telecommunications), and new opportunities in instruction and publishing. He predicted new advances and diversification of organizations in the fields of health and science. Nonprofit organizations should be in the forefront of what Toffler termed "[f]antastic scientific advances," yet ironically also very much involved in the resistance to new technology, being part of the organizational effort of "humanizing the technological thrust." He foresaw significant changes in healthcare delivery systems, with obvious implications for the nonprofit community.

Concerning the nation's political system, Toffler called for nothing less than the "design of new, more appropriate political structures." One of the pathways to this objective, he said, was "imaginative new arrangements for accommodating and legitimating diversity—new institutions that are sensitive to the rapidly shifting needs of changing and multiplying minorities." Nonprofit organizations will certainly be a part of this process, both as entities that help to design the new political process and as participatory elements of it.

In his wide-ranging analysis of life tomorrow, Toffler speculated on some of the needs in the future and on ways to satisfy them. Many of these ways would require the use of nonprofit organizations.

For example, Toffler discussed some of the problems that cannot be solved by national governments individually (such as inflation, activities of transnational corporations, arms trade, outer space governance, and interlocking currencies). He stated that "[w]e desperately need, therefore, to invent imaginative new institutions at the transnational level to which many decisions can be transferred" and called for "consortia and teams of nongovernmental organizations to attack various global problems."

Likewise, he wrote of the need to enable a variety of minorities to regulate more of their own affairs. To this end, he speculated, "We might, for example, help the people in a specific neighborhood, in a well-defined subculture, or in an ethnic group, to set up their own youth courts under the supervision of the state, disciplining their own young people rather than relying on the state to do so." He rationalized this suggestion in terms embodying some well-recognized tax law doctrines for such groups: "Such institutions would build community and identity, and contribute to law and order, while relieving the overburdened government institutions of unnecessary work."

In still another example of new nonprofit organization life forms, Toffler postulated the use of "semi-cults"—organizations that "lie somewhere between [the application of] structureless freedom and tightly structured regimentation." These groups were envisioned by him as a means to impose a certain degree of structure where and as long as it was required, yet persons would be able to return freely to productive life in society. He also suggests a variant of these entities to provide community services.

The conclusions of another futurist, John Naisbitt, parallel those of Toffler. Writing in *Megatrends*, Naisbitt also found, in the shift from an industrial society to an information society, the "evolution of a highly personal value system to compensate for the impersonal nature of technology," the transformation from national economics to a world economy, the emphasis on long-term concepts rather than short-term thinking, the change from centralization to decentralization, the shift from institutional help to self-help, the evolution from representative democracy to participatory democracy (within both government and large corporations), and the change from hierarchies to networking.

While Naisbitt, like Toffler, found no occasion to specifically address the future of nonprofit organizations as such, he foresaw growth in the human potential and self-help movements, massive changes in the delivery of education and healthcare, new political initiatives, the development of networking, and the emergence of new religions—all of which would inevitably utilize nonprofit organizations. Neither of these futurists wrote of any need to preserve tax exemption for nonprofit organizations—perhaps they simply assumed that it will continue. Toffler, for one, is not opposed to this type of utilization of the tax system, however; in his book, he calls for the application of tax incentives to help accomplish particular objectives.

This citation of futurists' suggestions and predictions is not intended to endorse any particular vein of futurist thinking or the necessary evolution of any particular form of tax-exempt organization, but only to suggest that unfolding societal needs are likely to heavily entail the active involvement of nonprofit (tax-exempt) organizations. Toffler's prognostications indicate an exciting and meaningful future, replete with a large dosage of the American tendency to create *associations*. The Toffler premise suggests that nonprofit organizations are an integral part of the American societal and political structure, and that the concern for the immediate future is not whether nonprofit groups are a dying breed but whether they are to be seriously endangered by evolving tax and fund-raising regulation policy.

It is projected that nonprofit (hopefully, tax-exempt) organizations will very much remain in the nation's future. The future holds considerable changes in tax law, fund-raising law, and other matters such as personal liability and compensation forms. These changes will govern the nation's nonprofit organizations well into the 21st century.

Glossary

S
ome of the terms listed here may seem deceptively simple. What could be plainer, for example, than "additional tax"? However, the law of nonprofit organizations has some complex and specialized definitions and applications for apparently ordinary terms. In some instances, it is inadvisable to try to paraphrase or "popularize" them. My best advice to readers, generally, is to supplement the Glossary by going directly to the Internal Revenue Code sections cited here and reading the original definitions and discussions. A key factor in successfully starting and managing a nonprofit organization is to know what the IRS says about a particular topic and what it means when it says it.

Abatement. In general, a decrease or diminution; in the nonprofit organization tax law context, relief from a tax liability. For example, the IRS has the ability to abate nearly all of the *excise taxes* imposed on *private foundations* (IRC § 4962).

Actuary. A specialist in projecting amounts of income, interest, or expense over future periods of time. Actuaries create the tables used in calculating *income interests* and *remainder interests*, which are important in implementing planned giving.

Additional tax. Under the tax rules that apply to private foundations, *initial* (excise) *taxes* are assessed first, on the foundations and their managers, as a method of enforcing the rules. If the offense is not corrected, *additional* (excise) *taxes* or "second-tier taxes" are added to encourage compliance with the rules.

Terms in italics appear elsewhere in the Glossary.

Adjusted gross income. In the case of an individual, the before-taxes amount that results when certain deductions are subtracted from his or her gross income (IRC § 62).

Advisory committee. A group of individuals who make their expertise and experience—and sometimes their celebrity—available to the *board of directors* of a *nonprofit organization;* a technique for attracting well-known persons to service for an organization without causing them to become involved in its actual governance.

Advocacy. The active espousal of a position, a point of view, or a course of action; it can include *lobbying, political activity,* demonstrations, boycotts, litigation, and various forms of program activity.

Agricultural organization. An organization described in IRC § 501(c)(5).

Alternative minimum tax. A federal tax intended to make certain wealthy and/or sophisticated taxpayers pay some taxes, even if only a minimal amount. It is an "alternative" tax in that it must be paid if its amount is larger than the *regular income tax* would be. The tax is determined, in part, by adding the value of a taxpayer's *tax preference items,* including the appreciation element in most *contributions* of *appreciated property* (IRC §§ 55–59).

Amateur sports organization. An organization formed and operated exclusively to foster national or international amateur sports competition, to conduct national or international competitive sports events, or to support and develop amateur athletes for national or international competition in sports (IRC § 501(j)).

Annual information return. The return that is required to be filed by most *tax-exempt organizations* annually with the IRS (Form 990).

Annuity. A regular payment of a set amount of money for a person's life (or persons' lives), or for a period of years. An annuity may be payable as the result of creation of a *charitable gift annuity* or a *charitable remainder trust.*

Apostolic association. A religious organization that has a common treasury or community treasury, even if it engages in business for the common benefit of its members. The members of the organization include in their gross income their entire pro rata shares, whether or not distributed, of the taxable income of the organization (IRC § 501(d)).

Application for recognition of exemption. The IRS form by which a *nonprofit organization* seeks recognition of tax-exempt status from the IRS (Form 1023 or 1024).

Appraisal. The determination of the fair market value of a property, as in the valuation of property that is the subject of a *charitable contribution.*

Appraiser. An individual who is in the business of making *appraisals*. An independent appraiser is mandated in connection with gifts of property with a value in excess of $5,000.

Appreciated property. Property that has increased in value so that its fair market value has become greater than its cost basis (IRC §§ 170(b)(1)(C) and 170(e)).

Appreciation element. The component of value that represents the difference between the cost basis and the fair market value of an item of property.

Articles of incorporation. See *articles of organization*.

Articles of organization. The generic term for the document used to create a *nonprofit organization*; "articles of incorporation" in the case of a corporation; a "constitution" in the case of an unincorporated association; a *"trust agreement"* or *"declaration of trust"* in the case of a trust.

Association. An organization, usually nonprofit and tax-exempt, that has a membership, whether of individuals and/or organizations.

Attorney. A word commonly used as a synonym for "lawyer"; anyone who is acting on behalf of another and who has the authority to do so (as in power of attorney).

Audit. The process whereby the IRS examines the books and records of an organization, and witnesses, in search of compliance with the internal revenue laws (IRC §§ 7601–7611).

Award. A gift of cash or property in recognition of an achievement, usually taxable to the recipient unless immediately transferred to a *charitable organization* (IRC § 74).

Bargain sale. A transaction whereby a person transfers property to a *charitable organization* for less than its fair market value, thereby making the transaction part sale and part gift (IRC § 1011(b)).

Basis. The cost amount for the acquisition of an item of property, plus certain subsequent expenditures (IRC § 1012).

Benevolent. A term sometimes used as a synonym for "charitable," although it is of broader scope than "charitable." Not formally used in the federal tax law rules, but sometimes found in state and local laws.

Benevolent life insurance association. An organization described in IRC § 501(c)(12).

Bequest. A gift of personal property made by means of a will.

Black Lung benefit trust. An organization described in IRC § 501(c)(21).

Board of directors. Two or more individuals who serve as the governing body of an organization; see *board of trustees*.

Board of trade. An organization described in IRC § 501(c)(6).

Board of trustees. The same as a *board of directors*, except that the organization involved is usually a trust and/or a *charitable* entity.

Business league. An organization described in IRC § 501(c)(6).

Bylaws. The document of an organization that contains its rules of operation; in some jurisdictions, the term "code of regulations" is used.

Byrd Amendment. This body of law restricts the use of federal funds that are awarded to recipients of federal contracts, grants, loans, or cooperative agreements. The funds received may not be used to pay persons to influence or attempt to influence government agency employees or legislative decision makers in connection with the awarding of any contract, grant, loan, or cooperative agreement. Certain reporting requirements are imposed as well.

Capital asset. Property held by a person, whether or not connected with a trade or business; does not include inventory, depreciable property used in a business, certain literary or artistic compositions, and certain publications of the United States Government (IRC § 1221).

Capital campaign. A *fund-raising* program designed to generate *contributions* for a *charitable* organization's capital, usually for a building, a major item of equipment, or an *endowment* fund.

Cause-related marketing. Fund-raising techniques used to generate nongift revenues, involving *related* and/or *unrelated* activities; the term usually includes *charitable sales promotions* and other forms of *commercial co-ventures*.

Cemetery company. An organization described in IRC § 501(c)(13).

Chairperson of the board. An individual selected, usually by a *board of directors*, to be the leader of the board; this is not usually an *officer* position, although it can be when so provided in *articles of organization* and/or *bylaws*; in some instances, an individual denominated "chairman" or "chair" of the board.

Chamber of commerce. An organization described in IRC § 501(c)(6).

Charitable. The description of a purpose, activity, or organization that the applicable law, such as the federal tax law (principally, IRC § 501(c)(3)), regards as meeting at least one of the required *charitable* objectives. (See Chapter 4.)

Charitable contribution. A *contribution* made to a *charitable* organization; sometimes, a contribution made to a noncharitable organization for a *charitable* purpose.

Charitable contribution deduction. A *deduction* available, under certain federal, state, and local laws, for an amount of money or property transferred to a *charitable* organization (e.g., IRC § 170).

Charitable gift annuity. An arrangement whereby property is transferred to a *charitable* organization in exchange for an *annuity*. The donated value of the property in excess of the value of the annuity is a *charitable contribution*.

Charitable lead trust. A trust used to facilitate the contribution of a *lead interest* or *income interest* to a *charitable organization* (IRC § 514(c)(5)).

Charitable organization. An organization that is formed and operated for what the applicable law, such as the federal tax law (principally, IRC § 501(c)(3)), regards as a *charitable* purpose.

Charitable remainder trust. A form of *split-interest trust* used to cause a deductible contribution of it easier to contribute a *remainder interest* to a *charitable* organization; a trust that is a charitable remainder annuity trust or a charitable remainder unitrust (IRC § 664).

Charitable sales promotion. An undertaking that essentially is the same as a *commercial co-venture*.

Charitable solicitation acts. State laws that regulate the process of soliciting *contributions* for *charitable* purposes.

Charity care standard. A standard of law that was once the basis of tax exemption for nonprofit hospitals. It is premised largely on the view that tax-exempt status for hospitals should be based on a definition of the term *charitable*, which emphasizes relief of the poor. Under this standard (which is the law in some states), a hospital, to be tax-exempt, must provide a substantial portion of its healthcare services without cost or on a reduced-rate basis.

Civic league. An organization described in IRC § 501(c)(4); also known as a social welfare organization.

Code of ethics. A statement of principles established by a nonprofit membership organization and used to affect the professional behavior of its members. Ethical principles are not necessarily the same as law; they tend to be loftier and idealistic. The ability of an individual or other person to remain a member of an organization may require compliance with its code of ethics.

Commercial. Conduct of an activity by a *nonprofit organization* in a manner similar to the way in which for-profit organizations conduct the same activity; the only federal law statutory illustration of this to date is the set of rules concerning *commercial-type insurance* (IRC § 501(m)).

Commercial co-venture. An arrangement between a for-profit organization and a *charitable* organization (sometimes more than one), whereby the for-profit entity agrees to make a *contribution* to the charitable entity, with the amount of the contribution determined by the volume of sales of products or services by the for-profit organization during a particular time period.

Commerciality. An emerging doctrine stating that an activity conducted in a "commercial" manner is deemed, for that reason alone, to be a nonexempt activity.

Commercial-type insurance. Generally, any insurance that is typically provided by commercial insurance companies. A *charitable organization* or a *social welfare organization* cannot be tax-exempt if a substantial part of its activities consists of the provision of commercial-type insurance (IRC § 501(m)).

Community benefit standard. The basis for the present-day rationale for the federal tax exemption of nonprofit hospitals; it is predicated on the fact that one of the definitions of the term *charitable* is the promotion of health. Thus, to be tax-exempt under federal law, a hospital must promote the health of a class of persons broad enough to represent an entire community, and must be operated to serve a public interest.

Community chest. One of the organizations described in IRC § 501(c)(3).

Consideration. The element of value in a bargain; something exchanged to receive something in return, as when both parties to a *contract* receive consideration.

Constitution. See *articles of organization.*

Constructive receipt. A doctrine that applies to tax funds received by an individual or other person, at the time he, she, or it has the right to possession of or access to the money. The person may not yet have actual receipt of the funds, but the law treats the person as if that were the case; this is also known as the rule of "economic benefit."

Consultant. One who provides services to an organization in a capacity other than as an *employee,* such as an accountant, fund-raising counsel, or lawyer; an independent contractor.

Contract. A set of promises between two or more persons that creates, revises, or eliminates a legal relationship; a set of promises underlain by *consideration.*

Contribution. A transfer by one person to another of money or property without an expectation of any material return; a transfer of money or property without *consideration.*

Contribution base. An amount equal to what is, essentially, an individual's *adjusted gross income;* used in computing the extent to which *charitable contributions* are deductible in a year (IRC § 170(b)(1)(F)).

Cooperative hospital service organization. An organization that performs, on a centralized basis, one or more specified services solely for two or more hospitals and is operated on a cooperative basis (IRC § 501(e)).

Cooperative service organization of educational organizations. An organization that is formed and operated solely to collectively invest in securities for the benefit of public and private schools, colleges, and universities (IRC § 501(f)).

Cooperative telephone company. An organization described in IRC § 501(c)(12).

Credit union. An organization described in IRC § 501(c)(14).

Crop financing organization. An organization described in IRC § 501(c)(16).

Cruelty prevention organization. One of the organizations described in IRC § 501(c)(3).

Damages. A form of compensation or restitution paid to a person, usually as the consequence of a lawsuit, for an injury or other loss (suffered personally in the case of an individual or by an organization, or caused by harm to property or violation of rights) occasioned by commission of an unlawful act or some failure to act.

Declaration of trust. A proclamation by a person of the existence of a trust; see *articles of organization, trust agreement.*

Declaratory judgment. A declaration by the U.S. Tax Court, the U.S. Court of Federal Claims, or the U.S. District Court for the District of Columbia as to whether an organization is tax-exempt as described in IRC § 501(c)(3), a *charitable* organization (IRC § 170(c)(2)), a *private foundation* or *public charity* (IRC § 509), or a *private operating foundation* (IRC § 4942(j)(3) and IRS § 7428).

Deduction. An item (usually an expenditure) that is subtracted from *adjusted gross income* to arrive at *taxable income.* An example is the *charitable contribution deduction.*

Defamation. The effect of one person's publishing something that injures the reputation of another; a written defamation is a "libel" and an oral defamation is a "slander."

Deferred compensation plan. A program whereby one or more employees of an organization are compensated for services rendered currently but the receipt of the compensation is deferred until a subsequent point in time (such as retirement).

Determination letter. A letter from the IRS indicating *recognition of tax exemption* for a *nonprofit organization*.

Development program. In many ways, a program that is the same as a *fund-raising* program, although this type of program usually emphasizes *capital campaigns* and/or planned giving programs.

Devise. A gift of real property by means of a will.

Direct lobbying. An attempt to influence the development of *legislation* by contact with legislators, their staffs, or staffs of legislative committees, such as by meetings, correspondence, and/or testimony at hearings. (See *grass roots lobbying.*)

Donor acquisition. A *fund-raising* program where the emphasis is on the acquisition of new donors to a *charitable organization* (who, hopefully, will continue to give); also known as "prospecting."

Donor renewal. A *fund-raising* program where the emphasis is on acquiring *contributions* from those who have previously given (the donor base) to a *charitable organization*.

Dues. Amounts of money paid to an organization for membership services; where these services are *consideration* and the organization is a *charitable* one, the dues are not deductible as *charitable contributions*.

Economic benefit. See *constructive receipt*.

Electioneering. The process of intervening or otherwise participating in a campaign for or against the election of a candidate for public office.

Employee. One who provides services to an organization (the "employer") where he or she is under the direct supervision and control of the organization; usually, the services are provided on the premises of the employer, using the resources of the employer, and under working hours and conditions set by the employer.

Employees' beneficiary association. An organization described in IRC § 501(c)(9).

Employer retirement claims. An organization described in IRC § 501(c)(22).

Endowment. An accumulation of *contributions* that are not expended for programs but are held for investment. The earnings (if any) are devoted to program activities, either generally or in a "restricted" manner.

Estate. A term with many meanings, including the property an individual owns at his or her death; federal tax law defines a "taxable estate" (IRC §§ 2051–2057).

Excise tax. In the *tax-exempt organizations* context, the sanctions sometimes used to enforce tax law prohibitions, for example, the private foundation rules and the *expenditure test* in the charitable organizations lobbying field.

Exclusion. In the tax context, an item of income that is excluded from the concept of *gross income*, such as a scholarship (IRC § 117).

Executive committee. A subgroup of directors of an organization that has particular influence over the affairs of the organization.

Executive director. An employee of an organization who is assigned the principal responsibility for administering the organization; sometimes termed "president" or "executive vice president"; this may be an *officer* position.

Exempt function revenue. Funds derived by a tax-exempt organization from the performance of an exempt function, such as revenue from the sale of publications or fees received for conferences or seminars.

Expenditure test. In the context of *lobbying* activities by *public charities*, a test that enables qualifying *charitable organizations* to elect to come under certain standards for more mechanically determining allowable lobbying (IRC § 501(h)).

Farmers' cooperative. An organization described in IRC § 521.

Federal Agents Registration Act. A body of law requiring lobbyists and other agents of foreign governments to register with and report to the Department of Justice.

Feeder organization. An organization, not tax-exempt, that distributes all of its net income of a tax-exempt organization (IRC § 502).

Felony. A criminal act of serious character—it is a graver act than a "misdemeanor." The punishment for the commission of a felony may be death or imprisonment for a period of time longer than one year; most of the state charitable solicitation laws contain penalties by which some violations of these laws are felonies.

Fiduciary. One who is bound to look after the affairs of another, using the same standards of care and prudence as he or she would use in attending to his or her own affairs, as in a trustee of a trust.

Foundation. See *private foundation.*

Fraternal society. An organization described in IRC § 501(c)(8) or § 501(c)(10).

Fund-raiser. One who is employed (see *employee*) or retained (see *consultant*) to assist a tax-exempt organization (usually a *charitable* one) in the raising of funds, conventionally in the form of *contributions* and grants, and more recently in the form of *exempt function revenue* or *unrelated* revenue; also known as "professional fund-raiser" or "professional fund-raising counsel."

Fund-raising. In the broadest sense, *fund-raising* is the process of soliciting and receiving contributions, usually for a *charitable organization;* there are several categories of fund-raising activities, most notably direct mail solicitation, in-person solicitation, private foundation grant solicitation, telemarketing, radio and television solicitation, special events (dinners, dances, auctions, and the like), and planned giving.

General partnership. A partnership in which all of the partners are equally liable for satisfaction of the obligations of the partnership.

Grass roots lobbying. An attempt to influence the legislative process by contacting the general public, or a segment of it, for the purpose of encouraging those individuals to contact the appropriate legislators; see *direct lobbying.*

Gross income. Except as otherwise provided in the IRC, all income from whatever source derived, including compensation for services (IRC § 61(a)); gross income does not include gifts (IRC § 102).

Homeowners' association. An organization described in IRC § 528.

Horticultural organization. One of the organizations described in IRC § 501(c)(5).

Identification number. A number assigned to organizations by the IRS; also termed an "employer identification number" (used even when the organization does not have any employees) (IRC § 6109).

Income interest. The right to receive all or some portion of the income from property for a stated period of time, either alone or with others.

Independent sector. The segment of U.S. society represented by nonprofit, principally *charitable,* organizations; also known as the "voluntary sector," "nonprofit sector," or "private sector."

Initial tax. Principally in the *private foundations* context, the *excise taxes* that are initially assessable in enforcement of the rules; also known as "first-tier" taxes.

Institutions. In the *tax-exempt organizations* context, entities such as churches, universities, colleges, schools, and hospitals; these entities are not *private foundations* (IRC § 509(a)(1)).

Internal Revenue Code. The statutory body of federal tax law developed by Congress and administered by the *Internal Revenue Service* (IRS). The current version of the law is the Internal Revenue Code (IRC) of 1986, as amended.

Internal Revenue Service. The agency of the federal government with the principal responsibility for regulating the activities of *tax-exempt organizations.* The IRS is a component of the Department of the Treasury.

Joint venture. An undertaking of two or more organizations and/or individuals for the accomplishment of a particular purpose; an arrangement closely akin to a *general partnership.*

Labor organization. One of the organizations described in IRC § 501(c)(5).

Lead interest. The same right to income as an *income interest;* so named because, in the planned giving context, an income interest precedes (leads) the *remainder interest.*

Legislation. General rules of human conduct that are consciously and deliberately stated by a law-making body; a declaration of general principles by a law-making body, to be applied (usually prospectively) to all persons or general classes of persons governed by the laws.

Limited partnership. A partnership comprised of at least one "general partner" and at least one "limited partner," the latter being one whose liability for acts of the partnership is limited to the amount of investment.

Literary organization. One of the organizations described in IRC § 501(c)(3).

Lobbying. An activity usually associated with an attempt to influence a legislative process; generically, it means being in the lobby, so it can also mean attempts to influence the outcome of executive branch or regulatory agencies' decisions, or actions of a legislative branch that are not *legislation.*

Modifications. Term used in unrelated business tax context to describe the rules that exclude certain forms of income, such as *passive income,* from taxation (IRC § 512(b)).

Mutual ditch and irrigation company. One of the organizations described in IRC § 501(c)(12).

Mutual telephone company. One of the organizations described in IRC § 501(c)(12).

Net earnings. Gross earnings less operating expenses; in for-profit organizations, net earnings are often passed along to owners (e.g., dividends paid to stockholders).

Nonprofit organization. An entity that is organized so that its *net earnings* do not inure to the benefit of individuals in their private capacity.

Not-for-profit activities. Activities for which a business expense deduction is not available (IRC § 183); often confused with "nonprofit" activities.

Officer. An individual who, by reason of an organization's *articles of organization* and/or *bylaws*, or by law, is assigned certain duties in the operation of an organization.

Operational test. Rules applied (most frequently in the IRC § 501(c)(3) context) to determine whether an organization's operations will merit IRS recognition of its tax-exempt status.

Organizational test. Rules applied (most frequently in the IRC § 501(c)(3) context) to determine whether an organization's *articles of organization* will merit IRS recognition of its tax-exempt status.

Paid solicitor. See *solicitor.*

Partnership. See *general partnership* and *limited partnership.*

Passive income. Income that is not generated from active participation in a business; usually annuities, capital gain, dividends, interest, rents, and royalties.

Person. An entity, either an organization (corporation, unincorporated association, trust, partnership, or estate) or an individual.

Political activity. Generally, activity to advance some political end. Some political activity can cause loss of tax-exempt status for charitable and some other types of tax-exempt organizations, if these activities usually have to constitute activities for the benefit of or in opposition to political candidates for a public office.

Political organization. An organization described in IRC § 527.

Pooled income fund. A form of *split-interest trust,* by which *contributions* of *remainder interests* in money or property are made to *charitable organizations* (IRC § 642(c)(5)).

Professional solicitor. See *solicitor.*

Private foundation. A *charitable organization* that is usually funded from one source (an individual, family, or business), that receives its ongoing funding from investment income (rather than contributions), and that makes grants for *charitable* purposes to other persons rather than conduct its own programs (IRC § 509(a)). See *private operating foundation* and *public charity.*

Private inurement. The doctrine, most prevalent in the IRC § 501(c)(3) context, that causes a *tax-exempt organization* to lose or be denied tax-exempt status because the organization is judged by the IRS to be operated for the private gain of a *person.*

Private operating foundation. A *private foundation* that operates one or more *charitable* programs (IRC § 4942(j)(3)).

Public charity. A *charitable organization* that usually is one of the *institutions* and thus not a *private foundation* (IRC § 509(a)(1)).

Publicly supported charity. A *charitable organization* that is not a *private foundation* because it receives the requisite amount of financial support from the public (IRC §§ 170(b)(A)(vi) and 509(a)(1) or 509(a)(2)).

Qualified amateur sports organization. See *amateur sports organization.*

Real estate board. An organization described in IRC § 501(c)(6).

Recognition of tax exemption. The process engaged in by the IRS in determining that a *nonprofit organization* is a *tax-exempt organization.*

Regular income tax. Term used to describe the basic federal income tax, to distinguish it from the *alternative minimum tax.*

Related activity. A program activity that furthers the purposes of a *tax-exempt organization* (IRC § 512).

Remainder interest. The element of an item of property that causes outright title of the property to pass to a person (usually a *charitable* one) after the *income interest* in the property has expired.

Restricted gift. A *contribution,* usually to a *charitable organization,* that is accompanied by documentation mandating that it must be applied to a particular purpose of the organization, rather than used for its general operations.

Royalty. Payment made for the right to use property, usually as a fixed amount paid each time the item of property is sold or otherwise used.

Self-perpetuating board. A *board of directors* that is elected to office by their own votes rather than those of a membership.

Shipowners' protection and indemnity association. An organization described in IRC § 526.

Social club. An organization described in IRC § 501(c)(7).

Social welfare organization. An organization described in IRC § 501(c)(4).

Solicitor. A *person* who is paid by a *charitable organization* to engage in the act of requesting *contributions* to the organization; also known as a "paid solicitor" or "professional solicitor."

Split-interest trust. A trust that is established for the purpose of creating an *income interest* and a *remainder interest* in one or more items of property (IRC § 4947).

Supplemental unemployment benefit trust. An organization described in IRC § 501(c)(17).

Supporting organization. A *charitable organization* that is not a *private foundation* because it has a supportive relationship to one or more other organizations. The supported organization or organizations usually are *institutions* or *publicly supported charities* (IRC § 509(a)(3)).

Tax preference item. A money amount, usually a deduction or credit, that enables a taxpayer to reduce taxable income for *regular income tax* purposes.

Taxable income. For individuals who elect to itemize deductions, *adjusted gross income* less itemized deductions and the personal exemptions; for individuals who do not itemize their deductions, *adjusted gross income* less the standard deduction and the personal exemptions (IRC § 63).

Tax-exempt organization. A *nonprofit organization* that is exempt from one or more federal, state, and/or local taxes, most frequently the federal income tax (IRC § 501); also known as "tax-exempt entities."

Teachers' retirement fund association. An organization described in IRC § 501(c)(11).

Testamentary trust. A trust created by a will.

Title-holding company. An organization described in IRC § 501(c)(2) or 501(c)(25).

Trade association. A form of *business league* that is attempting to improve conditions in a particular trade, business, or profession.

Trade or business. An activity carried on for the production of income from the sale of goods or the performance of services (IRC § 513(c)).

Trade show. A function, usually of a *trade association,* consisting of the exhibiting of products and services of interest to the association's membership; usually undertaken in conjunction with the association's annual membership convention.

Trust agreement. An agreement between two or more *persons* for the purpose of creating a trust; see *declaration of trust.*

Union. One of the organizations described in IRC § 501(c)(5).

Unrelated activity. An activity of a *tax-exempt organization* that is not undertaken in order to further the organization's tax-exempt purposes, other than most administrative, investment, and *fund-raising* activities (IRC § 512).

Veterans' organization. An organization described in IRC § 501(c)(19) or 501(c)(23).

Voluntary employee beneficiary association. An organization described in IRC § 501(c)(9).

Index